The Lesser Jihad

The Lesser Jihad

Recruits and the al-Qaida Network

Elena Mastors and Alyssa Deffenbaugh

ROWMAN & LITTLEFIELD PUBLISHERS, INC.
Lanham • Boulder • New York • Toronto • Plymouth, UK

ROWMAN & LITTLEFIELD PUBLISHERS, INC.

Published in the United States of America
by Rowman & Littlefield Publishers, Inc.
A wholly owned subsidiary of The Rowman & Littlefield Publishing Group, Inc.
4501 Forbes Boulevard, Suite 200, Lanham, Maryland 20706
www.rowmanlittlefield.com

Estover Road, Plymouth PL6 7PY, United Kingdom

Copyright © 2007 by Rowman & Littlefield Publishers, Inc.

British Library Cataloguing in Publication Information Available

Library of Congress Cataloging-in-Publication Data

Mastors, Elena, 1969–
  The lesser jihad : recruits and the al-Qaida network / Elena Mastors and Alyssa
Deffenbaugh.
    p.   cm.
  Includes bibliographical references and index.
  ISBN-13: 978-0-7425-5487-0 (cloth : alk. paper)
  ISBN-10: 0-7425-5487-2 (cloth : alk. paper)
  ISBN-13: 978-0-7425-5488-7 (pbk. : alk. paper)
  ISBN-10: 0-7425-5488-0 (pbk. : alk. paper)
1. Qaida (Organization) 2. Terrorists. 3. Terrorists—Recruiting. I. Deffenbaugh, Alyssa,
1978– II. Title.
  HV6432.5.Q2M37 2007
  363.325—dc22

                                                              2006031613

Printed in the United States of America

♾™ The paper used in this publication meets the minimum requirements of American
National Standard for Information Sciences—Permanence of Paper for Printed Library
Materials, ANSI/NISO Z39.48-1992.

For all those who believed in us when we said that studying recruitment was important.

Contents

CHAPTER 1

The Recruitment Dilemma

Our goal has to be to continue doing what we're doing on the global war on terror, and that is going well. We are capturing and killing a lot of terrorists. But we also have to think about the number of new ones that are being created.

—U.S. Secretary of Defense Donald Rumsfeld

Is This What the Future Holds for the United States?

It is 7:30 a.m. on a quiet November morning. Commuters in the Washington, D.C., metropolitan area begin the process of traveling by car, metro, train, and bus into the busy city. Travelers on I-395 heading north, the main highway leading into the city, suddenly stop. Commuters still miles from the city suspect there is a large accident ahead. This is just another typical day of driving in the metro area. But the story for those farther along on I-395, as it nears the Pentagon, is quite different. Police blockades are positioned across the highway. Emergency vehicles scream by at top speeds. Something is very wrong. Car-bound commuters are unaware that the metro trains have already come to a screeching halt, and metro riders are being quickly evacuated from the stations. Newscasters on the radio talk about some type of attack on the red, yellow, and blue lines of the metro. Reports are sketchy, but several hundred deaths are already suspected.

An hour later, three separate attacks on the metro line are being discussed. The information isn't complete because emergency officials have cordoned off access to all metro stations and evacuated all trains. The first attack occurred at 7:30 a.m., right as the blue-line train entered the Pentagon station. At least three bombs went off in packed train cars. Emergency workers suspect that the bombs were left underneath the seats of the cars and timed to go off. The attacks on the yellow and red lines indicated similar plots. Two explosions reportedly occurred at 7:35 a.m. at L'Enfant Plaza on the yellow line, and four explosions took place at Metro Center on the red line at 7:35 a.m. as well. An hour later, emergency officials report that the death toll is over four hundred and counting.

Several days later, the Federal Bureau of Investigation (FBI) reports that they have information about a cell in the United States that perpetrated the attack. Three of the ten individuals have been apprehended; the remaining seven are at large. Through their questioning of these three individuals, the FBI has learned that all of the individuals in the cell were born in the United States and were U.S. citizens. Two of the individuals were American Protestant converts to Islam, three were of Pakistani descent, one was of Egyptian descent, two were of Somali descent, and two were of Yemeni descent. There were eight men and two women in the cell. Their ages ranged from eighteen to thirty-six. Three were unemployed, two were teachers in a local school, and two were mechanics. Of the remaining three, one was a university professor, another, a student at a local university, and the last, a scientist. All of the members of the cell attended the same mosque in Virginia. They were heavily influenced by the teachings of the imam, who talked about the duty of jihad, depicted as a holy war, and the evils of the U.S. government.

While this story is obviously made up, the type of information it contains is really not so far from the truth. It provides an accurate depiction of the extremist threat, which is very real and very much a danger to the national security of the United States and its allies. This threat begins and ends with the recruits. The first question we ask when dealing with those individuals and groups who seek to harm the United States should be, what led them down this path? Some of these individuals belong to the al-Qaida network.

The Threat

At some point, while watching the evening news, reading a newspaper or magazine, perusing a book on terrorism, or having a discussion with friends and colleagues, we have seen, read, or heard such names, places, and things as Usama bin Ladin, Ayman al-Zawahiri, Muhammad Atta, Khalid Shaykh Muhammad, Richard Reid, Fazul Abdullah Muhammad, Khalfan Gailani, ricin, the Finsbury Park Mosque, the Milan Islamic Cultural Institute, and madrassahs. What do all of these people, places, and things have in common? In a strategic sense, they are significant parts of the same loosely affiliated network with global reach called al-Qaida.

For example, Usama bin Ladin, a wealthy Saudi, is the founder and head of al-Qaida. He has made it his mission in life to spend his considerable fortune attempting to roll back U.S. influence in the Muslim world and to advance his extremist brand of Islam with the hopes of establishing his conception of "true Islamic states" in Muslim countries. In a videotape broadcast in October 2001, bin Ladin admitted to al-Qaida's role in the 9/11 attacks on the Pentagon and World Trade Center in the United States. He described the attack on the World Trade Center as follows:

> We calculated in advance the number of casualties from the enemy who would be killed based on the position of the tower. We calculated that the floors that would be hit would be three or four floors. I was the most optimistic of them all. . . . Due to my experience in this field, I was thinking that the fire from the gas in the plane would melt the iron structure of the building and collapse the area where the plane hit and all the floors above it only. This is all that we had hoped for.[1]

Ayman al-Zawahiri, an Egyptian and trained physician, is considered bin Ladin's principal deputy in the network. Al-Zawahiri grew up in Maadi, a middle-class suburb of Cairo. He became involved with, and eventually led, the Egyptian extremist group Islamic Jihad. While operating with, and providing advice to, bin Ladin for many years, he only formally integrated himself and his staunchest supporters into the al-Qaida network in 1998, creating a formidable partnership. Muhammad Atta, also an Egyptian, became involved with al-Qaida while a college student in Hamburg, Germany. He participated in paramilitary training in Afghanistan, eventually killing thousands of people, including himself, when he flew a plane into the World Trade Center on September 11, 2001. The image of Atta's face, which was plastered over the papers during the days following this horrible attack on U.S. soil, is difficult to forget.

Khalid Shaykh Muhammad, a Kuwaiti, was a significant leader and operational planner in al-Qaida. Khalid Shaykh Muhammad is also the uncle of convicted 1993 World Trade Center bomber Ramzi Yousef. According to a news report, Muhammad directed the first World Trade Center attack and participated with Yousef in the planning of the failed 1995 Bojinka plot to down American airliners over the Pacific and crash a plane into the headquarters of the Central Intelligence Agency (CIA).[2] After 9/11, al-Jazirah reporter Yosri Fouda traveled to Pakistan, where he conducted an interview with Khalid Shaykh Muhammad and Ramzi bin al-Shibh, another significant operator in al-Qaida. In the interview, Muhammad discussed his role in the organization. He claimed to be the brains behind al-Qaida's 9/11 plot and referred to the attack as the "holy raids on Washington and New York."

Khalid Shaykh Muhammad was captured in March 2003 in Pakistan and remains incarcerated. Officials in the U.S. government claim that since his capture, he has provided valuable information on operatives and plots by the al-Qaida network.

Relying solely on the former examples would give the general impression that all members of the al-Qaida network are of Middle Eastern descent. Yet, nothing is further from the truth. On another continent, other al-Qaida members have been actively plotting against the United States. Born in the Comoros Islands, Fazul Abdullah Muhammad emerged to become a central figure in al-Qaida's East African network. He was indicted in absentia on September 17, 1998, for his alleged involvement in the 1998 bombings of the U.S. embassies in Dar es Salaam, Tanzania, and in Nairobi, Kenya. Fazul, still at large, continues to plan operations for al-Qaida and remains a central figure in the network. Khalfan Gailani, a Tanzanian, was also wanted for his part in the U.S. Embassy bombings. He was finally apprehended in July 2004 after a reported twelve-hour firefight with Pakistani authorities.[3] Others converted to Islam and joined the al-Qaida network. For example, shortly after the events on 9/11, British citizen and Muslim convert Richard Reid boarded a flight to the United States. On an al-Qaida mission, he attempted to light his explosive-laden shoes, intending to blow up the plane. However, alert passengers on board the aircraft thwarted his attempt, and he was later convicted for his role in the plot. Based on that incident, Reid became known as the "shoe bomber."

Years after 9/11, a stash of the poison ricin, derived from the beans of the castor plant, was discovered in a North London apartment. Several Algerians were arrested in connection with the discovery, and fears again came to light about al-Qaida's ability to use biological, chemical, and nuclear weapons. Several places of worship also became the focus of investigations and news stories. For example, the North London Central Mosque, more popularly known as the Finsbury Park Mosque, became implicated as a central node in the facilitation of terrorist activities worldwide. The same is true of the Islamic Cultural Institute in Milan, Italy, which came under close scrutiny due to its involvement in suspicious activities.

Finally, madrassahs are religious schools, and, unfortunately, some of these schools across the globe support or preach extremism. They have become the focus of intense observation, and the United States has put significant pressure on, for example, countries in South and Southeast Asia to rein in those madrassahs that are preaching extremist views and providing training to future extremists.

The Recruits

Now, consider the following two stories about al-Qaida recruits:

Our first story is about an individual whom we will refer to, for now, by his nom de guerre: Abdullah al-Muhajir. Al-Muhajir was born in 1970 in Brooklyn, New York; he was also born into a family of Catholics and is of Puerto Rican descent. Several years later, he and his family moved to Chicago. He eventually joined a gang called the Maniac Latin Disciples. At fifteen he landed in a juvenile center. He and his associate had mugged a man; when the individual tried to chase them down, al-Muhajir's associate stabbed the man in the stomach, al-Muhajir kicked him in the head, and the man subsequently died. According to a newspaper account, al-Muhajir kicked the victim in the head because he "felt like it."[4]

In 1991, al-Muhajir moved to South Florida with his family. Not long afterward, he ended up in prison when he fired a gun at another motorist's windshield after a traffic accident. After his release from prison in 1992, he found work at a fast-food restaurant and married another employee, a Jamaican. His boss, a Muslim named Muhammad Javed Qureshi, was one of the founders of the School of Islamic Studies. After attending Qureshi's mosque, al-Muhajir converted to Islam. Al-Muhajir eventually quit his job in 1993 and went in search of more money. He found employment doing maintenance at a country club. He also attended various mosques, becoming more involved in his newly embraced religion.[5] At the end of 1998, al-Muhajir left his American wife and went to Egypt—to study religion, he claimed. There he married an Egyptian woman and had two children. From Egypt he eventually found his way to the al-Qaida camps of Afghanistan. In May 2002, he boarded a flight in Zurich, Switzerland, to the United States and was arrested by U.S. authorities.

Our second story involves a Yemeni-born member of the al-Qaida network who was significantly involved in the 9/11 plot. He is believed to have been the intended twentieth hijacker in the plot, but failed to get a visa to the United States and was unable to carry out his mission.

This particular individual, known by the alias Ahad Sabet, was born in Yemen in 1972. We know that he came from Yemen to Germany in 1994 by ship. His stated reason for coming to Germany was political asylum, which he applied for upon his arrival in the country. In 1995, however, his application was rejected. While in Germany, he found employment at a company outside of Hamburg called the Hay Computing Service. Also working there were two other individuals involved in the 9/11 plot, Muhammad Atta and Marwan al-Shihi. In October 1998, Sabet moved to the now infamous apartment at 54 Marienstrasse, which was used by the Hamburg cell at the time. In 1999, he traveled to Afghanistan to participate in al-Qaida's training camps. He was captured during a raid in Pakistan in September 2002.

José Padilla is the recruit in the first story. He is accused of coming to the United States to execute a "dirty bomb" plot to kill Americans. Padilla is currently in U.S. custody and in November 2005 was charged "with providing—and conspiring to provide—material support to terrorists, and conspiring to murder individuals who are overseas."[6] Ramzi bin al-Shibh is the recruit in the second story. He is currently incarcerated at Guantánamo Bay, Cuba, and stands accused of being both an al-Qaida member and an integral part of the planning of 9/11.

All of the examples of the people and places provided above, as well as the profiles of the two recruits, demonstrate that al-Qaida members are of grave concern to the United States and its allies. They are the threatening pieces that comprise al-Qaida. The examples of Padilla and bin al-Shibh are provided up front to demonstrate al-Qaida's diversity: They demonstrate that two very different people can end up in the same network. Hopefully, these examples will help dispel some of the stereotypes associated with the individuals who make up the al-Qaida network.

But What Is the "Network" Exactly?

This book focuses on the recruitment of individuals into the wider al-Qaida network. The al-Qaida network is a widespread and loosely organized affiliation of individuals and groups who use violence as a strategy for achieving their objectives. The express purpose of those in this network is to strike blows against the United States and its perceived allies, who are seen as directly causing or contributing to the suffering of Muslims worldwide. They seek the demise of these "corrupt" regimes. Their alternative to these regimes is the creation of true Islamic states worldwide.

At times, certain groups in this network may use names other than al-Qaida. Furthermore, while some individuals and groups in the network may have a regional rather than a transnational focus, they do tend to share al-Qaida's core ideological views and goals; that is, the United States and its allies are to blame for Muslim ills worldwide. The indictments range from U.S. support for corrupt Arab regimes, particularly Saudi Arabia and Egypt, to the post-9/11 U.S. invasions of Muslim countries, notably Afghanistan and Iraq. Of significance to these groups as well is their clearly defined enemy Israel. The claim is that the United States provides unquestioning support to Israel, a country blamed for the immense suffering of the Palestinian people. Added to this list of indictments is the perceived invasion of Muslim lands by Western culture.

At times, participants in this network may act independently of each other. Often, they share the same logistical networks if, for example, one group has an already established, working route. The routes shared by several groups may also already be in use by other established criminal enterprises. Participants in the network may also share financial support. For instance, they may draw from the same funding sources, including Usama bin Ladin, Ayman al-Zawahiri, and those wealthy individuals and groups sympathetic to the cause. They may use the same banks and *hawalas*, unregulated international financing networks, to move money. They can also interact with certain organizations to provide cover for their extremist activities, including fundraising. Individuals and groups in the network may also share their training expertise through information sharing or joint exercises in camps. Individuals in these groups can also jointly engage in operational planning against a target of mutual interest. And, when all is said and done, all of these individuals and groups in the network pose a direct threat to the national security of the United States and its allies.

The Network Composition: That Was Then

Before 9/11 many groups in the network used Afghanistan as a base of operations and a training ground to launch their holy wars against their stated enemies. Due to the hospitality of the Mullah Omar and the Taliban, many of the fighters who participated in the war against the Soviets settled in Afghanistan, often bringing their families with them or finding brides and beginning their families. These individuals formed the base of al-Qaida. Those firmly entrenched had considerable expertise in fighting a foreign enemy. After all, they had fought against the Soviets and believed they had driven them from Afghanistan, allowing for the true Islamic government, the Taliban, to take hold of the country. These individuals represented those to be looked up to, the leaders of the struggle against the infidels, or unbelievers. They were the revered leadership.

Other individuals and groups, who were intent on waging their own battles in their countries at home, were also able to come to Afghanistan and interact with those already firmly entrenched in the network. North Africans, Arabs, Pakistanis, Africans, Uzbeks, Uighers, and many other ethnic or national groups could be found in Afghanistan. It has been estimated that between May 1996 and September 11, 2001, twenty thousand individuals trained at camps in Afghanistan, although far fewer are believed to have gone on to receive specialized training.[7] This base of operations in Afghanistan served to train individuals and groups so that they could take their fight back home in the name of Islam, with the hope of establishing what they claimed to be true Islamic governments. Others would unite with bin Ladin to plan against the enemy in a distant land, the United States. All shared the common understanding that Islam was the rightful path to changing a world order dominated by regimes that followed a different way from what they believed to be the rightful composition of the world.

The Network Composition: This Is Now

Unfortunately, historical accounts of the network do not provide us with information regarding its current makeup and composition. After 9/11, the al-Qaida base of operations in Afghanistan was decimated during Operation Enduring Freedom. Training camps were destroyed and many individuals who formed the core of the network dispersed to other places or went underground. Many other individuals in the network were captured or killed. However, as would become evident, taking away the base of operations in Afghanistan only marked the beginning of the fight against the network and its links worldwide.

After the Afghan base became less of a direct threat, countries across the world looked inward and embarked on efforts to destroy the functioning of the network, which extended far beyond the borders of Afghanistan into their own lands. Law-enforcement and intelligence agencies in numerous countries began trying to attack al-Qaida on all levels. Unfortunately, legislators and policymakers found that existing legislation was inadequate to hold or prosecute those apprehended for terrorist offences. Nevertheless, many countries, notably those in Europe, began arresting associated individuals and rolling up operational cell after operational cell. In Great Britain, for example, many North Africans were arrested and questioned. In another example, in 2004, Eisa al-Hindi, a leader in the network operating in Great Britain, was arrested. He allegedly had access to detailed surveillance of five financial institutions in Washington, D.C., New Jersey, and New York.[8] Great Britain was not the only country making arrests. Other European countries attempted to rout out cells as well. Countries outside of Europe followed suit when it became clear that these groups and individuals posed a direct threat to their survivability. One such country was Saudi Arabia, which begin to deal with attacks within its own borders conducted by home-grown extremists.

In addition, individuals who had been allowed to operate almost unfettered, such as those who served as "spiritual" guides for the network, were arrested or brought in for questioning. For example, in February 2003, Abu Hamza al-Masri, a fiery cleric who operated out of the Finsbury Park Mosque in London, was banned from preaching there. However, he continued to preach on the street outside the mosque. Al-Masri is in the process of appealing an attempt to deport him to the United States on charges pertaining to his links to terrorism in the United States.[9] Abdul Nacer Benbrika, also known as Abu Bakr, was charged by the Australian government in November 2005 with being a member of a terrorist group. Bakr, who claims he was only a teacher of the Koran and the Sunna, was born in Algeria, but had lived in Australia since 1989.[10] Indonesian cleric, Abu Bakar Bashir, long considered the spiritual guide for the group Jemaah Islamiyah, was arrested and questioned by Indonesian authorities. He was later convicted of conspiracy in the 2002 attacks in Bali.

Countries united in their efforts to attack al-Qaida's vast financial networks. The United States pressured countries to provide oversight of their lax banking practices, especially in the Middle East. The transfer of money was tracked, and assets known to support extremist activities were frozen. The *hawala* networks gained more attention from authorities because they allowed individuals to transfer cash (internationally or locally) without using a bank.[11] The use of these *hawalas* posed a significant challenge to law-enforcement agencies trying to track the money trail and shut down its sources.

Afghanistan certainly provided a place where the leadership could lead and plan operations and where training camps could be used to create the network's next generations of fighters and operatives. Now that this base has been destroyed, there have been a lot of discussions about where the next base of operations will be set up. Some have suggested Somalia, Yemen, Chechnya, and the northwestern frontier region of Pakistan as alternatives. Certainly, a base of operations would provide a place for the leadership to operate and train its recruits for its fight against its enemies. But they will not likely ever be able to replicate what was once the Afghan base of operations. The United States and other countries are too cognizant of what would happen if another al-Qaida base of operations were allowed to exist unencumbered and to operate freely to plan future attacks against the network's enemies. Furthermore, the network has proven adaptable in that it is carrying out operations worldwide without that base of operations: Training camps are still being set up, recruits are still being trained, money is still being raised and disbursed, and operations are still being planned.

In our effort to deal with the network, assets will continue to be frozen, banks will be regulated, and individuals will be captured or killed. The network will also continue to evolve and to adapt to these efforts to destroy it. New leaders will emerge as old ones die or are captured; training camps will emerge in different places; new technologies will be adopted to replace those that are figured out or otherwise compromised. Thus, it will always be difficult to talk about the exact nature of the network at a given time as we will always be racing to keep up with events.

Currently, many groups and individuals can be considered part of the al-Qaida network. Our treatment of the network here is purposefully broad in order to capture its essence and to provide an understanding of its diverse nature. Our discussion of the network is not intended to be exhaustive. As a result, there are obviously many more groups operating, which can be included under the al-Qaida network umbrella, than are mentioned. Additionally, to complicate matters, intragroup fighting at times generates offshoots that then emerge under different names. Therefore, these offshoots comprise the same players, just in different positions and under other names. Nevertheless, those groups discussed here provide a good representation of the types of groups that form the network and thus satisfy our purpose, which is to provide a general understanding of the breadth of the network. Therefore, the network includes, but is not limited to the following:

1. Core Network (the leadership and its direct supporters)
2. Middle East Network (i.e., Saudi al-Qaida, al-Qaida in Iraq)
3. Southeast Asia Network (i.e., Jemaah Islamiyah)
4. North Africa/Europe Network (i.e., Salafist Group for Call and Combat, Tunisian Combatant Group, Libyan Islamic Fighting Group, Moroccan Islamic Combatant Group, Salafiyah Jihadiyah, al-Muhajiroun)
5. Central Asian Network (i.e., Islamic Movement of Uzbekistan)
6. South Asian Network (i.e., Harakat ul-Mujahidin, Lashkar-i-Taiba, Jaish-i-Muhammad)

The Core

Chapter 2 will provide a detailed discussion of the evolution of al-Qaida's "core" network. This core comprises the central leaders of al-Qaida, as well as its core of supporters, who are usually not affiliated with any other group in the network. Prior to Operation Enduring Freedom, the core group operated from Afghanistan with a hierarchical command-and-control structure. Coalition efforts in Afghanistan essentially destroyed al-Qaida's primary operating base and forced the network to adopt a more decentralized structure. The network's leading figures, Usama bin Ladin and Dr. Ayman al-Zawahiri, continue to exert their influence over the global, loosely affiliated core network, calling for an international jihad against the United States and its allies. Yet, as already mentioned, other groups in the network can still act autonomously from the core. Having said that, however, the individuals and groups in the network can be so intertwined that is increasingly difficult to distinguish easily between those in the core and those on the periphery, especially due to overlapping memberships.

Middle East

Al-Qaida in Iraq is a network of various groups that joined together under the Mujahidin Shura Council. This network is leading the insurgency against coalition troops and the government in Iraq. The network conducts operations to undermine stability and decrease support for the coalition and the Iraqi government. Until his death in June 2006, the network was lead by Abu Musab al-Zarqawi, a Jordanian. Even though he ran the network in Iraq, he had an interest in overthrowing the Jordanian monarchy and had conducted operations there as well. Al-Zarqawi was succeeded by Abu Hamza al-Mujahir, an Egyptian, who has a history of involvment in Egyptian Islamic Jihad, Ayman al-Zawahiri's group. Perhaps this may impact the nature of future operations. Despite their common goal to drive out coalition forces and to destroy the Iraqi government, these individuals and groups in the Iraq network may have separate long-term interests. However, they tend to share the belief that they are creating the next Afghanistan, that is, a true Islamic government amenable to those likeminded in their pursuits around the world. Iraq is now viewed as a central node from which the network can wage international jihad.[12]

Before taking the reins of power in Iraq, al-Zarqawi operated within al-Qaida network circles and amassed a large network of contacts. He wasn't, by any stretch of the imagination, viewed as a rising leader in the network. He certainly was not someone who would be considered a successor for Usama bin Ladin or Ayman al-Zawahiri. An unfortunate aftereffect of the U.S.-led war in Iraq was the creation of an opportunity for members of the network to point to another example of infidel aggression against a Muslim country. It was also a rallying call for the recruitment of fighters and operatives.

Individuals poured in from all over the Muslim world to drive the U.S.-led coalition out of Iraq. Those who fought against coalition forces learned significant skills, including bomb making, and some have already returned to their countries as trained fighters. They have also built their own network of contacts from those who had also participated in the call to jihad, or holy war. This has become a serious cause for concern by governments already on al-Qaida's hit list: They see the beginnings of trained cells that will be one day turned against them.

Southeast Asia

Jemaah Islamiyah is al-Qaida's Southeast Asian affiliate. The group principally operates in Indonesia; however, it has connections throughout the region, notably in Malaysia and the Philippines. Jemaah Islamiyah's spiritual leaders and cofounders are Abu Bakar Bashir and Abdullah Sungkar. Bashir and Sungkar established the group in the early 1990s with the goal of overthrowing Suharto's regime in Indonesia and instituting an Islamic caliphate in Southeast Asia.

North Africa/Europe

The Armed Islamic Group (GIA) was formed in the early 1990s when the Algerian government cancelled elections due to the foreseeable victory of the Islamic Salvation Front. Consequently, the GIA set out on a violent campaign to overthrow the Algerian regime and to institute an Islamic state. In the mid-1990s, infighting within the GIA became a significant problem. Many members within the group and other extremist groups, notably al-Qaida, allegedly did not support the violent campaign that the GIA was waging on innocent Algerians.[13] Hassan Hattab and hundreds of fighters from the original GIA broke away and formed the Salafist Group for Call and Combat (GSPC). The GSPC shares the same objectives as the GIA, which are to overthrow the Algerian government and establish an Islamic state. Many members of the GSPC are closely affiliated with the al-Qaida network. This is especially true of the GSPC's network in Europe.

In 2000, Tarek Maaroufi and Saifallah Ben Hassine founded the Tunisian Combatant Group, whose objective is the removal of the Tunisian government and the creation of an Islamic state. They operate throughout North Africa and Europe and are closely aligned with the GSPC.[14]

In the mid-1990s, a group of Libyans who fought in the Afghan war with the support of the isolated clergy set up the Libyan Islamic Fighting Group

(LIFG).[15] Their primary goal is to overthrow Libya's leader, Muammar al-Qaddafi, and to establish an Islamic state. While their efforts have mainly focused on assassinating al-Qaddafi and fighting Libyan security forces, some members are also engaged in al-Qaida's international jihad against the United States.[16] The group mainly operates in Libya but has connections throughout North Africa and in Great Britain.

Former Moroccan fighters who fought in the Afghan war formed the Moroccan Islamic Combatant Group (MICG) in the late 1990s. They claim to want to institute an Islamic state in Morocco and also support bin Ladin's war against the West.[17] The group operates throughout North Africa and Europe. Salafiyah Jihadiyah is an extension of the MICG, sharing its goals and operating throughout Europe and North Africa.

In 1996, the Syrian cleric Shaykh Omar Bakri Muhammad founded the group al-Muhajiroun, whose goal is to establish a global Islamic state. Al-Muhajiroun's base of operations is Great Britain, yet it has global support. The group allegedly sent funds to the Taliban following 9/11, along with recruits to fight in Afghanistan.[18] Furthermore, Bakri openly supports bin Ladin and has called for British Muslims to join in the global jihad.[19]

Central Asia

The Islamic Movement of Uzbekistan (IMU), which operates in Central Asia, principally in Uzbekistan, is closely affiliated with al-Qaida. Tohir Yudalshev and Juma Namangani established the group in the late 1990s. The IMU's objectives are to overthrow Uzbekistan's government and to establish an Islamic state in the region. They are heavily involved in drug trafficking and allegedly focus on targeting U.S. military interests in the region.[20]

The Islamic Jihad Group is an offshoot of the IMU and operates in Central Asia. It has conducted numerous attacks in the region, and members of the group claim that the leadership shares a close relationship with bin Ladin.[21] When the group attacked the American and Israeli embassies in Uzbekistan in 2004, it released a statement claiming that the attacks were a demonstration of support for fighters in Palestine, Afghanistan, and Iraq.[22]

South Asia

Harakat ul-Mujahidin, or the "Movement of the Mujahidin," formerly known as Harakat ul-Ansar, originally focused its efforts in Kashmir. Fazlur Rehman Khalil and Masood Azhar led the group throughout the 1990s until it splintered.[23] Following the split, Fazlur Rehman Khalil and the Pashtuns extended their area of operations beyond Kashmir and into the international jihad. The group ran some of bin Ladin's camps in Afghanistan and, in 1998, was included in his International Islamic Front for Jihad against the Crusaders and Jews.

In 2000, a split occurred in Harakat ul-Mujahidin between Punjabis and Pashtuns.[24] The Punjabi faction, led by Masood Azhar, subsequently formed Jaish-i-Muhammad, or "Army of Muhammad." Jaish-i-Muhammad has orchestrated attacks not only in Kashmir but also within Pakistan. One attack in 2002 targeted a Christian church typically visited by Americans, demonstrating that the group's objectives extend beyond the conflict in Kashmir. The group has also concentrated its recruitment efforts among South Asian minority communities in Britain.[25]

The aim of Lashkar-i-Taiba, or "Army of the Pure," is to establish an Islamic state in India and Kashmir. However, the group is associated with the al-Qaida network, as is evidenced by bin Ladin's inclusion of the group in his International Islamic Front for Jihad against the Crusaders and Jews.[26] Despite reported crackdowns by Pakistani authorities, Lashkar-i-Taiba has executed numerous operations and allegedly provided support to al-Qaida members who fled to Kashmir.[27]

A Different Direction

A number of excellent books have been written about, or deal in part with, the al-Qaida network and its threat to the United States.[28] While we cannot do justice to all of these works here, a more detailed summary of some of the more popular titles is provided.

In *Inside Al Qaeda*, Rohan Gunaratna provides a comprehensive discussion of the al-Qaida network. He describes how the organization was originally structured and provides an understanding of how al-Qaida evolved into a decentralized global network. He identifies specific regions throughout the world where al-Qaida either penetrated already-established extremist groups or set up their own regional offices. For example, Gunaratna explains how al-Qaida invested significant time and resources in Great Britain, which ultimately became a primary recruitment location for the network. The book concludes with short-, mid-, and long-term military and nonmilitary responses to countering al-Qaida.[29]

In his account of al-Qaida, *Holy War, Inc.*, Peter Bergen relates his personal experience interviewing bin Ladin and many other extremists. He captures a unique perspective of al-Qaida and the man behind the organization. His interview with bin Ladin illustrates how bin Ladin has taken it upon himself to speak on behalf of all Muslims by publicizing their alleged hatred of the United States due to its foreign policy regarding the Arab world. Furthermore, Bergen explains how al-Qaida evolved into a global organization with all the modern technology that is typical of many American corporations. He describes how they have used modern technologies such as laptops, cellular phones, CD-ROMs, and the Internet, to wage a religious war on America that condemns Western culture and values. Bergen labels this phenomenon "Holy War, Inc."[30]

In *The Age of Sacred Terror*, Daniel Benjamin and Steven Simon provide a comprehensive picture of radical Islam's history and its development in the past century. The book describes the path bin Ladin's life took from his origins as the son of a Saudi millionaire to his leadership of the most significant movement that threatens U.S. national security today. Benjamin and Simon provide insight into how the U.S. government attempted to counter the threat from al-Qaida before and after the 9/11 attacks. However, they also discuss the ways in which the U.S. government failed to acknowledge the seriousness of al-Qaida prior to 9/11.[31]

In *The Cell: Inside the 9/11 Plot, and Why the FBI and CIA Failed to Stop It*, John Miller and Michael Stone provide insight into the extremists operating in the United States, beginning with the 1990 assassination of Rabbi Meir Kahane in 1990 by El Said Nosair, an individual born in Egypt. They also discuss at length the individuals who carried out the first World Trade Center attack, provide a discussion of 9/11, and give an account of the bureaucratic wrangling of the counterterrorism community and its apparent failure to prevent terrorist acts against the United States.[32]

In *Understanding Terror Networks*, Marc Sageman presents a view of how individuals join the network, which he refers to as the global Salafi jihad. From his perspective, the organization does not recruit individuals. Rather, through their own initiative, individuals seek out the network. In his view, recruitment occurs through three main steps: social affiliation with the jihad, intensification of the individual's beliefs, which leads to an acceptance of the global Salafi jihad ideology, and formal acceptance to the jihad through a link in the jihad network. Furthermore, Sageman highlights the importance of social bonds in this process. Building off this premise, he constructs the Salafi jihad's social network, which includes four clusters: the central staff, core Arabs, Maghreb Arabs, and Southeast Asians. Finally, he identifies ways in which the law-enforcement community, intelligence community, and other government agencies can counter the global Salafi terror network.[33]

In *Taliban: Militant Islam, Oil and Fundamentalism in Central Asia*, Ahmed Rashid explores how the relationship between bin Ladin and the Taliban in Afghanistan developed, as well as the role that Pakistan's Interservices Intelligence Directorate (ISID) played in forging this alliance. Specifically, he identifies the pragmatic nature of the relationship between the ISID, Taliban, and bin Ladin and his Arab-Afghans. He emphasizes how bin Ladin and the Taliban provided support to the ISID by training Kashmiri fighters, while ISID protected bin Ladin by not cooperating with the United States in the country's quest to capture him in the late 1990s. Conversely, he shows how the Taliban used bin Ladin for his money and initially attempted to use their knowledge of his whereabouts to their advantage when dealing with the United States in gaining their recognition as Afghanistan's ruling government. Rashid explains that when the Taliban didn't receive official recognition by the United States, they reacted by giving bin Ladin and his Arab-Afghans full protection. Furthermore, Rashid provides a comprehensive explanation of Pakistan's dealings with Afghanistan in the 1990s, specifically with regard to its attempt to control the Taliban. This eventually led to what he calls "Talibanization."[34]

In *Ghost Wars: The Secret History of the CIA, Afghanistan, and Bin Laden from the Soviet Invasion to September 10, 2001*, Steve Coll provides insight into the role that the United States, especially the CIA, played in supporting the Afghan resistance against the Soviets. He examines the relationships between the United States and Pakistan's ISID, Saudi Intelligence, and several different Afghan mujahidin groups and leaders throughout this period. He further discusses how these relationships changed over time as the interests of the United States changed. Coll explains how the United States remained unaware of the developing threat posed by Arab extremists operating in Afghanistan in the early 1990s to the stability and future of Afghanistan and, ultimately, to U.S. national security. Additionally, he explains America's "hands-off" policy with regard to Afghanistan from 1992 through late 2001, a period during which the United States had no policy for Afghanistan. Consequently, Coll builds the case that due to America's indifference to the region after Soviet withdrawal, the United States enabled the Arab extremists led by bin Ladin to build an infrastructure from which to attack the United States.[35]

In *Imperial Hubris: Why the West Is Losing the War on Terror*, Michael Scheuer, the former head of the bin Ladin unit at the CIA, gives an account of the dealings of the United States with the Arab-Afghans and the bin Ladin network. He indicts the United States for failing to understand the enemy and argues that attacks against the United States by Usama bin Ladin are the result of U.S. policies in the Muslim world, not of Muslim hatred of U.S. values.[36]

In *The Road to Al-Qaeda: The Story of bin Laden's Right-Hand Man*, Montasser al-Zayyat provides a portrait of Ayman al-Zawahiri and his ascendancy as bin Ladin's right-hand man.[37] Al-Zayyat met al-Zawahiri in an Egyptian prison after the Egyptian authorities rounded up al-Zawahiri and many other individuals following the assassination of Anwar al-Sadat in 1981. As a result, al-Zayyat is able to provide unique insights into al-Zawahiri's personality and dealings with other individuals in the Egyptian extremist groups. Al-Zayyat also sheds light on influences on al-Zawahiri's thinking, including the Egyptian dissident and writer Sayyid Qutb.

An interesting and new addition to the books on al-Qaida is Quintan Wiktorowicz's *Radical Islam Rising: Muslim Extremism in the West*.[38] Wiktorowicz deals with the British-based group al-Muhajiroun. Essentially, he uses this group as a case study and makes the argument that individuals participate in what he terms radical Islamic activism because they are "inspired by a cognitive opening that shakes certitude in previously accepted beliefs." Furthermore, he argues, "individuals must be willing to expose themselves to new ways of thinking and worldviews, and a cognitive opening helps facilitate possible receptivity."[39] He goes on to say that a number of things can spark a cognitive opening, including experiences with discrimination, socioeconomic crisis, and political repression. In his book, he also provides a thorough discussion of the type of information that the group uses to draw in its members.

Recruitment

So many different aspects of the al-Qaida network can be addressed and studied. This book is about individuals and recruitment into the al-Qaida network. Many things come to mind when the word "recruitment" is used, and there can be numerous parts to the so-called recruitment process. Just what is this book talking about with regard to recruitment? While this book could talk about many different aspects, it is mainly concerned with those aspects that tend to be the most misunderstood and aren't particularly well studied. Therefore, this is principally a book about the individuals, their experiences, and their reasoning and justification for participation in the network. Put another way, this book seeks to explain the why, how, and where of recruitment, which will provide a necessary understanding of one of the most important issues facing us today. To the best of our knowledge, even though recruitment is mentioned in articles and books, no book has yet provided a thorough assessment of this particular subject. Wiktorowicz comes closest in his focused treatment of individuals and their recruitment into al-Muhajiroun. It is not surprising that some of the same claims are made in our book. Both books see individuals as important, and both treat the information used to entice members as exceptionally important in a discussion of recruitment. However, our book differs from his in very important ways. He tends to be more process-oriented, while we focus solely on the individuals, their stories, and the wide-ranging types of information used in the network's propaganda machine, not on the process of recruitment. Additionally, his book is a case study of one group, while this book gives a more broad-brush treatment of the network. Finally, this book deals with a wide variety of solutions that can be used to ameliorate the problem of recruitment. Many of these solutions can be traced to individual motivation—the reason(s) individuals joined in the first place.

More specifically, our discussion of recruitment includes several aspects of the individual and the individual's information environment. With regard to the individual, particular aspects of recruitment are focused on, namely, the recruits' demographic backgrounds and their central motivation(s). In addition, we also look in great detail at the content of the information used to entice them, how they receive this information, and the places where this information is found. This book proposes to look at this issue in a different way, one that homes in on the root of the problem because, ultimately, our view of the problem shapes our policy responses. While a great deal can be learned by studying other aspects of recruitment, here lies the answers to the question, why do they want to hurt the United States and its allies? Unfortunately, if recruitment is allowed to continue at the same pace, more and more individuals will simply join this network bent on causing harm to the United States, its citizens, and its allies.

The Crazies among Us and Other Popular Views

Sadly, five years since that tragic day on September 11, 2001, the United States continues to be under threat by individuals very committed to harming its citizens both at home and abroad, as well as its allies. Since 9/11, there have been numerous discussions in op-ed pieces and journalistic articles about why people join extremist organizations, particularly the al-Qaida network. Oftentimes, these articles do not provide grounded evidence for their thinking on the subject, and generally speaking, they present emotional and biased views. They also usually revolve around four explanations: jealousy, insanity, brainwashing, and the battle between good and evil. Let's look at each of these a little more closely.

A frequent explanation is that individuals who join this network are simply jealous of the freedoms found in the United States. In other words, they hate our values. The answer, according to those who support this perspective, is very simple: To ameliorate this supposed jealousy, we need only provide them with all the things Americans hold dear, such as freedom and democracy. This argument harkens back to the old-school modernizationists found in political science departments in the 1960s, who claimed that the replication of the United States abroad would solve the world's ills. Even as this perspective was seriously challenged, it obviously did not die. Or if it did, it was somehow resurrected after September 11, 2001. Unfortunately, focusing on this explanation simplifies the complexity of the world, where social and political issues and the demands of citizens may not mirror exactly those in the United States. Dealing with those issues or finding solutions to problems in many countries may involve aspects that the United States and other Western countries will never understand if situations in other countries continue to be viewed through a Western lens.

In addition to these explanations, others argue that individuals in the network are simply crazy. Because they act in contravention to what is widely held to be acceptable behavior, they must obviously suffer from pathologies. As a case in point, consider the following letter to the editor printed in a popular U.S. magazine:

> Remembering the Dead and Waiting for Retribution . . . was right when concluding that the success of "twisted" men like [Abu Musab] Zarqawi [the self-proclaimed al Qaeda leader in Iraq] and their "hateful causes" will "over the long term . . . become impossible." I believe, however, that the media and the leaders within the Arab world have a duty to help expedite the downfall of terrorists by educating the misguided people who support al Qaeda. It is imperative that people like Zarqawi and bin Laden be viewed as demented psychopathic murderers inspired by Satan, not God. Only then will their support in the Arab world dwindle.[40]

Clearly, the writer suggests that sane individuals do not lead this network. Unfortunately, this isn't entirely the truth. Perhaps depicting extremists as crazy somehow makes us feel better that we still continue to be targeted by the network. There is absolutely no doubt that acts committed by al-Qaida extremists are atrocious on every level. However, to get us moving toward better solutions to the problems facing the United States and its allies, it is necessary to get beyond this "crazy" explanation. This idea is addressed more fully in chapter 4 on motivation, which, in addition to psychological issues, deals with some of the other reasons people join the network. For now, it is enough to say that an entire network of individuals cannot be dismissed as pathological. Some may be, and this should be noted when applicable, but it cannot be said that all of them are crazy.

Consider the perspective in the letter to the editor introduced above. The research for this book has found no compelling evidence that Usama bin Ladin is a psychopath. Granted, he may be a product of his own power designs, like many leaders, but that is a very different matter, and one that does not lend credence to the notion that he is a psychopath. On the other hand, Abu Musab al-Zarqawi is an interesting case, and given the preponderance of stories on the "normality" of those incarcerated for terrorism, he may also have been an exception to the rule. His criminal history certainly suggests that he simply may have found another outlet for his criminality by joining a terrorist organization. Whether this is an issue of pathology is open to debate. If he, as the press has reported, personally beheaded individuals in Iraq, looking into his psychological state may be warranted. Still, the explanation for this behavior may be found in the group-identity/social and political-psychological literature. In other words, when extreme stereotyping occurs, an enemy is vilified to the point where he or she is no longer seen as human, it is not surprising that individuals commit these types of atrocities against others. The examples of Bosnia, Kosovo, and the activities of the Shia militias in Iraq are cases in point. Unfortunately, with the death of Zarqawi, we may never know the full story of his psychological state.

Another popular explanation is that these individuals have been brainwashed. This view suggests a nefarious and calculating, cultlike phenomena that actively drags individuals away and reprograms their brains, after which they reemerge as committed fanatics. The family of a network bomber illustrated this perspective. After the July 2005 London bombings, the parents of one of the bombers gave their view on what had driven their son to commit such an act. In a statement through the police, they claimed that their son must have been brainwashed.[41]

The explanation that brainwashing causes recruits to join al-Qaida and attack the United States and its allies is faulty as well. It ignores the significant contribution that psychologists have made to our understanding of the functioning of groups, including issues of conformity. As will be discussed in chapter 4, individuals join the network for many reasons. Once an individual joins any group, including those in the al-Qaida network, pressures to conform are enormous; individuals lose their individualism and therefore will commit acts as part of a group that ordinarily they will not commit as individuals. This process, which psychologists call deindividuation, together with the act of extreme stereotyping of an enemy, explains significantly why individuals commit such atrocious acts on behalf of a group.

The final popular perspective we found is that there is a battle between good and evil; that is, all those opposed to the network are good, and all others are evil. It follows that evil must be destroyed by good. Unfortunately, this, like other perspectives, vastly simplifies the situation and can lead to some very dangerous courses of action, because actions aimed at destroying the network are seen as part of the greater struggle of good. Along the way, however, these policies may be doing more harm than good, especially in areas of law enforcement and intelligence.

Many who speak to this perspective do so in religious terms. This is evident in the letter to the editor presented above. In another example, then Crown Prince Abdullah of Saudi Arabia, now King Abdullah, described al-Qaida in an interview as "madness and evil" and "the work of the devil."[42] In the eyes of those who hold this view, their own religion is good, while the religion of their enemy is notably bad. This argument is entirely problematic because it brings the debate down to a level based on emotion and faith, not evidence. Furthermore, from a policy perspective, depicting a war of good versus evil in religious terms simply cannot be balanced with Western government statements asserting that this is not a war against Islam. As such, one of the goals of this book is to undercut such views and dispel the argument that religion is the recruits' only driving motivation.

The reality is that these arguments are not adequate to form the basis for solid policy. Advocating these perspectives is a very dangerous road to travel because it simplifies or misrepresents the most fundamental aspect of why individuals join the al-Qaida network and dedicate themselves to inflicting harm on Americans and their allies worldwide. These emotional responses only obscure the facts and oversimplify the issue of why individuals join such groups.

By writing about and advocating these views, the popular press perpetuates this flawed thinking and disseminates it to readers. The readers of these articles are mainstream, popular audiences, who on some level probably believe that there is at least some informed basis for these types of arguments. Needless to say, none of these explanations are solid or credible enough to rely upon. In fact, relying on emotional explanations will continue to drive U.S. policies and strategies in an increasingly dangerous direction. Only when the problem of why individuals join these networks is clearly outlined can we appropriately tailor our response.

The Academic View

Unfortunately, academics also cannot seem to settle on, or clearly articulate, a definitive reason why individuals continue to join the al-Qaida network, whose target of choice is the United States. When discussing the reasons for engaging in extremist activity, some scholars advocate psychopathological or personality-dysfunction explanations. Therefore, participating in extremism is not seen as normal behavior, and those engaging in such behavior are not representative of the norm in society. Terrorists are, according to this view, crazy, psychopathic, cold-blooded killers. A good representation of this type of approach is the work done by Jerrold Post. For example, Post maintains that political terrorists who commit violence do so in response to psychological forces. They use a "special psycho-logic" to rationalize such acts.[43]

Another theorist who advances this perspective is Abraham Kaplan. In his work, Kaplan traces extremist behavior to psychopathology, namely, a defective personality that stems from childhood experience of humiliation by an aggressor.[44] Those who identify personality disorders among extremists include Richard Pearlstein.[45]

Those academics familiar with the psychopathological literature can attest that it has certainly sparked a lot of discussion over the validity of such claims, particularly in the academic community. In dealing with this perspective, many academics tend to offer it as an explanation, then use it as a jumping-off point to clarify why this perspective is at best flawed and should be discounted. According to many academics and practitioners alike, there is simply not enough evidence to support this particular viewpoint, and many studies have indicated quite the opposite—that extremists do not suffer from pathologies at all.[46] For example, Andrew Silke argues that "research on the mental state of terrorists has found that they are rarely mad or crazy; very few suffer from personality disorders. But the body of research confirming this state of affairs has not prevented a steady and continuing stream of 'experts,' security personnel, and politicians from freely espousing and endorsing views to the contrary."[47] In addition, Clark McCauley argues that "Thirty years ago this suggestion was taken very seriously, but thirty years of research has found psychopathology and personality disorder no more likely among terrorists than non-terrorists from the same background."[48] These two statements tend to be more in line with the general perspective of this book.

Terminology

In this book, and from this point on, we have decided to avoid the value-laden term "terrorist." Terms such as "Islamic terrorist" or "Islamic extremist," which condemn an entire religious way of life for the deeds of a few, are also avoided. Using the word "Islamist" is also avoided because the term implies that those who are simply nonviolent Muslim activists should be grouped in with others who use violence to achieve their ends.

The word "extremist" is a suitable alternative for the purposes of this book and is defined here as a person who is "excessive and inappropriately enthusiastic and/or inappropriately concerned with significant life purposes, implying a focused and highly personalized interpretation of the world."[49] Later in this book, the word "Salafist" is introduced to describe the particular interpretation of Islam that these extremists are themselves using. We make exceptions to this rule on terminology only when paraphrasing or directly quoting an author. For obvious reasons, the original terminology used is preserved in such cases.

When necessary, a term that can be widely interpreted is defined to avoid confusion later. Finally, due to various translations, there are numerous spellings of the same word. We have attempted to be consistent in the spellings of certain terms; however, when quoting, we have left the original spellings intact, even if they differ from those in the written text. Also, the exact text as it appears in primary documents is used.

Organization of the Book

This book tackles the complexities of why individuals, regardless of the role they ultimately play, join a network that wants to attack the United States and its allies. There are some main issues that we must deal with. The first is why the al-Qaida network has chosen to focus on the United States and its allies. The second is why, how, and where individuals get involved in the network.

Who are the individuals of interest? For the purposes of this book, the al-Qaida network includes financial backers and fund-raisers, operators, logisticians, recruiters, trainers, and leaders. At some point, individuals filling these roles were recruited into the network. They all, in some way, shape, or form, contribute to the network, one that has explicitly sanctioned the killing of Americans and those perceived to be U.S. allies. A third and important component includes the potential strategies for dealing with the complexities of recruitment.

Chapter 2 largely deals with the first issue of why the network has chosen to focus on the United States and its allies. Here, we introduce and explain al-Qaida's background, a knowledge of which is essential to understanding the network itself and what it has evolved into today. This chapter discusses the relationship between bin Ladin and the United States during the Soviet-Afghan war and elucidates the underpinnings of his hatred for the United States. A brief history of bin Ladin's world travels and bases of operations before he went completely underground after the 9/11 attacks on the United

States is also provided. To give additional context, we deal with some of the more significant attacks by the al-Qaida network that demonstrate its breadth. Additionally, we discuss and dissect bin Ladin's fatwas (religious opinions), which, years later, lay out his well-considered argument for attacking the United States and its citizens. Through an unraveling of bin Ladin's politico-religious beliefs and arguments, the reader will gain significant insight into why bin Ladin hates the West, particularly the United States, and why he has specifically targeted the United States and its perceived allies.

The remainder of this book explains our proposed framework for understanding the why, how, and where of recruitment and the implications for dealing with it. Chapters 3 and 4 deal exclusively with individuals' attributes and recruitment. Specifically, chapter 3 addresses the demographics of the individuals who join the network, examining in particular an individual's country of origin, country of citizenship or residency, gender, age, occupation, education, and religion. This chapter discusses whether we can speak about actual demographic "profiles" of the recruits. Ultimately, we argue that while we can generalize about certain aspects, there is no "profile" of a typical recruit.

Chapter 4 specifically addresses individuals' motivations for seeking out alternatives to their lives, which ultimately leads them to join the network. Ascertaining their motivations provides us with a fundamental understanding of why individuals are vulnerable to joining the network in the first place. In the view of this book, recruits have one reason or several reasons for deciding that participation is an acceptable alternative to their present situations. These reasons vary across individuals. Specifically, we address personal, economic, social, and political motivations. Religion is relevant to all the categories. It is a central justification and a vehicle for participation. Taken together, chapters 3 and 4 provide the reader with a better understanding not only of the individuals' backgrounds but also of why they desire to join the al-Qaida network.

But this is only part of the story. This book is concerned with more than the demographics and motivations of individual recruits. Of keen interest is the type of information that these individuals rely upon in deciding to join the network. Additionally, an understanding of how and where these individuals obtain such information is discussed. This is the focus of chapter 5.

Knowing about the ways in which information is disseminated to individuals is extremely important. It helps us understand what individuals hear, read, or watch, which in turn aids them in making the decision to join. The methods focused on are speeches, fatwas, religious opinions and instruction, cassettes and audio recordings, videos, websites, chat rooms, magazines, books and essays, interviews, statements, leaflets and pamphlets, poetry, cartoons, and the personal approach. While this is not an exhaustive list of methods, it is sufficient to provide an overview of the type and content of information disseminated. Our central argument is that the motivated individual and the information converge, creating a recruit ready to take action against the United States and its allies in the name of the al-Qaida network. Thus, an individual must first be motivated before taking in the message propagated through the method and deciding to join the network.

Also significant is where this type of recruitment information is found. Determining the types of methods used by extremists in distributing this information provides us with an understanding of how recruits receive their information, while determining the locations helps explain where they acquired it. Thus, the entire environment, the methods used and the locations in which the potential recruit operates, is of interest. Indeed, the United States is up against a formidable opponent, one who has learned to infiltrate all avenues to disseminate its message. It will become readily apparent that the information is pervasive and found in many locations.

It is also important to understand that while one method may be used with one location in propagating the extremist message, at times a message is disseminated by one method through several different locations. Alternatively, a message can be disseminated through several methods in one location. For the purposes of this book, chapter 5 focuses on certain methods and provides examples of locations where these methods are found. Obviously, numerous other examples of methods and combinations within these categories by which information is spread are not mentioned.

Once an understanding of the motivation(s), methods, and locations—the environment—of the potential recruit is provided, we address ways to deal with recruitment itself. Suggested strategies are the central topic of chapter 6. These strategies include internal regime reform, changing U.S. policy, focusing on the extremist message, targeting the group, and encouraging personal interaction. Each is introduced and discussed in significant detail. It will be clear that many of these strategies can be traced back to our discussion of individual motivation, while others deal with the information found in chapter 5. None of these proposed strategies should be seen as a silver bullet that can solve the ills of the world. Some may take a significant number of years to implement, and others will face contentious policy battles. Some may never be possible or pragmatic. Many of these, especially those concerning U.S. policy change, are controversial in the eyes of many and always raise a litany of what-if questions. However, despite these challenges, all are discussed as possible solutions, and adopting any of them could aid us in our attempts to get down to the core of recruitment. The alternative is to do nothing and watch the recruits continue to pour into the network.

Having outlined the basic argument of the book, let's now turn to the historical basis of bin Ladin's hatred of the United States and some of the acts perpetrated in the name of the network.

Notes

1. Department of State, Washington File, "The 4,000 Jews Rumor," *U.S. Department of State*, October 30, 2004, available at http://usinfo.state.gov/media/Archive/2005/Jan/14-260933.html (last accessed March 10, 2005).

2. CBS. "The Mastermind," *CBS News*, March 5, 2003, available at www.cbsnews.com/stories/2002/10/09/60II/main524947.shtml (last accessed March 10, 2005).

3. Jason Burke, Paul Harris, and Martin Bright, "Suspect Arrested in Pakistan May Hold al-Qaeda's Secrets," *Observer*, August 8, 2004, available at www.guardian.co.uk/alqaida/story/0,,1278651,00.html (last accessed March 10, 2005).

4. Arian Campo-Flores and Dirk Johnson, "From Taco Bell to Al Qaeda," *Time*, June 24, 2002.

5. Campo-Flores and Johnson, "From Taco Bell to Al Qaeda."

6. ChargePadilla.org, "Padilla Indicted!" *ChargePadilla.org*, November 22, 2005, available at www.chargepadilla.org/index.html (last accessed April 15, 2006).

7. *Global Security*, "Terrorist Training Camps," *Global Security*, available at www.globalsecurity.org/military/world/para/al-qaida-camps.htm (last accessed March 10, 2005).

8. Dana Priest, "British Raids Net a Leader of Al Qaeda," *Washington Post*, August 5, 2004, available at www.washingtonpost.com/wp-dyn/articles/A40921-2004Aug4.html (last accessed March 10, 2005).

9. British Broadcasting Corporation, "Hamza Faces 11 U.S. Terror Charges," *BBC News*, May 27, 2004, available at http://news.bbc.co.uk/1/hi/england/london/3752257.stm (last accessed March 10, 2005).

10. British Broadcasting Corporation, "Profile: Abu Bakr," *BBC News*, November 8, 2005, available at http://news.bbc.co.uk/1/hi/world/asia-pacific/4416712.stm (last accessed April 15, 2006).

11. CBS, "Money-Transfer Systems, Hawala Style," *CBS News*, June 11, 2004, available at www.cbc.ca/news/background/banking/hawala.html (last accessed March 10, 2005).

12. Michael Ware, "Meet the New Jihad," *Time*, June 27, 2004, available at www.mafhoum.com/press7/200S30.htm (last accessed March 10, 2005).

13. Rohan Gunaratna, *Inside Al Qaeda* (New York: Columbia University Press, 2002).

14. Zachary Johnson. "Chronology: The Plots," *Frontline*, January 25, 2005, available at www.pbs.org/wgbh/pages/frontline/shows/front/special/cron.html (last accessed March 10, 2005).

15. Gary Gambill, "The Libyan Islamic Fighting Group (LIFG)," *Terrorism Monitor* 3, no. 6 (March 24, 2005), available at www.jamestown.org/publications_details.php?volume_id=411&issue_id=3275&article_id=2369477 (last accessed April 15, 2006).

16. Gambill, "The Libyan Islamic Fighting Group."

17. British Broadcasting Corporation, "Spain Names 'Bomb Suspect' Group," *BBC News*, March 30, 2004, available at http://news.bbc.co.uk/1/hi/world/europe/3583113.stm (last accessed March 15, 2005).

18. Colleen Gilbert, "War from Within," *Front Page Magazine*, July 26, 2005, available atwww.frontpagemag.com/Articles/ReadArticle.asp?ID=18901 (last accessed April 15, 2006).

19. Hannah Strange, "British Muslims Called to Take Up Jihad," *United Press International*, January 11, 2005, available at www.washtimes.com/upi-breaking/20050110-082616-6312r.htm (last accessed March 10, 2005).

20. Tamara Makarenko, "Central Asia's Opium Terrorists," *PBS*, 2005, available at www.pbs.org/wnet/wideangle/printable/centralasia_briefing_print.html (last accessed April 15, 2006).

21. Richard Boucher, "U.S. Department of State Designates the Islamic Jihad Group under Executive Order 13224," *U.S. Department of State*, May 26, 2005, available at www.state.gov/r/pa/prs/ps/2005/46838.htm (last accessed April 15, 2006).

22. Reuters, "Uzbekistan Arrests Blast Suspects: Suicide Bombers Hit U.S., Israeli Embassies; Death Toll Rises to 3," *Reuters*, July 31, 2004, available at www.msnbc.msn.com/id/5558327 (last accessed March 10, 2005).

23. Mariam Zahab and Olivier Roy, *Islamist Networks: The Afghan-Pakistan Connection* (New York: Columbia University Press, 2004).

24. Zahab and Roy, *Islamist Networks.*

25. Zahab and Roy, *Islamist Networks.*

26. Zahab and Roy, *Islamist Networks.*

27. Zahab and Roy, *Islamist Networks.*

28. See, for example, Yonah Alexandar and Michael Swetnam, *Usama bin Laden's al-Qaida: Profile of a Terrorist Network* (Ardsley: Transnational Publishers, 2002), Montasser Al-Zayyat, *The Road to Al-Qaeda: The Story of bin Laden's Right-Hand Man* (London: Pluto Press, 2004), Peter Bergen, *Holy War Inc.* (New York: Free Press, 2001), Daniel Benjamin and Steven Simon, *The Age of Sacred Terror* (New York: Random House, 2002), Yossef Bodansky, *Bin Ladin: The Man Who Declared War on America* (Roseville, CA: Prima Publishing, 2001), Steve Coll, *Ghost Wars: The Secret History of the CIA, Afghanistan, and Bin Laden from the Soviet Invasion to September 10, 2001* (New York: Penguin Group, 2001), Aukai Collins, *My Jihad: One American's Journey through the World of Usama Bin Laden—as a Covert Operative for the American Government* (New York: Pocket Star, 2002), Jane Corbin, *Al Qaeda: In Search of the Terror Network that Threatens the World* (New York: Nation Books, 2002), Natana Delong-Bas, *Wahhabi Islam from Revival and Reform to Global Jihad* (New York: Oxford University Press, 2004), Anthony Dennis, *Osama Bin Laden: A Psychological and*

Political Portrait (Lima, OH: Wyndham Hall Press, 2002), Steven Emerson, *American Jihad: The Terrorists Living among Us* (New York: Free Press Paperbacks, 2003), Rohan Gunaratna, *Inside Al Qaeda* (New York: Columbia University Press, 2002), Elaine Landau, *Osama bin Laden* (Brookfield, CT: Twenty-first Century Books, 2002), Walter Laqueur, *The New Terrorism: Fanaticism and the Arms of Mass Destruction* (Oxford: Oxford University Press, 1999), Abd Samad Moussaoui, *Zacarias, My Brother* (New York: Seven Stories Press, 2003), Ahmed Rashid, *Taliban Militant Islam, Oil and Fundamentalism in Central Asia* (New Haven, CT: Yale University Press 2001), Ahmed Rashid, *Jihad: The Rise of Militant Islam in Central Asia* (New York: Penguin Books, 2003), Marc Sageman, *Understanding Terror Networks* (Philadelphia: University of Pennsylvania Press, 2004), Michael Scheuer, *Imperial Hubris: Why the West Is Losing the War on Terror* (Dulles, VA: Potomac Books, 2004), Shay Shaul, *The Endless Jihad: The Mujahidin, the Taliban and Bin Laden* (New York: Livrenoir, 2002), Muhammad Sifaoui, *Inside Al Qaeda: How I Infiltrated the World's Deadliest Terrorist Organization* (New York: Thunder's Mouth Press, 2004), Quintan Wiktorowicz, *Radical Islam Rising: Muslim Extremism in the West* (Boulder, CO: Rowman & Littlefield Publishers, 2005), Mariam Zahab and Olivier Roy, *Islamist Networks: The Afghan-Pakistan Connection* (New York: Columbia University Press, 2004).

29. Rohan Gunaratna, *Inside Al Qaeda* (New York: Columbia University Press, 2002).

30. Peter Bergen, *Holy War Inc.* (New York: Free Press, 2001).

31. Daniel Benjamin and Steven Simon, *The Age of Sacred Terror* (New York: Random House, 2002).

32. John Miller and Michael Stone, *The Cell: Inside the 9/11 Plot, and Why the FBI and CIA Failed to Stop It* (New York: Hyperion, 2002).

33. Marc Sageman, *Understanding Terror Networks* (Philadelphia: University of Pennsylvania Press, 2004).

34. Ahmed Rashid, *Taliban Militant Islam, Oil and Fundamentalism in Central Asia* (New Haven, CT: Yale University Press 2001).

35. Steve Coll, *Ghost Wars: The Secret History of the CIA, Afghanistan, and Bin Laden from the Soviet Invasion to September 10, 2001* (New York: Penguin Group, 2001).

36. Michael Scheuer, *Imperial Hubris: Why the West Is Losing the War on Terror* (Dulles, VA: Potomac Books, 2004).

37. Montasser Al-Zayyat, *The Road to Al-Qaeda: The Story of bin Laden's Right-Hand Man* (London: Pluto Press, 2004).

38. Quintan Wiktorowicz, *Radical Islam Rising: Muslim Extremism in the West* (Boulder, CO: Rowman & Littlefield Publishers, 2005).

39. Wiktorowicz, *Radical Islam Rising*, 5.

40. *U.S. News & World Report*, "Letter to the Editor—Zapping Zarqawi," *U.S. News & World Report*, December 5, 2005.

41. Lynn Mcpherson, "London: Our Son Was Brainwashed to Do This Evil," *Sunday Mail*, July 11, 2005, available at www.rickross.com/reference/alqaeda/alqaeda63.html (last accessed April 15, 2006).

42. Cable News Network, "Voice Seems to Be al Qaeda Leader Calling for Uprising," *CNN*, October 1, 2005, available at http://edition.cnn.com/2005/world/meast/10/13/abdullah.abcinterview (last accessed April 15, 2006).

43. Jerrold Post, "Terrorist Psycho-logic: Terrorist Behavior as a Product of Psychological Forces," in *Origins of Terrorism*, ed. Walter Reich, 25–40 (Baltimore: Johns Hopkins University Press, 1998).

44. Abraham Kaplan, "The Psychodynamics of Terrorism," in *Behavioral and Quantitative Perspectives on Terrorism*, ed. Yohan Alexander and John Gleason, 237–57 (New York: Pergamon, 1981).

45. Richard M. Pearlstein, *The Mind of the Political Terrorist* (Wilmington, DE: Scholarly Resources, 1991).

46. Richard Braungart and Margaret Braungart, "From Protest to Terrorism: The Case of SDS and the Weathermen," in *Social Movements and Violence: Participation in Underground Organizations*, ed. Donatella della Porta, 45–78 (Greenwich, CT: JAI, 1992), John Horgan, "The Search for the Terrorist Personality," in *Terrorists, Victims and Society: Psychological Perspectives on Terrorism and Its Consequences*, ed. Andrew Silke, 4–27 (Chichester, UK: John Wiley and Sons, 2003), Andrew Silke, "Cheshire-Cat Logic: The Recurring Theme of Terrorist Abnormality in Psychological Research," *Psychology of Crime and Law* 4 (1998): 51–69, Andrew Silke, "Becoming a Terrorist," in *Terrorists, Victims and Society: Psychological Perspectives on Terrorism and Its Consequences*, ed. Andrew Silke, 29–53 (Chichester, UK: John Wiley and Sons, 2003), Andrew Silke, "Courage in Dark Places: Reflections on Terrorist Psychology," *Social Research* (spring 2004): 177–98.

47. Silke, "Courage in Dark Places," 177.

48. Clark McCauley, "The Psychology of Terrorism," in *Psychological Issues and the Response to Terrorism*, ed. Chris Stout (New York: Praeger Publishers, 2002), 5.

49. Maxwell Taylor, *The Fanatics: A Behavioral Approach to Political Violence* (London: Bassey's, 1991), 33.

CHAPTER 2

The Beginning and Context

The threat to all people, at any time, at any place in the world is real.

—British Prime Minister Tony Blair

For tragic reasons, he is one of the most infamous people of this century. Usama bin Ladin has spent many years of his life furthering an extremist view of Islam that specifically threatens the national security of the United States and its allies. He has managed to amass a significant following of individuals and groups sympathetic to his views and willing to join his network to fight his battle. Examining his life gives us an understanding of how his hatred of the United States and its allies developed and of the impact that this has had on American foreign policy. In constructing his background, we can also develop an understanding of the formation and development of the al-Qaida network. This will provide the necessary foundation for comprehending the how, why, and where of recruitment.

Bin Ladin's Early Years

In 1957, Muhammad Awad bin Ladin and Hamida al-Attas had their only son and named him Usama. Usama's father, Muhammad (now deceased), was from Yemen, and his mother, Hamida, is from Syria. Muhammad Awad bin Ladin had many wives and a total of fifty-two children. In the 1930s, he moved his family from Yemen to Saudi Arabia and eventually built his construction company into a multimillion-dollar corporation. He had a close relationship with the ruling Saudi House of al-Saud, which brought him immense financial success. At one point, Saudi king Faisal declared that all contracts would be given to the Bin Ladin Construction Corporation.[1] When Muhammad Awad bin Ladin died in 1968, Usama and his siblings inherited millions.

In 1973, after completing secondary school, bin Ladin traveled to Beirut. While there, he spent a great deal of his time frequenting bars and nightclubs. He was known to chase after women; in one incident, he found himself in a bar fight over a known prostitute.[2] In the mid-1970s, religion became more significant to bin Ladin. He returned to Saudi Arabia and participated in renovating two mosques. He started to question Western culture and felt that the problems in the Arab world were a result of Western influence. Furthermore, bin Ladin witnessed the defeat of the Arab world by Israel in the 1973 Yom Kippur War. The United States was viewed as Israel's most significant supporter during this time, which in bin Ladin's eyes further discredited the West.

In 1974, bin Ladin married Najwah Ghanim, who was also his first cousin. Bin Ladin would go on to marry several more times and allegedly has twenty-four children.[3] One of his most prominent sons, Saad bin Ladin, was born in 1979 and is also a member of al-Qaida. Also, during this time, bin Ladin studied management and economics at King Abdul Aziz University in Jiddah, Saudi Arabia. In 1979, he earned a degree in civil engineering from King Abdul Aziz University. His educational background in management and engineering would benefit him in later years, as he would become the leader of an international network and build up the infrastructures of several countries.

Soviet Invasion

When the Soviet Union invaded Afghanistan in 1979, the United States, perceiving the Soviet Union as its biggest threat, had a strategic interest in supporting the Afghan opposition. Thus, it was not surprising that the United States took this opportunity to back a group opposed to the Soviets. A significant amount of literature deals with the exact role played by the Central Intelligence Agency (CIA) in supporting the Afghans during the war.[4]

Bin Ladin arrived in Afghanistan in the early 1980s. He was just one of many Arab and Muslim men who traveled to Afghanistan to help the Afghans fight the Soviets. These men came to be known as the mujahidin (strugglers for Allah), and their goal was to defend Afghanistan and rid the country of the invading Soviet army. Bin Ladin was viewed very highly among the mujahidin because he sacrificed a comfortable life and his personal fortune for the Afghan cause. He used his financial resources and family connections in the construction business to support the Afghan fighters. For example, he built roads, dug trenches, and constructed training sites and hospitals, along with organizing the construction of many other necessary facilities.[5]

Abdullah Azzam

In Afghanistan, bin Ladin met two individuals who would significantly influence his life. One of these individuals was Shaykh Abdullah Azzam. Abdullah Azzam was born in Palestine in 1941. He received a bachelor's degree in Sharia (Islamic) law from Damascus University, and in the late 1960s, he received his master's degree in Sharia law from Al-Azhar University in Cairo, Egypt. Later, in 1973, he was awarded a scholarship from Al-Azhar and completed a Ph.D. in principles in Islamic jurisprudence. He then took a teaching position at King Abdul Aziz University. Azzam was deeply committed to advancing beliefs about jihad. He preached these beliefs and became devoted to creating an organized force that would embody this commitment to jihad.

At the beginning of the Soviet invasion of Afghanistan, Azzam moved to Pakistan and taught at the International Islamic University in Islamabad. In 1984, he and bin Ladin established the Mujahidin Services Bureau (Maktab al-Khadamat) in Peshawar. Bin Ladin was able to provide the financial means to start the bureau. This office provided support to the mujahidin by offering training to volunteers and creating and managing projects for the cause. Furthermore, the bureau worked to recruit individuals to come and fight in Afghanistan from all over the world.

Azzam became a mentor to bin Ladin.[6] His ability to recruit, organize, and manage a Soviet resistance network in Afghanistan laid the groundwork for how bin Ladin's al-Qaida group would initially operate. Thus, Azzam had es-

---

A Word on Jihad

The term "jihad" is perhaps one of the most controversial today. Numerous discussions have taken place regarding the true meaning of the word and its actual intent. It is not surprising, then, that there are different usages of the term. Literally, the word "jihad" means "to exert or strive."[1] To simplify the debate, many generally refer to the two types of jihad: the greater jihad (struggle against the self) and the lesser jihad (warring in the path of God). When the term "jihad" is used in this book, we are referring to the lesser jihad.

1. Reuven Firestone, *The Origin of Holy War in Islam* (Oxford: Oxford University Press, 1999), A. G. Noorani, *Islam and Jihad* (New Delhi: Left Word Books, 2002).

sentially imparted to bin Ladin the skills and tools he would need to become the front man in leading international jihad.

Azzam's commitment to the cause was evident in his willingness to live his life according to his beliefs. For example, he traveled throughout Afghanistan and participated in the fighting on the front line.[7] After his time in Afghanistan, he returned to Pakistan to gain further support for the Afghan jihad. Azzam was a master at mobilizing support for the Afghan jihad and had an abundant list of contacts.[8] He traveled throughout the Arab world in an attempt to inspire Muslims to participate in the jihad. In his work *Join the Caravan*, Azzam argues that jihad is a central duty. Drawing upon the work of scholar Ibn Taymiyyah, Azzam distinguishes between the collective duty, which is filled by the community, and the individual duty, which is the duty of every Muslim. According to him, if Muslims are unable to fight adequately against an invader, the onus is on the individuals nearest to the conflict to aid in the fight. For instance, the Afghanis were not able to repel the Soviets and had to rely upon the mujahidin. Thus, jihad is considered a duty of Muslims in defense of Muslim territory. On November 24, 1989, a car bomb killed Azzam and two of his sons in Peshawar. It is still uncertain who was behind the incident.

Dr. Ayman al-Zawahiri

Another individual who significantly influenced bin Ladin is Dr. Ayman al-Zawahiri. Al-Zawahiri was born in Maadi, Egypt, in 1951 and grew up in a

---

Foundational Thinkers: Ibn Taymiyyah and Sayyid Qutb

Ibn Taymiyyah (1268–1328) was a Syrian scholar who fought against the Mongols when they invaded the Middle East. Even though the Mongols had converted to Islam, Taymiyyah claimed that they did not follow Sharia, but Yasa, law. Taymiyyah railed against those who did not follow the correct path, arguing they were in a state of *jahiliyyah*, the pre-Islamic pagan era of disbelief and ignorance. Taymiyyah believed that engaging in jihad against such ignorance was permitted.

Sayyid Qutb was an Egyptian scholar who was imprisoned by President Gamal al-Nasir for his views and executed in 1966. Qutb wrote many books espousing his views, including *In the Shade of the Quran, Milestones, and Social Justice in Islam*. In *In The Shade of the Quran*, Qutb outlined his modern view of *jahiliyyah* and argued that Egypt was not an Islamic country, but one in a state of *jahiliyyah*. Through his reasoning, he was able to declare the Egyptian regime (although Muslim) apostate (as having abandoned Islam). Qutb advocated jihad to establish an Islamic state.

middle-class family. In fact, he came from a prominent family of religious scholars and professionals. His grandfather, Shaykh al-Ahmadi al-Zawahiri, was the imam of Al-Azhar Mosque in Cairo, and his father was a professor of pharmacology at Ein Shams University. His maternal grandfather was a professor of literature and president of Cairo University and served as an ambassador to Pakistan, Saudi Arabia, and Yemen.[9] However, al-Zawahiri would not follow in his family's footsteps by leading a professional life. At the age of sixteen, al-Zawahiri was already involved in a clandestine extremist cell whose aim was to overthrow the Egyptian government and establish an Islamic state.[10] In 1974, he received a medical degree and for a short time worked as a pediatrician. Al-Zawahiri then made his first trip to Pakistan to aid in the relief effort.

Following the assassination of Egyptian president Anwar al-Sadat in 1981, the Egyptian government arrested many individuals, including al-Zawahiri. He was sentenced to prison for three years because of a weapons charge and, while in prison, was allegedly tortured. While serving his time, al-Zawahiri became a voice for imprisoned extremists and exploited this to further his standing among his peers. Shortly after he was released from prison, al-Zawahiri left for Afghanistan. In *Knights under the Prophet's Banner*, al-Zawahiri notes,

> In Afghanistan the picture was perfectly clear: A Muslim nation carrying out jihad under the banner of Islam, versus a foreign enemy that was an infidel aggressor backed by a corrupt, apostatic regime at home. In the case of this war, the application of theory to the facts was manifestly clear. This clarity was also beneficial in refuting the ambiguities raised by many people professing to carry out Islamist work but who escaped from the arena of jihad on the pretext that there was no arena in which the distinction between Muslims and their enemies was obvious.[11]

While in Afghanistan, al-Zawahiri had also found a base of operations for his anti-Egyptian activities. He became the leader of the Egyptian Islamic Jihad (EIJ), which in essence grew out of the union of al-Zawahiri's compatriots and several other groups seeking to overthrow the Egyptian regime.[12] Eventually, al-Zawahiri would become bin Ladin's right-hand man. Al-Zawahiri merged his group with bin Ladin's in 1998, thus shifting his and his followers' focus away from the Egyptian regime onto the United States and its allies.

Birth of al-Qaida

In 1988, bin Ladin split from the Mujahidin Services Bureau and officially formed al-Qaida (the base). Many of its members were Arab mujahidin from

Afghanistan. Their objective was to establish a pan-Islamic state by fighting jihad in the name of Allah. Al-Qaida had a hierarchical structure. At the top was the Shura Majlis (consultative council), which made decisions for the organization. Bin Ladin was the leader, or emir, and strategically selected the leadership for the organization. Al-Zawahiri played a key role in influencing the individuals bin Ladin chose for leadership in the organization. Therefore, since al-Qaida's inception, Egyptians have played a central role in the leadership. Many of al-Zawahiri's associates were given key positions in bin Ladin's organization.[13] For example, Ali al-Rashidi (Abu Ubaidah al-Banshiri), an Egyptian and close associate of al-Zawahiri, was al-Qaida's first military commander. Muhammad Atef (Abu Hafs al-Masri), also an Egyptian, became the organization's second military commander when Banshiri was killed in a ferry accident in May 1996. Al-Masri was killed in 2001 in Afghanistan. There are numerous other examples of Egyptian al-Qaida leadership, such as Shaykh Said al-Masri, al-Qaida's financial officer, and Sayf al-Adil, a military commander.

After Afghanistan

After the Soviets withdrew from Afghanistan in 1989, bin Ladin returned to Saudi Arabia. For a short time, he worked in the family's construction business. Also, upon his return, he, like many mujahidin, was received as a hero for his work in Afghanistan.

When Iraq invaded Kuwait in 1990, the Saudi government found itself in a vulnerable position. The Saudis did not have the military strength to defend themselves if Iraq decided to invade them as well. Bin Ladin went to the Saudi government and offered his services, as well as the services of the mujahidin, to defend Saudi Arabia. He argued that the Saudis did not need the assistance of the American military and that his mujahidin could protect the Arabian Peninsula, just as they had defended Afghanistan against the Soviet Union. However, the Saudis not only decided to allow the Americans to use Saudi Arabia as a base for its military operations in the Gulf War but also declined bin Ladin's offer. This infuriated bin Ladin for two reasons. First, the Saudi regime allowed the Americans, who were unbelievers, or "infidels," into the Holy Land. Second, the Saudis refused the help of bin Ladin and his mujahidin. Bin Ladin began to criticize the Saudi government publicly, which led to his expulsion from the kingdom in 1991. Bin Ladin viewed this act by the Saudi government as the ultimate insult, which would serve as a seed of his hatred for both the Saudi government and the United States.

Sudan

Bin Ladin fled to Sudan, which provided him a new base for al-Qaida's operations. His decision to go to Sudan not only served his interests but also benefited the Sudanese government. Once again, bin Ladin was able to use his wealth and resources to build up the infrastructure of a Muslim country. For example, he invested in a construction business and an agriculture corporation. In return, he was allowed to set up training camps and was afforded protection by Hassan al-Turabi, the government and Islamic spiritual leader of Sudan. Bin Ladin used his new home as a base for planning and directing operations in other countries. For example, in 1993, al-Qaida was connected with the killing of eighteen U.S. soldiers in Mogadishu, Somalia.

In 1993, the first attack on the World Trade Center took place. While no substantial evidence indicates that bin Ladin planned or executed the attack, the individuals involved were later connected to senior al-Qaida leaders. For example, the lead planner and operator of the attack was Ramzi Yousef, nephew of 9/11 mastermind Khalid Shaykh Muhammad. Yousef was also involved in planning the Bojinka Plot, which was prevented due to the arrest of Yousef and other key operatives in his cell. The Bojinka operation was a complex plan, which involved simultaneously blowing up airborne U.S. commercial airliners departing from Asian countries over the Pacific Ocean. Despite their success in preventing Bojinka, Americans would later feel the effects of a very similar plot when Khalid Shaykh Muhammad incorporated similar tactics into his 9/11 operation.

By 1996, the United States and Saudi Arabia were putting pressure on the Sudanese government to expel bin Ladin, and in May 1996, Sudan finally acquiesced. After being expelled from the country, bin Ladin was left with few options in finding a base for his operations. He clearly could not return to Saudi Arabia, which had stripped him of his citizenship in 1995. Bin Ladin chose to flee to Afghanistan, where he would have the support and protection of the ruling Taliban.

Back to Afghanistan

In 1996, bin Ladin issued a fatwa entitled "Declaration of War against the Americans Occupying the Land of the Two Holy Places." In it, bin Ladin claimed that the Zionist-Crusader alliance had caused suffering to all Muslims. He referenced the Muslim blood spilled in Lebanon, Tajikistan, Burma, Kashmir, Assam, the Philippines, Fatani, Ogadin, Somalia, Eritrea, Chechnya, Bosnia-Herzegovina, Palestine, and Iraq. He further noted that the greatest offense to Muslims was the occupation by the American military of the land of the two holy places, Mecca and Medina.

Bin Ladin also depicted himself as a martyr suffering from the injustice of the Zionist-Crusader alliance. For example, he claimed that he and his men were driven from Pakistan, Sudan, and Afghanistan and into the Hindukush Mountains in Khurasan, Afghanistan. He mentioned that it was at Khurasan that the Soviets, the largest infidel army, had been destroyed by the mujahidin. Bin Ladin proclaimed that it was from this location that he and his men would lead Muslims to take action against the Zionist-Crusader alliance.

Furthermore, he criticized the Saudi government and blamed King Fahd for leading the country into disaster. He declared the economic, social, and military failures of the Muslim world to be the result of the policies of apostate Arab regimes, specifically the occupation of the Holy Lands by U.S. forces. For example, he stated that merchants and contractors were complaining about not being paid by the Saudi government in the amount of hundreds and thousands of millions of riyals (Saudi currency).

This fatwa called on Muslims to engage in jihad against the Americans and to boycott American products so that the U.S. economy would also suffer. Throughout his fatwa, bin Ladin referenced the scholar Ibn Taymiyyah, who wrote that "to fight in defense of religion and Belief is a collective duty; there is no other duty after Belief than fighting the enemy who is corrupting the life and religion." Bin Ladin sought to provide religious justification in order to gain credibility for his call for jihad. Essentially, bin Ladin outlined an underlying problem and provided a simple solution: U.S. occupation represented the underlying problem of the Muslim world, and in order to rectify the situation, Muslims needed to wage jihad against the United States.

In February 1998 bin Ladin released yet another fatwa that was issued on behalf of the World Islamic Front for Jihad against Jews and Crusaders. This fatwa was signed by bin Ladin, Ayman al-Zawahiri, and several other groups. The fatwa clearly reflected the signatories' hatred of the United States and Israel. It called upon all Muslims to kill Americans and their allies in order to remove Americans from the Holy Lands in Saudi Arabia and Jerusalem. The fatwa did not distinguish between civilians and military personnel in its calls for Muslims to kill Americans. Thus, the fatwa was used to wage an international war between the Muslim world and the United States. The signatories stated,

> No one argues today about three facts that are known to everyone; we will list them, in order to remind everyone: First, for over seven years the United States has been occupying the lands of Islam in the holiest of places, the Arabian Peninsula, plundering its riches, dictating to its rulers, humiliating its people, terrorizing its neighbors, and turning its bases in the Peninsula into a spearhead through which to fight the neighboring Muslim Peoples. If some people have

formerly debated the fact of the occupation, all the people of the Peninsula have now acknowledged it. The best proof of this is the Americans' continuing aggression against the Iraqi people using the Peninsula as a staging post, even though all its rulers are against their territories being used to that end, still they are helpless. Second, despite the great devastation inflicted on the Iraqi people by the Crusader-Zionist alliance, and despite the huge number of those killed, in excess of 1 million . . . despite all of this, the Americans are once against trying to repeat the horrific massacres, as though they are not content with the protracted blockade imposed after the ferocious war or the fragmentation and devastation. So now they come to annihilate what is left of this people and to humiliate their Muslim neighbors. Third, if the Americans' aims behind these wars are religious and economic, the aim is also to serve the Jews' petty state and divert attention from its occupation of Jerusalem and murder of Muslims there. The best proof of this is their eagerness to destroy Iraq, the strongest neighboring Arab state, and their endeavor to fragment all the states of the region such as Iraq, Saudi Arabia, Egypt, and Sudan into paper statelets and through their disunion and weakness to guarantee Israel's survival and the continuation of the brutal crusade occupation of the Peninsula.[14]

The official partnership between bin Ladin and al-Zawahiri that was demonstrated by the release of the 1998 fatwa also led to the reorganization of al-Qaida. The organization was restructured into four committees: military, religion, finance, and the media.[15] Each of these operational committees had specific responsibilities in the organization and its own chain of command. The military committee provided recruitment and training and facilitated the planning and support of operations. The religious committee was responsible for issuing rulings based on extreme interpretations of Islam to validate the organization's role in violent attacks. The financial committee monitored financial resources to facilitate all of the organization's operations. Finally, the media committee was responsible for propagating information that supported the organization.[16] Bin Ladin still oversaw all of the committees and maintained control of the organization.

In placing the blame squarely on the United States, bin Ladin and al-Zawarhiri were indeed going to bring the fight to a faraway enemy. The terms "near enemy" and "far enemy" are often used to describe this shift in focus. In modern, practical terms, the near enemy refers to apostate Arab regimes, and the far enemy refers to the United States. Historically, Azzam's goal was to unite Muslims by exhorting them join the jihad to liberate Afghanistan from the Soviet army. However, he also spoke out against the corrupt regimes of the Arab world and their Western influences. He urged Muslims to take up jihad within their own lands, especially in Palestine. Azzam's focus was clearly on removing the near enemy and establishing Islamic rule throughout the Arab world. However, throughout the 1990s, bin Ladin and al-Zawahiri both shifted the focus of international jihad from the near enemy to the far enemy, which they defined as the United States. Bin Ladin's 1996 fatwa was the first indication of this shift. He was able to outline why Muslims should unite in attacking Americans on the Arabian Peninsula. While he targeted the Saudi regime in his fatwa, his primary focus was to highlight the fact that Americans' presence in the Holy Land was the single greatest offense to Islam. Al-Zawahiri also became a supporter of targeting a more distant enemy than Arab regimes. According to Montasser al-Zayyat,[17] in the early and middle part of the 1990s, al-Zawahiri was leading the EIJ against the near enemy by calling for attacks on the Egyptian regime. In 1996, al-Zawahiri stated that the near enemy had priority because it was a closer enemy, but in 1998 he shifted his focus from the near enemy to the far enemy.

Al-Qaida Attacks

Soon after the release of the 1998 fatwa, bin Ladin's threats against the United States became a reality. On August 7, 1998, two attacks were carried out within minutes of each other at the U.S. embassies in Dar es Salaam, Tanzania, and Nairobi, Kenya. More than 220 people died, which demonstrated al-Qaida's ability to inflict massive casualties and damage in simultaneously executed attacks. The United States was quick to respond to the embassy bombings. President Bill Clinton ordered cruise missiles to strike at targets in Afghanistan and Sudan. In Sudan, cruise missiles destroyed the El Shifa Pharmaceutical Industries factory, where it was alleged that bin Ladin was storing chemical weapons. The locations hit in Afghanistan were believed by the U.S. government to be al-Qaida compounds and training facilities. Unfortunately, the U.S. response caused little damage to al-Qaida's infrastructure and furthered elevated al-Qaida's confidence in its own abilities.

On October 12, 2000, in Aden, Yemen, two men drove an explosive-laden boat into the USS *Cole*, a U.S. Navy destroyer, killing seventeen American sailors. Just prior to this, bin Ladin had released a videotape calling for attacks in Yemen. Al-Qaida viewed this attack as a huge success, considering that it had been able to strike a U.S. naval warship. In 2004, six men were charged for their involvement in the attack. Abd al-Rhim al-Nashiri, a Saudi, and Jamal al-Badawi, a Yemeni, received death sentences for their planning of, and involvement in, the attack. A Yemeni court ruled that these men, along with the other four men charged in the attack, were all linked to al-Qaida.

On September 11, 2001, America's national security was tested as it had never been tested before. Nineteen extremists, all of whom were affiliated with al-Qaida, hijacked four American commercial planes. American Airlines Flight 11 hit the North Tower of the World Trade Center at 8:46 a.m. Only seventeen minutes later, at 9:03 a.m., United Airlines Flight 175 hit the South Tower. American Airlines Flight 77 then crashed into the Pentagon at 9:37 a.m. By 10:03 a.m., the final plane that had been hijacked, United Airlines Flight 93, crashed into a field in Shanksville, Pennsylvania. Nearly three thousand people were killed; it was the single worst attack on American soil. Furthermore, this attack was designed to strike at America's economic, military, and political infrastructures. Bin Ladin did not immediately take credit, but he eventually claimed responsibility for the attack in Arab press. Nonetheless, bin Ladin's network had delivered a devastating blow to its biggest enemy and had accomplished it within that enemy's homeland.

Obviously, 9/11 was not the first attack on the United States by al-Qaida, but it was the first attack on United States soil. For those Salafists who condone the use of violence in the conception of jihad, 9/11, including the death of innocent civilians, was justified. Qunitan Wiktorowicz and John Kaltner explain the mindset of what they call the jihadi Salafis:

> In general, most Salafis agree that the United States is waging a war of aggression against Muslims through its actions in Afghanistan, Pakistan, Iraq and elsewhere. Differences emerge, however, over the proper response and course of action. Jihadis once again call for violence, while the non-violent Salafis promote other means, including public announcements of opposition to a U.S. presence in the Middle East, prayer, and advice to Arab and Muslim leaders. This is the context in which one should understand al-Qaeda's 2002 justification for September 11 and the purposeful targeting of civilians. The document is part of a discursive contest over the proper methodology for fulfilling religious obligations. As a result, it reflects a carefully constructed case to undermine the legitimacy of non-violent solutions. In this respect, it makes three important arguments. First, proponents of non-violent response to the United States are corrupt, ignorant and/or hypocritical, and therefore are not credible religious mediators. This is contrasted with the scientific, independent and religiously authentic interpretation of the jihadi Salafis. Second, the United States is waging a war against Islam. Therefore, violence is a *defensive* jihad that is incumbent upon all Muslims. And third, there is no unconditional prohibition against killing civilians in Islam. In fact, civilians can be purposely targeted under certain conditions, and these conditions are met in the current climate.[18]

Thus, once again, bin Ladin sent a strong and violent message to the United States.

Ayman al-Zawahiri and the Jihad

In October 2002, the *Qoqaz* website published an interview with al-Zawahiri. The following excerpt from the interview shows al-Zawahiri's views on dialogue versus violence and the strength of the movement.

QUESTION: Some of those who are affiliated with the Islamic call claim that resisting America militarily is impossible and that the solution is through dialog and attempting to convince it, of our rights. Also they claim that the present state is the stage of "preparation" and not the time for battle. What is your view?

AL-ZAWAHIRI: One is not amazed by the falsehood of such claims, but one is amazed that they continue to be repeated, even after the entire world witnessed the great events in Afghanistan. Here, in Afghanistan, the course of history changed, when the Soviet Union, the largest land-based military force in the world, was dashed to pieces on the boulders of the Afghan jihad. The Afghan nomads, villagers, and their young comrades from the Arab and Islamic world, who destroyed the empire of the Soviet tyrant, were, Praise be to Allah, not affected by these opinions. For if they had [been], then the Soviet forces would today be in the Arabian Peninsula. It is only by the blessings of Allah that the Islamic resistance in Palestine was not affected by such thought. Otherwise, Israeli tanks would today be in Medina, Cairo, and Damascus in realization of the goal of Greater Israel. These claims feign ignorance of the significant power of love of death for Allah's cause. It was the mujahideen's desire for martyrdom that was the unique advantage, which resulted in the stealthy raids on New York and Washington—by the grace of Allah. Nineteen mujahideen who desired death were able to inflict damage upon America, such as it had never before witnessed in its history. This effective force is also apparent in the battle between Islam and disbelief currently taking place in Palestine. Israel sustains hundreds of killed and injured yearly as a result of martyrdom operations. These claims provide the greatest service to the American propaganda in actively discouraging Muslims. It keeps them in a state of impotence, paralysis, and submission to the American and Zionist tyranny. If we have reached this state of inability, then let us act according to the saying of the poet: "If there is no escape from death, then due to incapability you will die as a coward." As for the saying of those who sit back from jihad that the period is one of "preparation" and not battle, there is a simple reply. It is to say to them that the unassuming men who destroyed the Soviet Union by the Grace of Allah did not go—Praise be to Allah—through the "preparation" at all! Then, we ask them, do you not know that Palestine has been occupied for more than eighty years? Do you not know that the Islamic caliphate fell at about the same time? Do you not know that the Islamic world has been under Western influence for more than a century? What was your "preparation" during those long decades? Then, we further ask ourselves, what is the actual effort that you have put forward while your hairs turned grey in humiliation? What "preparation" has been made for fighting the enemies of Islam? Or is your share from the "preparation" to defame and slander the mujahideen? Or is it making the Muslim nation despair of Jihad and making peace with the oppressive, sinful rulers? Is this your jihad in your opinion? In reality, the most knowledgeable people regarding the requirements of the "preparation" and war are the people of jihad. These are the people who are implementing it practically. This is because, in this field of jihad, they are the people of *Ijtihaad* [Islamic jurisprudence reasoning], which made them the foremost people to give Islamic rulings. . . . They are the scholars who are practically living the realities of these current affairs, and this makes them more suitable for fatwas . . . as proven by the great scholar of Islam, Ibn Taymiyyah, may Allah have mercy on him, in his book [*Fatawa Kubra*]. While some of these people have taken this "preparation," which is in reality a way to gather military force and consolidate its strength, to something that has become a hindrance to the way of Jihad. The continual attacks on the American system have finally pulled the biggest Satan to the arena of jihad. This is after it had remained hidden for a long time behind its various agents. Once in the arena of war, it will start feeling its own losses. Then, it will start paying the price for its support of Israel and its agents in our own countries. Our weapon in this battle is patience [*sabr*], perseverance [*mussabara*] and reliance upon Allah [*tawakkul*] in our fight against America. By the permission of Allah, this war will continue until the bleeding of America will result in its own collapse. If America possesses advanced weapons of mass destruction and well-equipped armies, then it should be known that we possess what they cannot: the love of death in the path of Allah. American weapons, as we have witnessed by our own eyes in Tora Bora and Shahiekoot, hide their shameful cowardliness. It is the love of death in the path of Allah that is the weapon that will annihilate this evil empire in America, by the permission of Allah. The mujahid youth will compete with each other to die in the path of Allah. It is this "great" America that has been built from oppression, arrogance, and deviation from the methodology that Allah is pleased with.[1]

---

1. Azzam Publications, "Interview with Egyptian Islamic Jihad Leader Dr. Ayman al-Zawahiri," *Qoqaz*, October 11, 2002, available at www.qoqaz.net (last accessed November 5, 2002).

Post-9/11

In October 2001, the United States launched Operation Enduring Freedom in Afghanistan, and U.S. forces began an offensive campaign against bin Ladin's al-Qaida network and the Taliban, which was harboring them. The U.S. campaign aimed to destroy al-Qaida's infrastructure and capture its leaders. While the Taliban was decimated, it was able to regroup and continue to attack U.S. and allied forces and the Hamid Karzai regime in Afghanistan.

Since October 2001, and to the credit of U.S. and allied forces, many of the original al-Qaida leadership has been killed or captured, and its infrastructure in Afghanistan has been destroyed. The first significant capture was Abu Zubaydah, a senior leader in the organization. Also significant was the capture of Ramzi bin al-Shibh in September 2002. Bin al-Shibh was a senior al-Qaida operative and key planner of the 9/11 attacks. The mastermind of 9/11, Khalid Shaykh Muhammad, was captured in Islamabad on March 1, 2003. Abu Faraj al-Libi, another key operational planner, was arrested in Pakistan in May 2005. Each arrest of a senior leader impacted the al-Qaida network hierarchy. As a result, it seems, unqualified and unseasoned junior members in the network had to step up into more senior positions. Additionally, the network had to modify its communication methods, which impacted its leadership's command and control of different cells. The leadership has had to find alternative methods for communicating with the network to avoid detection by coalition forces.

The al-Qaida Network

Since 9/11, the most significant change to al-Qaida has been to its overall structure. Al-Qaida is no longer a centralized group operating from within Afghanistan and executing attacks on Americans worldwide. It has evolved into a loosely affiliated global network that provides a framework for extremist groups with similar beliefs and objectives. Several of these were mentioned in chapter 1 when the network was outlined. These groups are all part of the al-Qaida-affiliated network whose purpose is to strike at America, its interests, and its allies. Even though there has not been an attack on the same scale as 9/11, there have been multiple al-Qaida-affiliated attacks since the conclusion of Operation Enduring Freedom, demonstrating the breadth of the network. These include, but are not limited to, those in Casablanca, Bali, Madrid, multiple cities in Saudi Arabia, Sharm al-Shaykh, Amman, and London.

Casablanca Attacks

On May 16, 2004, a series of suicide bombings took place in Casablanca, Morocco, killing thirty-three victims and twelve bombers. According to Moroccan authorities, Moroccan extremists, members of the group Salafiyah Jihadiyah, were responsible for the attack; however, authorities claimed that Abu Musab al-Zarqawi was behind the attacks as well. According to Director of Moroccan National Security Gen. Hamidou Laanigri, "in 2002, the Moroccan jihadists [holy warriors] asked bin Laden to give them financial help. Al-Zarqawi, who believed in them, pulled a few strings."[19]

Bali and Jakarta Attacks

Bali, an island in Indonesia known for its sunny beaches and picturesque scenery, was the last place one would expect the network to strike. However, on October 12, 2002, two bombs blasted through a nightclub section on this tropical island. The attacks, conducted by al-Qaida's affiliate Jemaah Islamiyah, killed 202 people; Australians, Indonesians, Britons, Swedes, Germans, Dutch, and Americans were among the victims. Authorities were quick to react and over the next year arrested key members of Jemaah Islamiyah, including its notorious spiritual leader Abu Bakar Bashir, key operational planner Riduan Isamuddin (a.k.a. Hambali), and operatives Imam Samudra and Ali Gufron (a.k.a. Mukhlas). In November 2002, bin Ladin praised the attacks, calling the bombers "zealous sons of Islam."[20] Bin Ladin's statement demonstrated his support for Jemaah Islamiyah conducting attacks in this area of the world, especially those targeting Westerners.

Not even a year later, Jemaah Islamiyah conducted another attack in Indonesia. On August 5, 2003, a car bomb exploded outside the Jakarta Marriott, killing at least thirteen and injuring 150 individuals. The Marriott bombing occurred just prior to the announcement of the verdict in the trial of a suspect in the Bali bombings, Amrozi bin Nurhasyim.[21] Jakarta unfortunately would see more violence the following year. In September 2004, a bomb exploded at the Australian Embassy, killing nine. Even though the group was targeting Australians, the bombing killed only Indonesians. On a website, Jemaah Islamiyah claimed responsibility for the attacks and told Australians in Indonesia to leave the country, citing Australia's involvement in Iraq.[22]

On October 1, 2005, another series of attacks occurred in Bali. This time, three suicide bombers detonated bombs in two cafés near Jimbaran and one at a restaurant in Kuta's main square. The suicide bomber, wearing a backpack in the restaurant bombing, was captured on amateur video. Nineteen people died and more than one hundred were injured. Indonesian antiterrorism official Maj. Gen. Ansyaad Mbai attributed the planning of the attacks to Jemaah Islamiyah's leading members Azahari bin Husin and Noordin Muhammad Top.[23]

Madrid Attacks

On March 11, 2004, ten bombs were set off on commuter trains in Madrid, killing 191 people and wounding more than 1,800. It was the single worst terrorist attack ever on Spanish soil. The perpetrators of the attacks claimed they did so in response to Spain's collaboration with the United States in support of the Iraq war. Several people were arrested, including several Moroccans. The perpetrators were members of the Moroccan Islamic Combatant Group. In the aftermath of the bombings, Spain held its scheduled elections, which resulted in the defeat of the ruling Popular Party. The Socialist Party gained control, and its leader, Jose Luis Rodriguez Zapatero, became the next Spanish prime minister. Zapatero then announced he would withdraw Spain's thirteen hundred troops from Iraq. In response, al-Qaida was able to claim that it had influenced the outcome of the Spanish election with the bombings.

Saudi Arabia Attacks

The Saudi al-Qaida network operates principally in Saudi Arabia with the goal of overthrowing the Saudi regime and expelling Westerners from the kingdom. This part of the network is particularly important, given that bin Ladin is a Saudi and was expelled from the kingdom. Additionally, the ruling al-Saud family and the United States are perceived to have a close relationship.

On May 12, 2003, Saudi al-Qaida attacked three residential compounds in Riyadh, killing thirty-five people. This attack within Saudi Arabia was a wake-up call to the al-Saud that the al-Qaida network was a formidable threat in its own backyard. The Saudi government realized the seriousness of the threat and responded with an aggressive counterterrorism campaign. This campaign included multiple tactics such as counterterrorism operations, the publication of the names of wanted extremists with the hope of attaining public support in identifying them, and the institution of an amnesty program in June 2004 that turned in approximately sixty-one extremists. Saudi counterterrorism operations have had some significant successes such as arresting or killing many key members of the group, including Yusuf al-Ayiri, its revered leader, Abdul Aziz al-Muqrin, Khalid Ali Hajj, Abdul Karim al-Mejatti, and Younis Muhammad Ibrahim al-Hayari.

Despite these successes, Saudi al-Qaida has executed many attacks since the May 2003 bombings. The following are some of the attacks that have occurred since this time. In November 2003, suicide bombers hit a housing compound in Riyadh, killing at least seventeen, including Westerners and Saudis. The group then targeted Saudi Arabia's most prized resource, the oil infrastructure. Gunmen stormed an oil company compound in Khobar in May 2004, killing twenty-two people. Later, in June 2004, Saudi al-Qaida kidnapped and beheaded American Paul Johnson. This tragic event heightened the Saudi security forces' efforts to combat al-Qaida. Security forces went on the offensive and quickly tracked down and killed the leader of the cell, Abdul Aziz al-Muqrin.[24] While this dealt a significant blow to the network, Saudi al-Qaida was able to adapt. In December 2004, Saudi al-Qaida stormed the U.S. consulate in Jiddah, killing nine individuals. Bin Ladin allegedly praised the attacks in a video distributed on the Internet. In the video, bin Ladin stated, "God bless our brothers who stormed the American consulate in Jiddah. . . . Those who were killed were our brothers. We ask God to accept them as martyrs."[25] Thus, bin Ladin acknowledged al-Qaida's affiliation with the attack, and by publicizing this statement, he showed his support for future attacks targeting Americans within the kingdom. In mid-2005, Saudi al-Qaida claimed responsibility for an attack that burned three helicopters in al-Qasim airport in May.[26] Again, Saudi al-Qaida continues to prove itself an active organization that can adapt to Saudi counterterrorism efforts by replacing captured or killed senior leaders and adjusting operations based on current capabilities.

Egypt Attacks

Several attacks have occurred in Egypt, including the Taba and Sharm al-Shaykh bombings. On October 7, 2004, car bombs targeted two holiday resorts in the popular tourist destination of Taba. The bombs killed thirty-two individuals, mostly Israelis. Another attack occurred on July 23, 2005, this time in the resort town of Sharm al-Shaykh. Eighty-eight people were killed when three bombs were detonated. One occurred in the old market, and two targeted a hotel.

London Attacks

On July 7, 2005, during rush hour, four coordinated explosions rocked London, notably during the G-8 summit taking place in Scotland. Three of the explosions took place on tube trains, and one was on a metro bus. Each of the bombs weighed less than ten pounds and was set off by a timer. Over fifty people were killed, and at least seven hundred were injured in the attacks. On the Internet, the Organization of al-Qaida in Europe took credit for the attack and claimed it was a response to Great Britain's "massacres" in Iraq and Afghanistan. In addition to the human toll, the general impact of the attack on the transportation system was also very significant. Furthermore, the financial markets were disrupted. A few weeks later, another coordinated bombing attack of the tube and metro bus system was attempted; however, this time the effort was unsuccessful.

Enter Iraq

In April 2003, U.S.-allied forces entered Iraq with the intention of deposing Saddam Husayn, whom the United States depicted as a grave threat to its national security. On May 1, 2003, President George W. Bush declared an end to major hostilities. Not long after, however, the U.S. and allied forces were embroiled in a full-fledged insurgency. Today, numerous groups are participating in the uprising, including those affiliated with al-Qaida. The significance of Iraq with regard to recruitment cannot be overstated. The presence of Western allied forces in Iraq serves to bolster al-Qaida's argument that the West is bent on invading Arab and Muslim lands and seeks to oppress Muslims worldwide. This serves as a rallying cry for individuals to join the network and fight jihad against the invading infidel army.

Jordan Attacks

On November 9, 2005, three hotels in Amman, Jordan, were bombed. Sixty people were killed, including several members of a wedding taking place in one of the hotels. As justification for the attacks, Abu Musab al-Zarqawi announced on his website that the hotels were serving as bases for Jewish and American security services. This was not the first incident to take place in Jordan. On August 19, 2005, rockets were launched against two U.S. warships in the port in Aqaba. The rockets missed the ships but hit a Jordanian military warehouse, killing one guard. The other rocket allegedly landed in Israel and didn't cause any casualties.[27] In addition to these incidents, on October 28, 2002, U.S. Agency for International Development official Lawrence Foley was assassinated as he was walking to his car in front of his house.

Conclusion

The al-Qaida network continues to target the United States and its allies, both at home and abroad. Bin Ladin strategically makes use of his position in the network by providing guidance on, and giving his blessing to, operations targeting the United States and its allies. However, due to his inaccessible location, he is somewhat out of touch with the network and is therefore probably unable to make significant tactical decisions for the organization. Despite the many arrests of members of the network by the United States and allied forces, individuals are able to continue to plan and execute operations. In part, this is due to the network's ability to recruit individuals successfully. Furthermore, the network's ability to adjust to the arrests of senior leaders and fill their positions with junior members demonstrates not only its flexibility but also the significant threat that extremist recruitment poses to the national security of the United States and its allies. Let's now turn to examining the types of individuals who have joined this network.

Notes

1. Elaine Landau, *Osama bin Laden* (Brookfield, CT: Twenty-first Century Books, 2002).

2. Landau, *Osama bin Laden*.

3. David Ensor, "Wives, Mother May Hold Key to Bin Laden's Whereabouts," *CNN*, March 12, 2002, available at http://archives.cnn.com/2002/US/03/12/gen.binladen.wives (last accessed March 10, 2005).

4. Peter Bergen, *Holy War Inc.* (New York: Free Press, 2001), Yossef Bodansky, *Bin Ladin: The Man Who Declared War on America* (Roseville, CA: Prima Publishing, 2001), Rohan Gunaratna, *Inside Al Qaeda* (New York: Columbia University Press, 2002), Elaine Landau, *Osama bin Laden* (Brookfield, CT: Twenty-first Century Books, 2002).

5. Landau, *Osama bin Laden*.

6. Daniel Benjamin and Steven Simon, *The Age of Sacred Terror* (New York: Random House, 2002).

7. Abdullah bin Omar, "The Striving Sheik: Abdullah Azzam," *Nida'ul Islam*, July–September 1996, available at www.islam.org.au/articles/14/azzam.htm (last accessed March 10, 2005).

8. Jonathan Fighel, "Sheikh Abdullah Azzam: Bin Laden's Spiritual Mentor," *Institute for Counter-Terrorism*, September 27, 2001, available at www.ict.org.il/articles/articledet.cfm?articleid=388 (last accessed March 10, 2005).

9. Nimrod Raphaeli, "Al-Zawahiri: The Making of an Arch Terrorist," Inquiry and Analysis Series No. 127, *MEMRI*, March 11, 2003, available at http://memri.org/bin/articles.cgi?Page=archives&Area=ia&ID=IA12703 (last accessed March 10, 2005).

10. Montasser Al-Zayyat, *The Road to Al-Qaeda: The Story of bin Laden's Right-Hand Man* (London: Pluto Press, 2004).

11. Ayman Al-Zawahiri, "Knights under the Prophet's Banner," *Al-Sharq al-Awsat*, December 2, 2001, 10.

12. Al-Zayyat, *The Road to Al-Qaeda*.

13. Gunaratna, *Inside Al Qaeda*, 26.

14. Usama bin Ladin, "Text of Fatwah Urging Jihad against Americans," *Al-Quds al-'Arabi*, February 23, 1998, available at www.ict.org.il/articles/fatwah.htm (last accessed March 10, 2005).

15. Gunaratna, *Inside Al Qaeda*.

16. Evan Thomas, "Cracking the Terror Code," *Newsweek*, October 15, 2001, available at http://msnbc.msn.com/id/3668484 (last accessed March 10, 2005).

17. Al-Zayyat, *The Road to Al-Qaeda*.

18. Qunitan Wiktorowicz and John Kaltner, "Killing in the Name of Islam: Al-Qaeda's Justification for September 11," *Middle East Policy* 10, no. 2 (summer 2003): 80.

19. *News24*, "'Al Qaeda Financed Casablanca,'" *News24*, August 5, 2004, available at www.news24.com/News24/World/News/0,,2-10-1462_1523957,00.html (last accessed March 10, 2005).

20. British Broadcasting Corporation, "Timeline: Bali Bomb Trials," *BBC News*, August 24, 2004, available at http://news.bbc.co.uk/1/hi/world/asia-pacific/3126241.stm (last accessed March 10, 2005).

21. British Broadcasting Corporation, "Bomb Wrecks Top Jakarta Hotel," *BBC News*, August 5, 2003, available at http://news.bbc.co.uk/2/hi/asia-pacific/3124919.stm (last accessed March 10, 2005).

22. Maria Ressa, "JI 'Claims Jakarta Bombing': Website Says Blast Targeted Australia for Iraq Policy," *CNN*, September 9, 2004, available at www.cnn.com/2004/WORLD/asiapcf/09/09/indonesia.blast (last accessed March 10, 2005).

23. John Aglionby and Maria Ressa, "Security Tightened after Bali Suicide Bombing," *CNN*, October 2, 2005, available at www.cnn.com/2005/WORLD/asiapcf/10/02/bali.blasts (last accessed April 15, 2006).

24. Craig Whitlock, "Saudis Facing Return of Radicals: Young Iraq Veterans Join Underground," *Washington Post Foreign Service*, July 11, 2004, available at www.washingtonpost.com/wp-dyn/articles/A41375-2004Jul10.html (last accessed March 10, 2005).

25. MSNBC, "Purported Bin Laden Tape Posted on Web," *MSNBC*, December 17, 2004, available at www.msnbc.msn.com/id/6722361 (last accessed March 10, 2005).

26. *Arabic News*, "Prince Nayef Discloses Investigations into al-Qaida Burning Three Copters in al-Qasim," *Arabic News*, June 17, 2005, available at www.arabicnews.com/ansub/Daily/Day/050617/2005061719.html (last accessed April 15, 2006).

27. Erich Marquardt, "Intelligence Brief: Aqaba Attack," *Power and Interest News Report*, August 30, 2005, available at www.pinr.com/report.php?ac=view_report&report_id=356 (last accessed April 15, 2006).

CHAPTER 3

The Demographics of Extremists: Is There a Profile?

We are building a women's structure that will carry out operations that will make the U.S. forget its own name.

—Umm Osama, female trainer of mujahidin

What type of individual joins the al-Qaida network? In thinking about this question, many of us invariably conjure up certain images of the "typical" member. Odds are, most of us surmise that they are young, male, and probably Middle Eastern in origin. This is our idea of the quintessential "Arab terrorist." But the question remains, is this assertion true? Are most extremists who join the al-Qaida network young, male, and of Middle Eastern descent? Furthermore, can we even speak of demographic commonalties among al-Qaida recruits? And, if there are commonalties, then what are they exactly?

This chapter, in seeking to address these questions, sheds light not only on where the recruits were born and raised but also on their educational background, what jobs, if any, they held, and their religious preferences. Specifically, when discussing demographics, this chapter is principally concerned with an individual's country of origin, country of citizenship or residency, gender, age, occupation, education, and religion. Each of these demographic aspects is discussed below. Overall, the chapter aims to dispel existing stereotypes and demonstrate that recruits come from many different places and walks of life.

Country of Origin, Country of Citizenship, and Country of Residency

Generally speaking, when we mention a person's country of origin, we are referring to the country in which he or she was born. An individual's country of citizenship is the country where an individual holds legal citizenship. Finally, a country of residency is one in which an individual was not born but has chosen to live, without desiring or being granted legal citizenship for whatever reason.

It is important to note the distinctions between origin, citizenship, and residency, especially when attempting to talk about the commonalties of where extremists "come from," which may or may not exist. If this can't be sorted out, then how can we possibly discern where extremists are coalescing and plotting?

Many recruits are born and raised in the same country and one day join an extremist group operating in their country of origin. However, this is not the case for all, especially because more and more people are leaving their countries of origin and settling elsewhere. The following example illustrates the quagmire generated when discussing extremism solely in terms of birthplace and also points out the numerous complexities involved in this demographic category alone: an Algerian moves to France at age nineteen, becomes a citizen of France, and joins the al-Qaida network in France at age twenty-four. Invariably, in the press, this person will be described as an Algerian, conjuring up images of a person who fought in the Algerian "jihad," then brought his fight to the shores of France. In reality, his story may be very different. In fact, this person may have emigrated to France legally, found France to be less than accommodating to North Africans, and joined al-Qaida's network in France because he felt discriminated against even as a French citizen. To those engaged in the "global war on terrorism," knowing that a person joined in France would ultimately lead them to focus on networks in France, not Algeria.

Let's examine another brief example: if asked, an individual may claim to be Yemeni specifically because of tribal roots. However, this person may have long-standing familial roots in Saudi Arabia and hold citizenship there and for that reason have been influenced and recruited by the network in Saudi Arabia. Thus, dealing with this and similar individuals would realistically indicate the need to concentrate on networks in Saudi Arabia and not Yemen.

The major point here is that in our efforts to deal with the extremist threat, it is important to know where individuals were recruited and indoctrinated, not simply where they were born, especially if there is no actual connection between individuals' birthplaces and their extremist activities. This is not to suggest we should ignore the fact that the person in our first example is also an ethnic Algerian. This becomes very important in determining patterns. At first glance, we may not discern much in the way of patterns, but they do exist. In other words, in this example, the fact that a large number of Algerians with no previous extremist ties are joining extremist networks in France due to perceived discrimination has serious social and political implications for France, as well as for developing French counterterrorism policy. The same could be true for Yemenis who live in Saudi Arabia, with similar implications for Saudi Arabia.

Can we actually determine the extent of the extremist threat by focusing on this particular demographic category? It is probably too difficult to ascertain accurately how many individuals are recruited in certain countries. While we can rely on expert "estimates" or comb the news for arrests, focusing on the former can be unreliable because we don't really know how many people are actually associated with the al-Qaida network (as financial backers, fund-raisers, operators, logisticians, recruiters, trainers, and leaders). In our view, this is merely the nature of a secretive extremist network and attempts to estimate membership accurately are essentially futile. In addition, as noted above, accounts of extremists in the press frequently mix up national origin with residency and citizenship. In other words, the press commonly reports on French extremists. Further research reveals that these individuals were actually North Africans (a mix of Moroccans, Algerians, and Tunisians) who began their descent into extremism long before they hit the shores of France. Along the same vein, "combing arrests" is also unreliable. For example, from combing arrests it can be ascertained from the news in the spring and summer of 2004 that Moroccans dominated the al-Qaida network and that they were all concentrated in Spain. Similarly, the press would have us believe, given its attention to Saudi Arabia's extremist problem, that the entire country is overrun with people intent on destabilizing the regime. Furthermore, given the press coverage, we could conclude that Iraq is the only country experiencing an internal conflict. Our perceptions are shaped by the interests of the news disseminators, not by an actual reflection of the reality of the extremists and their networks. This is very unfortunate, but true.

In short, in our view, no country is immune to extremism. Nuances such as origin versus citizenship or residency become very important in addressing where the recruit embraced extremism in the first place.

Gender

At first glance, the gender of those who join the al-Qaida network would seem to be the most straightforward of all demographic characteristics. The members of the network are frequently talked about in the news, which shows pictures of the men. Generally speaking, the majority of the individuals who make up the al-Qaida network are men. In addition, the entire leadership structure of the network was, and still is, dominated by men.

Focusing on men is not meant to suggest that the network is devoid of women or that women play no role. While it is true that some women are unaware of the activities of their spouses, others are clearly cognizant of the roles their spouses play.

Many women are aware of their spouses' extremist activities and support them, as best they can, within the constraints of cultural norms. Thus, women are very important to the network in the support function. For example, the wife of one al-Qaida member and suicide bomber articulated her support for her husband's mission. She testified, "My husband had a mission to carry out, to place a bomb and end up as a martyr."[1] Others help out with financial matters. Saraah Olson, who knowingly married an Egyptian member of al-Qaida, admitted she drew up papers for a fake charity used to channel money overseas.[2]

Another example of the role of women is demonstrated in a letter submitted to *Sawt al-Jihad* (Voice of Jihad), al-Qaida's online magazine, allegedly by the wife of a deceased Saudi extremist killed by Saudi security forces. The letter, entitled "A Letter to the Wife of Slain Pagan Paul Johnson from the Wife of One of the Martyrs," discusses the killing of Paul Johnson, who was an American hostage in Saudi Arabia. In the letter, she wrote, in part,

> When my husband was killed you certainly were not interested, nor did you know about it; and if you had known, you probably would have been pleased that he was killed before he reached your husband and his countrymen. However, I find solace in the fact that the Mujahideen were able to reach their target with precision, and they killed your husband by slaughtering him. By Allah, on that day I rejoiced a lot because the real terrorist was killed having been gorged with the blood of our Muslim children.[3]

Women are encouraged by the network to play a support function. For instance, *Al-Khansa*, an al-Qaida women's magazine published by al-Qaida's Arabian Peninsula Women's Information Bureau, called for women to participate in jihad. Their call, entitled "Our Goal Is Paradise," articulated the following:

> We stand shoulder to shoulder with our men, supporting them, helping them, and backing them up. We educate their sons and we prepare ourselves. May Allah know of the honesty of our intentions and of our good deeds, and [may

he] choose us and make us *Shahids* [martyrs] for His sake, as we charge forward and do not retreat and as Allah is pleased with us. We will stand covered by our veils and wrapped in our robes, weapons in hand, our children in our laps, with the Koran and Sunna of the Prophet of Allah directing and guiding us. The blood of our husbands and the body parts of our children are the sacrifice by means of which we draw closer to Allah, so that through us, Allah will cause the *Shahada* for His sake to succeed.[4]

In addition, women are encouraged to keep themselves physically fit and to keep their views to themselves. They are also expected to help recruit others.[5]

Extremist groups survive in part because of their secretive nature. One way to aid in this is through marriage ties. For example, senior members of the network will offer their sisters or other relatives to new recruits.[6]

In many ways al-Qaida has proved to be a pragmatic network. Thus, its members have most likely recognized the need to adapt to a changing security environment and to bring women into the fold. It is possible then that women will steadily gain a much more prominent role as money couriers, messengers, and even operatives in the network as law-enforcement and intelligence agencies continue to focus on men. According to Mia Bloom, "The stereotype exploited by terrorists is that women are gentle, submissive and nonviolent. Women evade most terrorist profiles because they are perceived as wives and mothers, victims of war-torn societies, not bombers. But terrorist organizations are increasingly employing women to carry out the most deadly attacks."[7]

One does not need to look too far in the news to recognize the face of Aafia Siddiqui, a suspected facilitator, who is currently on the FBI's wanted list. Born in Pakistan, she was educated in the United States and holds a doctorate in neurological science. Another example is Sajida Mubarak Atrous al-Rishawi, an Iraqi who was a suicide bomber in the November 2005 bombings in Amman, Jordan. She had a limited education. Her brother-in-law was a top aide of al-Zarqawi, and her brothers were also members of the network.[8]

Age

When looking at the age of recruits, we must determine when recruitment actually took place. This is not always an easy endeavor. For our purposes, recruitment into the network occurs when the person has made the decision to participate in activities supporting the al-Qaida network. Numerous individuals have spent years fighting jihad in notable places like Chechnya, Bosnia, Afghanistan, and now Iraq, eventually joining the network in their later years, after they have gained their "jihadi" credentials. In addition, many individuals join the organization without ever having fought jihad.

There are many news reports on the ages of the individuals being sought, arrested, or accused of participating in al-Qaida-related activities. The ages can start with the early teens and include those who were well into the thirties before joining. Thus, the age range for recruitment is fairly wide. For example, Operations Chief Riduan Isamuddin (a.k.a. Hambali) was a teenager when he became involved in Jemaah Islamiyah. One of the participants in the 2004 Madrid bombings was sixteen years old when he was sentenced for his role.[9] Ayman al-Zawahiri became involved in his first Egyptian extremist cell at the age of sixteen. Abdul al-Aziz al-Muqrin, a member of the Saudi network, was only nineteen when he embarked on his extremist journey.[10] Richard Reid, the "shoe bomber," was thirty when arrested after his attempt to blow up an airliner in 2001. He fell in with extremists after his release from prison in 1996, which suggests that he joined at around twenty-five years old.

September 11 hijacker Muhammad Atta, an Egyptian, was well into his twenties before he made the decision to join the network. Zacarias Moussauoi, a Franco-Moroccan who is being held in the United States on charges related to 9/11, was in his early thirties when arrested in the United States. Given what is known about his activities prior to his arrest, he was likely in his late twenties when he became involved in the network.

Occupation

Unfortunately, like age, it is also difficult to generalize about the occupations of individuals before they joined the network. There are a wide range of occupations in the network, from the unemployed to teachers and professionals.

Some individuals who turn to the al-Qaida network were unemployed or engaged in criminal activity to support themselves. For example, Ahmed Ressam, an Algerian who became known as the "millennium bomber" for his plot to blow up the Los Angeles Airport during the millennium celebrations, was primarily a thief prior to leaving for al-Qaida's training camps. Jamal Ahmidan, one of the bombers in the March 2004 Madrid attacks, grew up in a poor Moroccan city and came illegally to Spain, where he became a hashish dealer.[11]

Others were students, including at religious schools, having attained differing levels and differing degrees before joining the network. However, these individuals will be addressed in the education section below.

Some were members of the military or the police. For example, Khalid al-Azmi, who appeared in an al-Zarqawi network propaganda video called *The*

Winds of Triumph, served in the Kuwaiti navy. Faisal Said al-Mutairi, who also appeared in the video, was a Kuwaiti police officer.[12] Juma Namangani, deceased former head of the Islamic Movement of Uzbekistan, was a Russian army paratrooper who served in Afghanistan in the mid-1980s.[13]

Many recruits had everyday jobs as teachers or laborers or were employed in the service industry before entering into their life of extremism. For example, Jean-Marc Grandvisir, who was involved in a plot to blow up the U.S. Embassy in Paris, had a job counseling "wayward youths."[14] Muhammad Sidique Khan, one of the perpetrators of the July 2005 London attacks, was a teaching assistant. Muhammad Haydar Zammar, a Syrian who came to Germany as a child and became influential in the Hamburg cell involved in the 9/11 attacks, was a trained motor-vehicle mechanic.[15] Muhammad Sadique Khan was a teacher of children with special needs.[16]

Others members of the network were professionals, doctors, scientists, and engineers, who left their primary professions to pursue the goals of the network. Muhammad Noor Khan, now detained, was a graduate of Nadir Eduljee Dinshaw Engineering University in Karachi, Pakistan. He was considered a key link in the network between top leaders and operational cells.[17] Mamdouh Mahmud Salim is another key figure in the network. He served on the advisory Shura Council and Fatwa Committee and was an electrical engineer.[18]

Some members naturally use their learned professional skills to augment the organization. For instance, Ayman al-Zawahiri is a trained doctor and is said to still function as bin Ladin's physician. Kamel Daoudi, a Franco-Algerian with a knack for computers and aspirations to be an aeronautics engineer, was able to leverage these skills when he joined the network.[19]

Education

Like age and occupation, education too varies in the network. Education levels vary from little or no formal education to postdoctorate degrees. For example, several of those involved in the 9/11 attacks were college students, many in the engineering fields. Khalid Shaykh Muhammad attended an agricultural and technical college in the United States. As we already noted, al-Zawahiri was a trained doctor, and many of his Egyptian compatriots were educated professionals as well. Ouoassini Cherifi, who was arrested in 2000 for providing money and false documentation to network members, is a Frenchman of Algerian descent who earned a degree in mathematics and computer science. Dr. Azahari bin Husin, a Malaysian and bomb-making expert for Jemaah Islamiyah, has a doctorate from Britain's University of Reading. He then became a university lecturer in Malaysia.[20] Shehzad Tanweer, one of the participants in the 2005 London bombings, was a university graduate who studied sports science.[21]

Others did not have a complete education. For example, Abu Musab al-Zarqawi dropped out of school in the ninth grade.[22] Shoe bomber Richard Reid allegedly dropped out of school at the age of sixteen. Abdul al-Aziz al-Muqrin, a now deceased senior Saudi al-Qaida, was a secondary school dropout; he left school before he went to Afghanistan at the age of seventeen.[23] Serhane ben Addelmajid Fakhet, considered the ringleader of the 2004 Madrid bombings, studied economics at Madrid University but never finished his degree.[24]

Others were religious students, or had pursued religious studies. This is true of Saudi Khalid al-Harbi, a prominent figure in the network. He surrendered to Saudi authorities in July 2004. Several members of Jemaah Islamiyah, who were involved in the 2004 Bali bombings, were the products of religious schools. Another example is Omar Bakri, a Syrian and an extremist imam who grew up in Syria and studied at Al-Azhar University in Cairo. Finally, Muhammad Rashid Daoud al-Owhali, a Saudi born in Great Britain, was attending a religious university in Saudi Arabia prior to his involvement in the network.[25]

Religion

There are far too many terms to describe the religious philosophies of individuals who are part of the al-Qaida network. We settled on the term "Salafists," which we broadly use to describe those Sunni Muslims in the network who believe that they are the most devout of the ancestors of the prophet Muhammad, his followers, and the subsequent two generations that followed Muhammad. Ultimately, Salafists believe in the establishment of "true Islamic states." However, not all Salafists believe in the use of violence to achieve those ends.[26] Since the al-Qaida network does advocate violence, this chapter considers those Salafists who are part of the network supportive of the use of armed confrontation. Therefore, unless otherwise indicated, when we use the term "Salafist," we are referring to those who advocate or support violence.

The Salafists, in part, draw their inspiration from Islamic scholars such as Ibn Taymiyyah and Sayyid Qutb and have influenced many individuals associated with the al-Qaida network, such as Abdullah Azzam, Ayman al-Zawahiri, and Usama bin Ladin.

We are concerned with three subsets of this religious category in this chapter. The first includes individuals born into the religion who adopt the Salafist interpretation of Islam. Many times this occurs from birth when parents are already indoctrinated and their children are socialized into this Salafist way of thinking. The second category comprises "born-agains." Islam was not central to the lives of born-agains, and when they do "rediscover" their Muslim roots, they do so with zealousness. Thus, many then adopt the views of the Salafists. The third category includes converts who were not born Muslims, choose to convert to the religion, and adopt a Salafist perspective.

As already noted, born-agains are born Muslims who were before neither practicing nor strict Muslims. At some point, they seek to rediscover their religious roots and attend to it with a zeal not manifested in the past. Over time, the individual becomes more extreme in his or her views. According to many accounts, the style of dress may change to appear more traditional, the length of the beard is extended, and the individual often verbalizes intolerance of views outside of the Salafist brand of Islam. However, this change in appearance may not take place because often the zealous embracing of Islam occurs with engagement in extremist activities, and it is incumbent upon individuals to exercise discretion and maintain a low profile in order to hide their affiliation.

There are many examples of born-agains who have gone on to engage in extremist activities. A notable example is Nizar Trabelsi, a Tunisian professional soccer player in Germany who fell into drugs and alcohol and was even a petty drug dealer. Eventually, he came into contact with extremists, rediscovered his Muslim roots, and was slated to become a suicide bomber in a plot to blow up the U.S. Embassy in Paris, France.[27] Another example is that of Ihsan Garnaoui, a German with Tunisian roots.

> After almost two years of being a recruit in the holy war, no one realized the change from the open-minded Muslim to the fanatic Islamic fundamentalist. Garnaoui, who has been in prison since last March [2003] for allegedly planning an attack in Germany, is considered to be a kind of mover between the first and second generation. His personal jihad began in the small town of Velten in Brandenburg's Oberhavelland. In his refrigerator at home, he only allowed meat to be stored that was slaughtered by Islamic rules. After he moved to Berlin, his daughter's baby food also had to be selected strictly according to God's law. Garnaoui's ex-wife, who had met her husband in 1995 in Sousse in Tunisia on vacation, remembered, "My whole life, my schedule was geared to Islam."[28]

Another notable born-again individual is Lebanese-born Ziyad Jarrah, pilot of the plane that crashed into the field in Pennsylvania on 9/11. Jarrah went to Germany in 1996 to attend a language course, and according to accounts of his life, he was known to drink and enjoy the nightclubs. He later moved to Hamburg to enroll in the university. Jarrah also had a serious girlfriend, Aysel, whom he called from the cockpit of the plane before it crashed. At some point, Jarrah met his future accomplices and began to embrace their extremist views. He disappeared in 1999 and emerged in the United States to take flight training in 2000.[29]

Our final example is Yasin Taher, an American of Yemeni descent who was part of what the media termed the Lackawanna cell, named after the city in New York in which its members lived. Taher, who graduated from high school in 1996, married his high school sweetheart. According to his friends, it wasn't until his early twenties that he became more interested in Islam. In the spring of 2001, Taher left for Afghanistan to attend an al-Qaida training camp.[30]

In addition to those who were born Muslims are those who at some point in their lives convert to Islam. Before their conversion, they may have been Christians, Jews, atheists, agnostics, or members of any other religious affiliations.

Individuals convert to Islam for many reasons. First, they may convert due to sheer curiosity about the religion, which oftentimes leads the individual to attend a mosque or cultural center to become better informed. In other words, an individual may wonder what happens in the mosque and what the religion has to offer. These visits may eventually lead to conversion. Others develop a self-professed camaraderie with Muslims, especially those Muslims they see as oppressed by the West. Some are attracted to the structure that the religion provides in their lives. Others want to change their lives, and Islam fills a void. Conversion can also occur through marriage ties. In other words, when a man wants to marry a Muslim woman, the parents may insist that he convert and vice versa.

Thus, individuals convert for a variety of reasons. Unfortunately, in some cases, individuals attend a mosque or engage in discussions with those in the neighborhood, local café, university, or prison who are proselytizing the Salafist version of Islam. As a result, conversion occurs shortly before or almost simultaneously with the joining of the extremist group. In the latter cases, the motivations for joining the al-Qaida network and converting to Islam are blurred. This motivational aspect of joining the network will be addressed in the next chapter.

Other times, individuals convert years before they make the actual decision to join the extremist network. This can happen for two reasons. First, an individual may hold Salafist views but not yet be motivated to join the network. Second, an individual may not at first hold Salafist beliefs but adopt them gradually through association with them. For now, suffice it to say that not all converts take on a Salafist bent, and it is those who adopt the violent extremist viewpoint for whatever reason, during whatever time frame, that interest us in this book.

Why should we be concerned about converts? The simple answer is that converts are coveted by the network and therefore are a cause for concern. They are coveted because they are able to blend in more effectively and avoid the "profiling" pitfalls that others in the network are likely to encounter. In addition, converts are likely to carry Western passports and can theoretically travel more easily than their counterparts from scrutinized countries. For these reasons, they are a greater threat to the security of the United States and its allies. It is important to note, however, that the number of converts who turn to extremism represents a small percentage of converts overall. For example, the French government estimates that of the 50,000 converts in the country, 1,110 had adopted an extremist viewpoint.[31] The proportion of individuals who actively participate in the network is probably much smaller.

Unfortunately, all converts are new to Islam and are therefore vulnerable to the Salafist version of the religion. Additionally, converts can come into contact with Salafists and can be influenced by them in any place and at any time. Salafists do not articulate alternative views of Islam to the convert; instead, converts are taught that this is the only and, indeed, the correct way. "The force of any given passage of Qur'an or Hadith, not blunted by culture or familiarity, can be presented to whoever instructs the convert with any spin the teacher might favor."[32] In addition, converts are more likely to embrace their newfound religion zealously because they were not born into it. In other words,

> The Salafists, who demand a pure and original interpretation of the sacred texts, suggest as religious referents clerics from Islamic universities of the Muslim world, notably Saudi Arabia and Syria. Some of them teach a real break from Western values, declared enemies of Islam. The converts, who suffer a deficit in terms of legitimacy compared to those of Muslim origin, sometimes seek to compensate by a total engagement, in studies and in religious journeys.[33]

It is not surprising then that in addition to proving their religious knowledge, converts also must pass a series of steps to further prove their commitment. According to one French analyst, Western converts in particular followed a path and, like any recruit, had to prove their worth.

There are numerous examples of high-profile converts. David Hicks, an Australian captured in Afghanistan in December 2001, is a good example. A father of two, Hicks held various types of jobs, from rodeo rider to ranch hand. In 1999, he decided to fight with the Muslim Kosovo Liberation Army against the Serbs. He then became interested in Islam. Upon returning, he attended various mosques and adopted the nom de guerre Muhammad Dawood. From there Hicks went to Pakistan to fight in Kashmir against the Indians and then to Afghanistan, eventually becoming embroiled in the world of al-Qaida.[34] Another example is Adam Gadahn (a.k.a. Yahiye), a Jewish American who became interested in Islam and eventually attended an Orange County Islamic Center in California, where he interacted with extremists.[35]

Another example is the case of Jerome and David Courtailler, sons of a French butcher. The two brothers were raised as Roman Catholics. Their parents divorced, and the brothers abused drugs. "I couldn't see a way out" was David's explanation for turning to a London mosque, where he claimed he saw serenity on the faces of those inside.[36] They then decided to attend training in Afghanistan; David decided not to pursue training, which he found "tiresome," while his brother continued on, eventually becoming involved in a plot to bomb the U.S. Embassy in Paris.[37]

Christian Ganczarski is another example of a European convert. Ganczarski, a German, grew up as a Roman Catholic. Completing only seventh grade, he became an apprentice welder, then went on to work in a company that employed many Muslims. During his discussions with them, they influenced him to read the Koran. He converted to Islam when he was twenty.[38]

On the other hand, Richard Colvin Reid, a British citizen and the son of an English mother and Jamaican father, converted to Islam while in prison in Great Britain for robbery. After his release, he attended London mosques, notably the Finsbury Park and Brixton mosques, eventually traveling to Afghanistan to participate in al-Qaida's training. José Padilla, an American of Puerto Rican descent, converted to Islam while in an American prison. Padilla was being held in the United States as an enemy combatant for al-Qaida-related activities; however, his prosecution was turned over to the criminal justice system.

Certainly, after Operation Enduring Freedom, the Afghan base of operations was decimated. However, we can assume that the same principle of proving oneself a worthy convert still applies. And, as noted above, converts have taken their place alongside Muslim-born recruits.

Conclusion

The demographics of the recruits are indeed complex. Given the differentiation among recruits, it isn't possible to come up with a particular profile of the quintessential extremist. For one, while males have dominated the network, the role of women should not be overlooked. Recruits also come from all ages, backgrounds, and walks of life. For example, the employment situation of recruits is diverse, and there are no significant commonalties regarding employment type before individuals join the al-Qaida network.

Shedding light on recruits' backgrounds, however, invariably leads us to question our own long-held assumptions or to examine the individuals more closely. For example, it is commonly stated that economics are the driving force behind recruitment, but we have seen that other factors are important as well, and in some cases, economics are not important at all. As more and more data is gathered on the backgrounds of such individuals, it may be possible to make more definitive judgments about where certain characteristics may be coalescing. At the same time, a demographic profile alone does not provide us with a full picture as to why people join. In other words, while a recruit may be unemployed, we cannot simply assume that his economic situation is a motivating factor. Having said that, we will now turn to an examination of recruits' motivations.

Notes

1. Marcella Andreoli, "Under Orders from Usama," *Milan Panorama*, April 22, 2004, 2.

2. Brian Ross and David Scott, "An American Married to Al Qaeda," *ABC News*, December 23, 2004, available at www.abcnews.go.com (last accessed March 10, 2005).

3. Middle East Media Research Institute, "A Letter by an Alleged Wife of a Martyr to the Wife of Paul Johnson," Special Dispatch Series No. 758, *MEMRI*, August 5, 2004, available at http://memri.org/bin/articles.cgi?Page=archives&Area=sd&ID=SP75804, 2 (last accessed March 15, 2005).

4. Middle East Media Research Institute, "Al-Qaida Women's Magazine: Women Must Participate in Jihad," Special Dispatch Series No. 779, *MEMRI*, September 7, 2004, available at http://memri.org/bin/articles.cgi?Page=archives&Area=sd&ID=SP77904, 1 (last accessed March 10, 2005).

5. Abd-al-Muhsin al-Murshid, "Fundamentalist Websites Publish Physical Fitness Training Programs for al-Qa'ida's Women and Some of Them Urge Organization's Elements to Reduce Intake of Kabsat," *Al-Sharq al-Awsat*, October 4, 2003.

6. Kelly McEvers, "Jemaah Islamiyah Uses Women, Marriage to Strengthen Ties," *Straights Times*, January 19, 2004.

7. Mia Bloom, "Terror's Stealth Weapon: Women," *Los Angeles Times*, November 29, 2005, available at www.latimes.com/news/opinion/commentary/la-oe-bloom29nov29,0,3416302.story?coll=la-news-comment-opinions (last accessed April 15, 2006).

8. Rana Sabbagh-Gargour, "Failed Suicide Bomber 'Acted out of Revenge,'" *The Times*, November 15, 2005, available at www.timesonline.co.uk/article/0,,251-1872491,00.html (last accessed April 15, 2006).

9. British Broadcasting Corporation, "Madrid Bombing Suspects," *BBC News*, March 10, 2005, available at http://news.bbc.co.uk/1/hi/world/europe/3560603.stm (last accessed March 10, 2005).

10. Faris Bin-Hazzam, "Profile of 'Local Leader' of Al-Qaida in Saudi Arabia," *Al-Sharq al Awsat*, December 10, 2003.

11. Bruce Crumley and Scott MacCloud, "The Madrid Bombings One Year On," *Time*, March 13, 2005, available at www.time.com/time/europe/html/050321/story.html (last accessed April 15, 2005).

12. *Global Terror Alert*, "The Foreign Martyr's of Iraq," *Global Terror Alert*, 2003–2004, available at www.globalterroralert.com/pdf/0105/iraqmartyrs04.pdf (last accessed March 10, 2005).

13. Rohan Gunaratna, *Inside Al Qaeda* (New York: Columbia University Press, 2002).

14. Sebastian Rotella and David Zucchino, "Embassy Plot Offers Insight into Terrorist Recruitment, Training," *Los Angeles Times*, October 22, 2001, available at http://www.norwalkadvocate.com/news/nationworld/sns-worldtrade-embassyplot-lat,0,3646484.story?page=1&coll=sns-newsnation-headlines (last accessed March 10, 2005).

15. Dominic Cziesche, Georg Mascolo, Sven Roebel, Heiner Schimmoeller, and Holger Stark, "As If You Were at War," *Der Spiegel*, March 22, 2004.

16. *Daily Mail*, "Suicide Bomber Profile: The Family Man," *Daily Mail*, July 13, 2005, available at www.dailymail.co.uk/pages/live/articles/news/news.html?in_article_id=355621&in_page_id=1770&in_a_source= (last accessed April 15, 2006).

17. Jason Burke, Paul Harris, and Martin Bright, "Suspect Arrested in Pakistan May Hold al-Qaeda's Secrets," *Observer*, August 8, 2004, available at www.guardian.co.uk/alqaida/story/0,,1278651,00.html (last accessed March 10, 2005).

18. Howard Chua-Eoan, "Is He Osama's Best Friend?" *Time*, November 12, 2001, available at www.time.com/time/archive/preview/0,10987,1001170,00.html (last accessed March 10, 2005).

19. Jean Chichizola, "The Afghan, the Convert, and the Unknown Kamikaze," *Le Figaro*, March 18, 2004.

20. British Broadcasting Corporation, "Bali Bomb Maker's Luck Runs Out," *BBC News*, November 10, 2005, available at http://news.bbc.co.uk/2/hi/asia-pacific/4423960.stm (last accessed April 15, 2006).

21. *Manchester Evening News*, "Suicide Bomber 'Had All to Live For,'" *Manchester Evening News*, July 13, 2005, available at www.manchesteronline.co.uk/men/news/s/165/165813_suicide_bomber_had_all_to_live_for.html (last accessed April 15, 2006).

22. Jean Charles Brisard, *Zarqawi: The New Face of Al-Qaida* (New York: Other Press, 2005).

23. Faris Bin-Hazzam, "Profile of 'Local Leader' of Al-Qaida in Saudi Arabia," *Al-Sharq al Awsat*, December 10, 2003.

24. British Broadcasting Corporation, "Piecing Together Madrid Bombers' Past," *BBC News*, April 5, 2004, available at http://news.bbc.co.uk/1/hi/world/europe/3600421.stm (last accessed March 10, 2005).

25. Benjamin Weiser and Tim Golden, "Who and Where Are al-Qaida?" *Houston Chronicle*, October 17, 2001, available at www.chron.com/cs/CDA/printstory.mpl/side/1074253 (last accessed March 10, 2005).

26. Qunitan Wiktorowicz and John Kaltner, "Killing in the Name of Islam: Al-Qaeda's Justification for September 11," *Middle East Policy* 10, no. 2 (summer 2003): 76–92.

27. Benjamin Orbach, "Usama Bin Ladin and Al-Qa'ida: Origins and Doctrines," *Middle East Review of International Affairs* 5, no. 4 (December 2001), available at http://meria.idc.ac.il/journal/2001/issue4/jv5n4a3.htm (last accessed March 10, 2005).

28. Dominic Cziesche, Georg Mascolo, Sven Roebel, Heiner Schimmoeller, and Holger Stark, "As If You Were at War," *Der Spiegel*, March 22, 2004.

29. *Der Spiegel*, "The Warriors from Pearl Harburg," *Der Spiegel*, November 26, 2001.

30. Roya Aziz and Monica Lam, "Profiles the Lackwanna Cell," *Frontline*, October 16, 2003, available at www.pbs.org/wgbh/pages/frontline/shows/sleeper/inside/profiles.html (last accessed March 10, 2005).

31. Piotr Smolar, "Converts to Radical Islam, a Growing Minority of Activists," *Le Monde*, June 4, 2004.

32. Robert Spencer, "Why American Muslim Converts Turn to Terrorism," *Human Events*, June 3, 2004, available at www.humaneventsonline.com/article.php?id+4063, 1 (last accessed March 10, 2005).

33. Piotr Smolar, "Converts to Radical Islam, a Growing Minority of Activists" *Le Monde*, June 4, 2004, 2.

34. Richard Leiby, "Taliban from Down Under," *Washington Post*, March 10, 2002, available at http://pqasb.pqarchiver.com/washingtonpost/access/110332251.html?dids=110332251:110332251&FMT=ABS&FMTS=ABS:FT&fmac=&date=Mar+10%2C+2002&author=Richard+Leiby&desc=Taliban+From+Down+Under (last accessed March 10, 2005).

35. Amy Argetsinger, "Muslim Teen Made Conversion to Fury," *Washington Post*, December 2, 2004, available at www.washingtonpost.com/wp-dyn/articles/A26447-2004Dec1.html (last accessed March 10, 2005).

36. *Newsweek*, "Bin Laden's Invisible Network," *Newsweek*, October 29, 2002, available at www.msnbc.com/news/645596.asp (last accessed March 10, 2005).

37. Josh Lefkowitz and Lorenzo Vidino, "Al Qaeda's New Recruits," *Wall Street Journal*, August 28, 2003, available at http://online.wsj.com/article/0,,SB106202472928168100 (last accessed March 10, 2005).

38. Stephan Brown, "White Terror," *Front Page Magazine*, July 31, 2003, available at www.frontpagemag.com/Articles/ReadArticle.asp?ID=9173 (last accessed March 10, 2005).

CHAPTER 4

Individual Motivation:
The Push to Extremism

We should not investigate the monetary flows of al-Qaida, but rather analyze its way of thinking.

—Syrian Grand Mufti Ahmad Bader Hassoun

One of this book's central goals is to address why individuals join groups whose principal goal is political or social change through violence. To help explain this phenomenon, this chapter will provide a detailed discussion of the role of individual motivation in recruitment. In many circles, individual motivation is not seen as important. Alternatively, it is simply overlooked as part of the discussion. Focusing on the individual is not always the preferred level of analysis; thus, it is often passed over in favor of group-level analysis to explain what are really individual-level phenomena. Our suspicion is that, for some, delving into anything resembling individual psychology is uncharted territory, oftentimes referred to as psychobabble and even perceived as voodoolike. Therefore, addressing individual motivation can be unappealing because it relies upon, as its core, a different literature and perspective from the more traditional case study and descriptive approaches to studying extremism. These unfortunately represent a comfort zone for many, and while they have contributed significantly to the literature, they have not provided a solid basis from which to understand why individuals join extremist groups. To us, an individual's motivation is fundamental, and without discussing it, we lose the opportunity to understand why individuals want to join the network in the first place, as well as to understand the individuals themselves. As will become evident below, we believe that the only way to really understand motivation is to take a look at individuals' stories; otherwise, we are left with only the same conjecture about why individuals join extremist groups like al-Qaida.

Defining Motivation

For our purposes, motivation is defined as the reason or reasons why individuals look for alternatives to their present life situations. As a result of motivating factors, they are drawn to, and eventually join, the al-Qaida network. Yet, as chapter 1 explained briefly, the motivation to join the network is only one-half of the recruitment puzzle this book is attempting to unravel. Motivation is simply what we describe as "the push" to join the network. The recruitment environment, methods, and locations—what we call "the pull," are also necessary to complete the process of joining the network. This aspect of the recruitment puzzle is more fully addressed in chapter 5, while this chapter focuses solely on motivating factors.

The Normality of Extremists

Before beginning a detailed explanation of our own framework, one major point that emerged from our discussion of the psychology of extremists in chapter 1 needs to be reiterated: Generally speaking, the types of individuals who join the al-Qaida network and other groups are, for the most part, "normal." That being said, as with any group, it is statistically likely that some individuals drawn to the network are sociopaths, psychopaths, or suffering from some very disturbing psychological problems. This could be true of any group, not just those engaged in extremist activities. In the case of al-Qaida, some individuals may have found a venue for fulfilling violent aspirations in an extremist group. But, again, they are not the norm and therefore are not the central focus of this chapter or this book. Instead, we focus on the everyday people who join the network and the wide variety of motivations that lead them to join the al-Qaida network. While psychological issues do play a role, they are still a small part of the overall picture.

Our discussion also does not concentrate solely on the recruitment of those individuals who become suicide bombers. The network and the individuals involved in it are much more complex than a subset of individuals who desire to commit suicide for a particular cause. The answer to why they want to kill themselves is not the focus of this book because that is a different question from why they want to join an extremist group. Furthermore, solely focusing on suicide bombers misrepresents the differentiation within, and the complexity of, the network. Not all individuals are actually willing to kill themselves for the cause. It is more likely that only those most committed to the group, or those looking for a way to end their lives, will do so.

Understanding Motivation: A Framework for Analysis

Our framework seeks to provide a simplified, yet rich, explanatory categorization of motivation, complete with descriptive attributes. In general, our argument is that motivation is central to the decision to join the al-Qaida network. Again, motivation is defined as an individual's reason or reasons for seeking an alternative to his or her present life situation; it is what we have already described as the push to a network like al-Qaida.

There are numerous ways to categorize motivation. To aid in our discussion, our framework is first presented in general terms, as categories of our choosing. Subsequently, the framework is presented at the observable-indicator level in order to provide a detailed discussion of what was actually going on in these individuals' lives before they joined the network. Thus, while we chose the categories to facilitate organization, the more specific indicators were observed in the stories of the recruits.

The Role of Group Factors

Before introducing our individual-level framework, it is necessary to make a few important comments about group-level factors. What is the role of group factors? Joining the network fills a void in an individual's life. It is important to emphasize that individuals eventually join the al-Qaida network in response to the particular motivating factor or factors present in their lives before they decide to join. Therefore, they are seeking to compensate for, or deal with, a motivating factor or factors (the push). In seeking this outlet, they encounter an enticing group (the al-Qaida network). This network, as chapter 5 discusses, has significant recruitment methods (the pull). This all converges when a motivated recruit meets a resonating message. Ultimately, the network, with its great appeal, satisfies an individual's need to belong to something meaningful. In other words, the network provides the individual with an identity. He or she is now an important member of a group with a great cause. The network provides the structure and becomes the outlet through which the individual can address his or her motivational factors. While individuals can be conscripted into an organization, this chapter focuses on those who either actively seek membership or are sought and vetted for membership by existing members of the network.

The individuals who join the network experience the pressures of conformity. Those who join are now pressured, generally speaking, to conform to the rules of the group. For example, roles, or expectations of how a person ought to behave, are made known to the recruit, as are norms, or expectations about how all members should behave. Individuals will be forced to conform, to change their beliefs or behaviors to be consistent with those laid out by the group. What makes individuals conform? Studies have shown they do so because they want to be liked, because they want to be "right" (motivation to be correct is high), and even because they want to avoid rejection by their peers.[1] After all, no individual member wants to be ostracized or expelled from the group.

Ultimately, as part of a group, individuals engage in extremist activities that they probably wouldn't have as individuals. As will become evident in chapter 5, the rationales for doing so are provided in great quantities by the network itself. In joining the group, an individual now feels absolved of any wrongdoing for participating in violence.

Once an individual joins and is pressured to conform, leaving the group becomes a difficult proposition indeed. Pressures from other members may thwart any ideas of leaving the trusted network. There may even be fear of retribution against the individuals themselves or family members and other associates.

The Role of Emotion

In addition to group factors, the importance of emotions cannot be discounted. Our view is that cognition and emotions go hand in hand.[2] Therefore, individuals do not simply have cognitive processes devoid of emotion. More importantly, however, there is an emotional component to the decision to join a group in the first place, and emotion plays a role in the push to the network. Anger, frustration, contempt, disgust, resentment, jealousy, guilt, shame, envy, pity, fear, anxiety, and pride are some of the emotions that can be relevant. But the role of emotion does not stop there. Emotions are especially important when the influential methods (the pull) are factored in. There is a deliberate emotional content to all of the methods used to draw individuals to the network. Appealing to an individual's emotions helps not only to draw in new members but also to sustain old ones.

Individual Motivation: The Specifics

Our framework divides motivation into four categories: personal, social, economic, and political. Under each of these categories our real-world indicators are listed. At this level, our most basic reasons for why people are primed to join the al-Qaida network are provided.

- Personal motivations: absent fathers, the alleviation of boredom, camaraderie, the desire to fit in, disputes with parents, desire for fame/status/recognition, family influence, lack of purpose, marital problems, parental divorce, peer pressure, poor academic performance, poor job performance, desire for adventure, a traumatic event, vengeance
- Social motivations: alcohol abuse, cultural alienation, drug abuse or addiction, societal alienation, wanting a cause
- Economic motivations: criminal activity, financial problems, lack of motivation to seek employment or work, underemployment, unemployment
- Political motivations: acts by an imperial country, cultural imperialism, an imperial country's support for a defined enemy, objectionable government policies, oppression of the identity group

Motivation or Motivations?

In digesting these motivational categories, it is also important to point out that these categories and the indicators within them should not be taken as mutually exclusive. Therefore, individuals can have one or more motivating factors. For example, one individual may just have unemployment as an economic motivating factor, while another individual can have academic failure and divorce as personal motivating factors. Likewise, individuals can have more than one indicator across categories. Thus, an individual may have personal (divorce) and economic (unemployment) motivations, and another may have personal (divorce) and political (oppression of an identity group) motivations. Alternatively, an individual may have multiple personal (divorce, academic failure) and economic (unemployment, financial problems) motivations. Finally, certain indicators within the categories can actually influence each other. For example, a person who engages in criminal activity and gets caught and imprisoned may feel a lack of purpose in life when released.

These motivational attributes are present in virtually every society, but they have also been observed in our research on the individuals who join the al-Qaida network. Obviously, not all people will act on these motivations and join the network, but, as will be revealed in chapter 5, when motivated individuals are also exposed to an appealing message, they are more likely to join the network.

Personal Motivation

Our observation is that particular individuals join the network for a variety of personal motivations. It should be clear from the number of indicators under this specific category that it happens to be most commonly observed motivational factor in individuals' stories.

First, vengeance can be a powerful motivation for some individuals, who may have felt personally wronged or witnessed the mistreatment or death of a close friend or family member. They then turn to a group that they perceive will allow them to carry out that vengeance. Other individuals are severely impacted by such problems as personal divorce or the divorce of their parents. A life-changing event such as a divorce can leave many individuals looking for ways to bounce back from the stressful experience. Other traumatic events, such as death and illnesses, can also be influential motivators. Finally, some individuals experience marital difficulties but see no socially acceptable way out of the marriage. Joining a group that takes one far away from the problem can help temporarily absolve the person from dealing with personal marital problems.

In addition, many individuals look for alternatives when experiencing significant family issues, such as power struggles or disputes with parents, particularly fathers. Other individuals are left with a significant void in their lives after the death of a father or the loss of parental influence and guidance. For some, this void results from the total absence of a father's influence in their lives. Still others have poor academic or job performances, leading to a great sense of personal failure or disappointment. These feelings are sometimes shared by others within the family, notably fathers, further complicating the situation.

Undeniably, some individuals simply lack any sense of structure or purpose in life and are looking for something to provide them with that structure and purpose. In these cases, groups, particularly those with an appealing message, can provide that structure and purpose that the individual desperately seeks.

The desire to fit in or for camaraderie can also be an important motivating factor. The discussion on group factors above applies here as well. Wanting to go along with the group to avoid being ostracized can be a powerful motivating factor. There are also those who eventually join a group because they are actually being pressured by their peers to do so. While this may sound like camaraderie, it is slightly different. The pressure placed on the individual by others can often be a negative experience. Fitting in with friends and feeling camaraderie have more to do with going with the flow, but not necessarily being pressured to do so. However, both camaraderie and pressure can certainly occur at the same time. Family members can also assert these types of pressures. Typically, these family members are already either involved in, or support the notion of, joining an extremist group. Out of fear, perhaps, or to avoid disappointing the family, an individual can be driven to join a group designated as worthy, even if he or she has absolutely no desire to do so.

Certain individuals are simply on a quest for adventure. Typically, these individuals are bored with their current circumstances and are looking for an alternative to alleviate that boredom. What better way to alleviate boredom than to join a potentially exciting group? Oftentimes, they view the hoops they must jump through to join as thrilling challenges rather than hardships to be endured.

Some individuals are motivated by the quest for some sort of personal fame. These individuals want to believe that they are important. Self-esteem is a contributing factor here; an individual can actually have too much or too little. These individuals want to be viewed as important to others, whether within their peer group or family or outside them (i.e., by the group they join or even the world). Related to this are those individuals who want to achieve personal status or gain recognition. Still others want to lead or be in charge of something seen as important. One way to achieve this is to seek out a group that will allow them to actualize their desires for leadership and power. Many of these types join to go straight to the top. Some are more patient than others about "doing their time." Others simply want to work toward a goal or achieve something. These individuals will be attracted to groups that can convincingly argue that their goal is worth committing to and working toward.

Finally, while we have argued above that psychological issues are not the norm among recruits in the al-Qaida network, our framework does not discount that they are influential in the lives of some. Aside from serious psychological issues, certain individuals may simply be depressed and looking for an outlet to deal with that depression. In many instances, depression, especially among men, is not acknowledged or dealt with. If individuals are sinking into depression, they may look for a way to deal with the feelings associated with the disease.

There are numerous examples of the role that personal motivations play in the lives of al-Qaida members. For example, the unfortunate participation of two young men in extremist activities provides us with particular insight into the influence of family. Shalali bin Shalali is an Algerian imam in a neighborhood mosque located in the basement of a residential building in Venissieux, France. The imam's son Murad and Murad's friend, Nizar Sasi, went to Afghanistan in June 2001. U.S. forces captured both Murad and Nizar, and both are being held in Guantánamo Bay, Cuba. Murad's father is known for his outspoken political views, notably on Palestine, Chechnya, George W. Bush, and Jacques Chirac. Another of the imam's sons, Munad, is part of the al-Qaida network and is believed to have been influential in his brother's life choices as well.[3] Family was also influential in a case far away from France. On October 12, 2002, twelve blasts set by Jemaah Islamiyah erupted in Bali, Indonesia. Thirty-four individuals were detained after the bombing. Among those arrested was an individual named Ali Gufron (a.k.a. Mukhlas). Mukhlas attended an Islamic school run by the spiritual leader of Jemaah Islamiyah, Abu Bakar Bashir. At this school, Mukhlas claimed to have met the group's infamous operational planner, Hambali. He also met Usama bin Ladin in Afghanistan in the late 1980s.[4] Mukhlas became a teacher at a religious school in the town of Ulu Tiram in southern Malaysia.[5] He was influential in recruiting many individuals, including his two brothers and other relatives and friends, into Jemaah Islamiyah.[6] The story of Azizbek Karimov is another example of the influential role of family. In hopes of receiving leniency for his participation in an Islamic Movement of Uzbekistan (IMU) plot to blow up the U.S. Embassy in Afghanistan, Karimov has provided keen insight into his life leading up to his decision to join the group. Born in Andizhan, Uzbekistan, Karimov was, by his account, from a broken home. In fact, when his was seven, his parents divorced, and he became the victim of a family struggle that, he says, "left him deeply scarred." He came under the influence of his mother's uncle, who had "taken up religion."[7] Karimov attended the Juma Mosque in Andizhan. In 1995, the Uzbek authorities shut down the mosque, presumably because of extremist activities that were taking place. Karimov fell in with extremists who convinced him to travel to Chechnya to get military-type training.[8] His comrades would eventually lead him on the path to the IMU.

Different personal issues play a role in the lives of others. For example, Salih Muhammad al-Awfi was a member of Saudi al-Qaida killed during a police raid in Saudi Arabia in August 2005. Al-Awfi was born in Medina, Saudi Arabia. After completing his basic studies, he took a course in prison affairs and graduated in 1988 as a private first class in the prison service. However, reports on his background indicate that he was known as a "troublemaker" and was disciplined for "unbecoming conduct."[9] While he continued working in the system, he was dismissed after three years due to "troublemaking and frequent absenteeism." In the early 1990s, he left Saudi Arabia to participate in jihad, eventually ending up in Chechnya. He then carried over his participation in jihad by joining al-Qaida.[10] The story of Kamel Daoudi was also partly personal, but reflected a different type of troubled past. Daoudi was arrested for his involvement in a plot to blow up the U.S. Embassy in Paris. The issues in Daoudi's life, although complex, shed light on his decision to embrace extremism as an outlet for his problems. Daoudi was born in Algeria. His father worked in Paris, and when Kamel was almost five, the family moved from Algeria to France to join his father. Daoudi claims that his father was demanding, pushing him to excel in school and beating him with a wooden paddle. He also noted his feelings of cultural alienation while in France. For example, he claimed he was often the only Arab in class and that the children made fun of him because of his first name.[11] According to several accounts of his life, Daoudi was a good student with a bright future, yet he found his university courses in math and computer science difficult.[12] Daoudi, who was Internet savvy, married a Hungarian woman from Romania, whom he met and courted in an Internet chat room.[13] He worked as an instructor in a cybercafé but soon became associated with extremists. He eventually left France for Great Britain and began to attend extremist mosques.[14]

The background of Azahari Husin also demonstrates the role that stressful personal issues can play. Husin was, until his death in 2005, a senior bomb maker for Jemaah Islamiyah. He was called the "demolition man" in Malaysian newspapers. He is implicated in several bombings, including the 2002 Bali nightclub and August 2003 and September 2004 Jakarta attacks. In the late 1970s, Azahari studied engineering in Australia for four years. He subsequently received a doctorate in land management from Reading University in England. He taught at Malaysia's University of Technology until 2001. Azahari had a wife and two children; however, his wife found out she had throat cancer after the birth of their second child. In the early 1990s, Azahari left his wife with the words that he had a greater cause of God to serve.[15] Finally, the actions taken by Sajida Mubarak Atrous al-Rishawi in Jordan can be traced to the role of not only personal pain but also family ties to extremists. Al-Rishawi was a thirty-five-year-old married woman without children who came from a family of al-Qaida members. Her brother-in-law and her two brothers were members of al-Zarqawi's network. Her brother-in-law was killed in Ramadi, and her two brothers were killed in Fallujah.

All of them died during U.S. military operations.[16] She was committed to killing herself and her husband at a wedding reception in a hotel in Amman, Jordan, in November 2005. Her husband's belt detonated, and he was killed, but she survived when her belt did not detonate. As she explained during her confession on Jordanian television, "My husband wore a belt and put one on me. He taught me how to use it, how to pull the [primer cord] and operate it."[17]

Essam Muhammad Hafez Marzouk is an Egyptian member of the al-Qaida network responsible for training the bombers of the 1998 East African embassy attacks. He served as an instructor in bin Ladin's training camps in the early 1990s. Marzouk was the son of a Cairo businessman and grew up in the wealthy El Mohandeseen neighborhood. He also served in the Egyptian military and, after his discharge, spent his time working out in the gym. There, he met an individual who told him about jihad in Soviet Afghanistan and how to join.[18] Thus, given that he had just left the military, and was spending his time at the gym, there was very likely a personal or economic motivation (or combination) for why he made the decision he did. Others such as Marwan al-Shihi needed acceptance. Al-Shihi, a member of the 9/11 Hamburg cell, came to Germany from the United Arab Emirates to be a student, not an extremist. He was described as financially secure and was on a military scholarship sponsored by his government. A teacher described him as immature and aimless but not a zealot. When he became acquainted with others in the Hamburg cell, it seems as though al-Shihi was looking for acceptance and found it with this particular group of individuals bent on striking a severe blow to the United States.

Social Motivation

A variety of social issues can impact the lives of individuals. The most notable are drug and alcohol abuse. At times, individuals engage in such seemingly destructive behaviors and are often cognizant of the impact that these abusive behaviors have on them. To deal with their recognized problem, they seek out alternatives, namely, a group that does not condone engaging in such behavior and will help them abstain from, or fix, their abusive tendencies.

Another important social motivation is cultural alienation. Many individuals are attempting to find a place in their societies, particularly in Western countries, to which individuals come from all over the world, settling into a country very different from their own. This can also be true of first- and even second-generation children whose families have retained their culture, customs, and religion but live in a society with a seemingly alien culture. As a result, some individuals feel that they don't have a foot squarely placed in either camp. In other words, they are not truly part of the dominant nation but neither are they truly part of their "other" nation. Yet, even though they don't think of themselves as being fully of a different culture, they may experience significant discrimination, which in turn leads them to feel a sense of cultural alienation. Those who are culturally alienated are looking for grounding, a sense of identity, which they haven't found in either camp. In their quest for identity, they will encounter groups that claim to accept and want them for who they are and what they can contribute.

Other individuals experience a different form of cultural alienation. They feel alienated in their own societies where cultural tradition and modernity may clash. In other words, they may believe that negative outside influences on their country are threatening their cultural identity. The government, which is believed to have allowed such infiltration, is perceived as complicit in this threat. Finally, some individuals simply believe that the government doesn't care about, or understand, the needs of the generation of which they are a part. This is essentially a problem caused by a generation gap, where the misunderstood are seeking to rebel against authority.

Hasib Mir Husayn, one of the participants in the 2005 London attacks, is a good example of the impact that cultural alienation can have on an individual. Husayn was eighteen years old when he blew himself up on a London bus. According to accounts of his life, Husayn grew up in Leeds, England, and is of Pakistani origin. One of his school friends recounted that Husayn's time at Matthew Murray High School was difficult: "It was always whites against Asians, and there were so many fights. Hasib was really quiet and didn't get into any fights, but he was in the thick of gangs that did. Maybe that played a part in making him feel alienated from the country of his birth and Western society."[19] A few years later, those around him witnessed his transformation after a trip to Pakistan to visit relatives; he began to wear robes and a topi hat from the mosque, and he grew a beard.[20] After the London attacks, apparently shocked by his participation, his family commented that he "was a loving and normal young man who gave us no concern."[21]

Another telling example of cultural alienation is in the life of Zacarias Moussaoui. Moussaoui is currently in U.S. custody for his involvement in the 9/11 plot. His case is extremely pertinent to understanding the personal challenges individuals face, as well as the cultural identity of Muslims in Europe. His struggle to find an identity was highlighted in a book by his brother.[22]

Born in France and of Moroccan descent, Moussaoui had, by his brother's account, a tumultuous upbringing. His parents divorced when he was young, and his mother, unable to care for them financially, put him and his three siblings in an orphanage. Eventually, his family was reunited, but he went on to be raised by his seemingly abusive mother. In France, he was also subject to discrimination, being referred to as "dirty nigger," which he perceived to be the cause of his inability to advance academically (having been forced into a vocational track) and to find employment. Yet, his mother never made an effort to educate her children about their religion or their ethnicity. The father of his French girlfriend was not pleased with him either. Thus, Moussaoui could not identify with being a Frenchman or a Moroccan, as he perceived his being ethnically Moroccan as the reason for the discrimination he faced. Moussaoui became resentful of his life and left for London in search of something better. There, he found an outlet, became radicalized, and eventually joined the ranks of al-Qaida's network.

Others such as Jack Roche struggled with substance abuse. Roche, a British convert to Islam, was a member of Jemaah Islamiyah. In 2004, he was convicted on charges of a plot to blow up the Israeli Embassy in Canberra, Australia, and received a nine-year sentence. Roche is originally from England but moved to Sydney, Australia, in the late 1970s. In Sydney, his life was on an empty path. He worked in a factory and battled a drinking problem.[23] Roche saw Islam as the solution to his problems and converted in the early 1990s. In 1996, Jemaah Islamiyah operational leader Hambali recruited Roche into the network. In 2000, he sent Roche to meet with al-Qaida. After he spent time in Pakistan and Afghanistan, senior al-Qaida leaders directed Roche to return to Australia and conduct surveillance on possible targets. He was also instructed to recruit individuals into the network. Following the Bali, Indonesia, bombings in 2002, he was arrested in Australia.

Richard Colvin Reid, better known by his nickname, "the shoe bomber," had a criminal background and was a product of the prison system. Reid was found guilty of trying to blow up an American Airlines flight from Paris, France, to Miami, Florida, by lighting his explosive-laden shoes on fire. Reid, a British citizen, is the son of a Jamaican father and British mother. His father was in jail for car theft at the time of his birth, and his parents divorced when he was eleven.[24] Reid had dropped out of secondary school by the time he was sixteen. Between 1992 and 1996, he served time in prison for a series of crimes, including muggings. He served one of his sentences at Feltham Young Offender's Establishment in London. During this time, he converted to Islam. According to Reid's father, he was instrumental in his son's conversion. His father converted himself in prison to deal with the racial discrimination he experienced. His father says he asked Reid, "Why don't you become a Muslim? They treated me all right."[25] Upon his release from prison, Reid began to attend the Brixton Mosque. He studied Islam and Arabic. Reid came under the influence of extremists who attended the mosque. He then began to attend the Finsbury Park Mosque.

Economic Motivation

Economic factors are important in any discussion of motivation. They are also the most heavily cited reasons, particularly in the press, for why individuals join the al-Qaida network. While economic motivations are important, this assertion needs some clarification. Unemployment, that is, the inability to find a job, can be a powerful motivation to seek alternatives, particularly when individuals believe that their unemployment is no fault of their own. Typically, they think the government or society is to blame for their circumstances. Alternatively, underemployment is another important economic motivation and is clearly distinguishable from unemployment. Either an individual is employed in a low-paying job that doesn't allow him to make ends meet or is, for example, a trained engineer who works driving a taxi or selling vegetables in a market because he can't find a job in his field. Both situations could cause resentment. Additionally, some individuals simply lack the motivation to find employment. The reality is that some believe they are too good to work, or they simply don't want to work. Usually, then, they are bored, financially secure, and looking for alternatives. Enter the group with an alternative to spare.

Many individuals want to stop engaging in, or seek to atone for, their participation in criminal activity. Other individuals simply want to change their economic situation or make money. This can be a powerful motivating tool not only for those who are economically deprived but also for those who perceive that they deserve something better from life.

There are several examples of the role economic motivations can play in the lives of extremists. Ahmed Ressam is currently incarcerated for his role in the Millennium Plot in which he sought to blow up Los Angeles International Airport in December 1999. In his court testimony, Ressam claimed he went to Montreal, Canada, in 1994 in order to "improve my life situation and improve my life in general." While there, Ressam found employment distributing advertising leaflets and turned to welfare and theft (robbing tourists) for financial support. In 1998, he found another outlet to change his life and attended training in basic weapons, advanced explosives, and poisons in Afghanistan. His contacts there helped him lay the groundwork for what eventually became the Millennium Plot.[26] Riduan Isamuddin (a.k.a. Hambali) has been called the Usama bin Ladin of Southeast Asia. His name is taken from Imam Hambali, an eighth-century Islamic saint.[27] Hambali was a key operational planner and figure in Jemaah Islamiyah and is believed to have been involved in many extremist plots, including the attack on the USS *Cole*, 9/11, and many bombings in Indonesia. Another example can be found in the background of Hambali. Hambali was born in West Java in 1966. He was from a poor family "that fought poverty on a daily basis."[28] While a teenager, he became involved in local extremist activities against the ruling Suharto regime in response to perceived religious repression. However, due to those activities, he was forced to relocate to Malaysia. In his early twenties, he traveled to Afghanistan to participate in the jihad against the Soviets. When he returned, he resumed his extremist activities. He was arrested in Thailand in August 2003.

The participation of Abu Musab al-Zarqawi in extremist activities was likely the result of a combination of several motivating factors. Al-Zarqawi, now deceased, was the leader of al-Qaida in Iraq. Al-Zarqawi's is the story of a man who always embraced the most extreme path in any situation he found himself in. He grew up in Zarqa, a poor suburb of Amman, Jordan. Al-Zarqawi spent his youth playing sports and was described as someone who liked to fight. He dropped out of high school at of seventeen and began drinking heavily and getting tattoos.[29] In his earlier twenties, he was in and out of trouble with the law, much to the disappointment of his father, who was a leading figure in the city.[30]

Al-Zarqawi was desperate to get out of Zarqa and felt he had finally found his path when he left for Afghanistan in the late 1980s. Unfortunately, he missed both the war and a chance to make a name for himself. He spent the next few years as a reporter, traveling around Afghanistan and interviewing jihadists. Still seeking an identity, he returned to Jordan in 1992 with nothing but jihad on his mind. He and his mentor, Abu Muhammad al-Maqdisi, formed a group called Bayaat al-Imam to spread their beliefs and to plan operations against Israel and the Jordanian government.[31]

In 1993, he was arrested for his role in Bayaat al-Imam and sentenced to Suqawah prison, where he fully embraced extremism. He spent his time in Suqawah lifting weights, immersing himself in the Koran, and bullying other inmates, who were subservient to him. In time he had created his own network within the prison walls. When the Jordanians released him under an amnesty program, al-Zarqawi found himself lost and without any purpose in his homeland. Thus, he returned to Pakistan and eventually Afghanistan, determined to position himself to join the leadership ranks of the al-Qaida network.

Political Motivation

Our last category is political motivation. While all of our categories have an emotional component to them, the emotions associated with this category can be highly charged. Oftentimes, this category seems to work in conjunction with other categories. For example, a person with one or more personal motivations can also have certain strongly held beliefs about what is right or wrong with their present political situation and the world and who is responsible for them.

Generally speaking, this category encompasses many perceptions about the nature of the world order and domestic politics and can include many elements. Individuals may focus on one, a few, or all of these elements. The imperial image[32] is central to this category. An imperial country is perceived as having superior capabilities and a "sophisticated and dominating" culture. An imperial group can also be highly threatening. When an imperial power is perceived as threatening, the threatened group or country is not likely to challenge the imperial if this group or country accepts its status. On the other hand, a group or country may actually believe it can change its status vis-à-vis the imperial and perceives an opportunity, not a threat. The imperial is viewed as being in decline. Its culture and capabilities are perceived to be equal, or in some cases inferior, to those of the challenging group or country.

In the case of al-Qaida recruits, individuals determine that the acts of another imperial country or group are simply unacceptable. Obviously, those who join a group that aims to defeat the imperial power believe that the imperial power can and should be challenged. Others hold these beliefs but never act upon them. The former are the concern of this book.

Individuals will often focus on outside countries or groups that they perceive to be not only imperialistic but also supportive of a very threatening enemy. According to Martha Cottam,

> The enemy is a familiar image. In its stereotypical extreme it is the evil empire. It is led by a cabal of evil geniuses and is as strong as one's own country. Culturally, it is one's equal. Although its moral characteristics may be foul and its values rotten, it is smart, it has the ability to carry out its plans, it knows science, and is extremely dangerous.[33]

Others believe that outside groups or countries, which can be either imperialists or enemies, are oppressing their own identity group. This identity group can be self-defined as religious, ethnic, cultural, or belonging to some other category. Others object to the actual politics of an internal group, usually the ruling elite. This group can be seen as cavorting with the enemy, imperial power, or simply threatening the individual's identity group. Finally, many point to cultural imperialism as a motivating factor. This involves perceived attempts made by an enemy or imperial power to supplant an individual's identity and replace it with one foreign and objectionable in nature.

While our purpose is not to reiterate what will be discussed in chapter 5 on recruitment methods, we will say that the above generally translates into the perception that an imperial power, namely, the United States, is oppressing Muslims. Not only is the United States a threatening imperial power, but it is also seen as supporting Israel, an established enemy. Israeli activities in Palestine and the Arab world are seen as an extension of U.S. policy. Or, alternatively, the United States is seen as taking its direction from Israel. Either way, U.S. support for Israel is a serious source of contention. Many cite other U.S. policies, such as the United States' stationing of troops in Muslim countries and bolstering of corrupt Arab regimes. Others point to specific jihads as evidence of Muslim oppression, such as Bosnia, Chechnya, Afghanistan, and now Iraq, where the United States is seen as the oppressor. Still others dislike the regimes and policies in their own countries. Finally, U.S. cultural imperialism and the perceived destructive influence it has on Muslim countries is also an issue. Of course, the United States is not the only country accused of being imperialistic. However, it receives more intense focus than others because of its prominence in international affairs.

We have found that those motivated by a political indicator can have some very strongly held beliefs about the world. When they are bombarded with the information discussed in the next chapter, their beliefs are simply reinforced. The next chapter will also show that the al-Qaida network's propaganda machine continually relies upon and reinforces these beliefs. Other individuals, however, don't have any sophisticated knowledge or conception of the world around them. When these individuals are introduced to the al-Qaida network's message, they then begin to form their belief systems about what is right and wrong with their circumstances and the world. Even if a person has only cursory knowledge and poorly defined beliefs about what is right and wrong with the world, the al-Qaida network will step in to fill in the blanks.

The actions by Ryan Anderson and Ahmed al-Haznawi illustrate the role of political motivation. Anderson, a convert to Islam, served in the U.S. National Guard. According to Anderson, he was against being sent to Iraq and aiding the United States and was upset at the denigration of Muslims and Arabs by fellow soldiers. He publicized his views on the Internet. In a statement recorded on a video taken by federal investigators posing as al-Qaida recruiters, he stated, "While I love my homeland, I believe the leaders have taken this horrible road. I have no belief in what the American army has asked me to do. They have taken me from my family and sent me to die."[34] He also advised his perceived al-Qaida recruiters on how to defeat the U.S. military.

Saudi 9/11 hijacker Ahmed al-Haznawi appeared in a videotape in April 2002 that was aired by the al-Jazirah news network entitled "The Wills of the New York and Washington Battle Martyrs." In a demonstration of his hatred of the United States, al-Haznawi declares on the tape, "It is time to kill the Americans on their own ground among their sons and next to their soldiers and intelligence agencies. . . . The truth is that we will fight them on their own ground."[35]

Pulling It Together

This chapter has explained that several factors motivate individuals to seek alternatives in their lives and then membership in a network like al-Qaida. When these attributes are present in conjunction with influential messages, it is not surprising that individuals join this extremist network. As was discussed in chapter 3, it is difficult to speak of a demographic profile of a typical recruit. This also holds true for individual motivations. Before concluding our discussion of motivation, we need to address one more important factor, the role of religion.

The Religious Justification

We have deliberately not discussed so far the role of religion and its connection to individual motivation. In our view, the roles of religion and motivation warrant separate treatment because of religion's obvious importance to recruits in this particular network. We believe that religion is intricately involved in each one of these motivational categories. However, it is not a central motivation. Rather, religion is the important justification used by the recruits for their participation in the network.

That religion is so important should come as no surprise, given that individuals who join the network are repeatedly told, through a variety of methods, that they are doing so for their religion. Thus, the al-Qaida network principally uses religious terminology in its philosophy and as a justification for its actions. Religion is the main vehicle used by the network to entice these recruits to join. As a result, religion is a fundamental attribute that always stands out. This is a significant part of the pull.

Oftentimes, recruits take on the arguments of the methods that were influential in their own recruitment, often parroting the religious justifications and statements they have seen, read, heard, or been told by others and invariably taking on this religious justification as their explanation for why they joined the network and participated in extremist activities in the first place. Thus, statements such as the following, made by one of the bombers in the 2005 London attacks and aired by al-Jazirah, are typical of an al-Qaida network recruit:

> I, and thousands like me, have forsaken everything for what we believe. Our driving motivation doesn't come from tangible commodities that this world has to offer. Our religion is Islam—obedience to the one true God, Allah, and following in the footsteps of the final Prophet and Messenger, Muhammad, Allah's blessings and prayers upon him. This is how our ethical stances are dictated. Your democratically elected governments continuously perpetuate atrocities against my people all over the world, and your support of them makes you directly responsible, just as I am directly responsible for protecting and avenging my Muslim brothers and sisters. Until we feel security, you will be our targets, and until you stop the bombing, gassing, imprisonment, and torture of my people, we will not stop this fight. We are at war, and I am a soldier. Now you too will taste the reality of this situation. I myself, I make du'ah to Allah, to raise me amongst those whom I love, like the Prophets, the Messengers, and the martyrs, and today's heroes, like our beloved Sheik Osama bin Laden, Dr. Ayman Al-Zawahiri, and Abu Mus'ab Al-Zarqawi, and all the other brothers and sisters that are fighting in Allah's cause.[36]

An Irish member of the network made a statement to the same effect. This statement was aired on al-Arabiyah TV: "The Muslim world is not your backyard. The Muslim world is not Germany, Japan, or South America. The honorable sons and daughters of Islam will not sit down, watching you spread your evil and immorality and infidelity to our land."[37]

In an interview, a British-born convert who was accused of plotting to blow up the Israeli Embassy in Australia had the following to say with regard to the United States: "If someone punches you, you are allowed to punch them back. I am very concerned about my brothers and sisters of Islam who are being punched by these people."[38]

Saudi Testimonials: The Religious Justification

In their attempt to deal with the recruitment of Saudi nationals, Saudi television stations air interviews with members of al-Qaida. The following are statements pertaining to the religious justifications that they expressed or were told by recruiters.[39]

- *Testimonial*: "They told us that Islam will only be well with the collapse of this infidel, hypocritical, apostate country, which shields Jews and Christians, and the Jews hide behind it. . . . They kept repeating these things all the time—that Allah had shown us that many Muslim and Arab countries are infidel, but that this [Saudi Arabia] of all countries, alone among these countries, is a great evil, and is more evil and more dangerous than the rest."
- *Testimonial*: "The emir of the Uzbek mujahideen in Afghanistan came to Taif, where I worked. I wanted to meet with Taher Kahn, so I found him and talked to him about my strong desire to go to Afghanistan or to any region where there is fighting for the sake of Allah, under a clear banner. He said that, Allah willing, he would take me with him. He said, 'You may not be able to bear it, since you live.'"

Unfortunately, the use of religious justifications causes analysts and scholars to deal with the network by focusing almost entirely on Islam and Islamic arguments rather than on the background and motivations of the individuals who join the al-Qaida network. Our perspective is that while focusing on the religious arguments is crucial to understanding the pull, the backgrounds and motivations of the individual recruits need to be taken into account in order to get an accurate understanding of why they join.

Motivation versus Demographics

How do the motivational categories relate to our demographic categories? Our separate treatment of demographics and motivation is purposeful. Again, while our argument is that there is no "typical" profile of an extremist, we can learn a lot of interesting things by looking into recruits' backgrounds. However, a demographic profile may not necessarily link up with a motivational profile. Our thinking is best illustrated by an example of a young, male, highly educated, and satisfactorily employed recruit. Upon examination, his motivation is determined to be purely personal in nature. In other words, two members of his family, both with extremely strong influence over him, are members of the network. Therefore, he joins because of family pressures to do so. Motivation provides our reasoning for why he joined, and the demographic profile gives us his background. That is not to say that motivation and demographics will never link up; at times they may. Take another example of a recruit who is male, young, and unemployed; upon examination, we determine that he joined because he was unemployed and saw no prospects for his future.

Conclusion

Motivation is undeniably an important aspect of recruitment. Looking at motivation at a very basic level gives us some interesting insights into why individuals made the choices they did. Oftentimes, the motivations are complex, and more than one attribute is at play in a person's life. Yet, demographics and motivation make up only one-half of the picture. Our discussion now turns to the influence of the extremist message, a glimpse of which was provided in our discussion of the religious justification. When these methods collide with the motivated individual, the eventual result is a new recruit to the network.

Notes

1. Martha Cottam, Beth Dietz-Uhler, Elena Mastors, and Tom Preston, *Introduction to Political Psychology* (Mahwah, NJ: Lawrence Erlbaum and Associates, 2004).

2. Cottam et al., *Introduction to Political Psychology*.

3. Uthman Tazghart, "Al-Majallah Goes to Minguettes, the Neighborhood of Islamic Radicalism in France," *Al-Majallah*, January 4, 2004.

4. Simon Elegant and Jason Tedjasukmana, "The Jihadis' Tale," *Time*, January 20, 2003, available at www.time.com/time/asia/covers/1030127/story.html (last accessed March 10, 2005).

5. Simon Elegant, "The Family behind the Bombings," *Time*, November 25, 2002, available at www.time.com/time/asia/covers/1101021125/story.html (last accessed March 10, 2005).

6. Andrew Perrin, "One More Down," *Time*, December 9, 2002, available at www.time.com/time/asia/magazine/printout/0,13675,501021216-397545,00.html (last accessed March 10, 2005).

7. Peter Baker, "A Confessed Bomber's Trail of Terror: Uzbek Details Life with Islamic Radicals, Turn Back to Violence," *Washington Post*, September 18, 2003, available at www.uzbekconsul.org/news/Trail.pdf (last accessed March 10, 2005).

8. Tashkent Uzbek Radio 1, "Ex-Militant Reveals Details about Uzbek Islamic Movement," *Tashken Uzbek Radio 1*, September 7, 2003 (last accessed April 15, 2006).

9. British Broadcasting Corporation, "Profile: Saudi al-Qaeda Leader," *BBC News*, August 19, 2005, available at http://news.bbc.co.uk/1/hi/world/middle_east/4166612.stm.

10. British Broadcasting Corporation, "Profile: Saudi al-Qaeda Leader."

11. Elaine Sciolino, "Kamel Daoudi," *New York Times*, September 22, 2002.

12. Bruce Crumley, "The Boy Next Door," *Newsweek*, November 5, 2001.

13. Crumley, "The Boy Next Door."

14. Michael Elliot, "Hate Club: Al-Qaeda's Web of Terror," *Time*, November 4, 2001.

15. Agence France Presse, "Professor Bombmaker—and Fanatic," *AFP*, November 10, 2005.

16. Rana Sabbagh-Gargour, "Failed Suicide Bomber 'Acted out of Revenge,'" *The Times*, November 15, 2005, available at www.timesonline.co.uk/article/0,,251-1872491,00.html (last accessed April 15, 2006).

17. Jamal Halaby, "Iraqi Woman Confesses on Jordan TV," *SF Gate*, November 13, 2005, available at http://sfgate.com/cgi-bin/article.cgi?f=/n/a/2005/11/13/international/i081557S62.DTL (last accessed April 15, 2006).

18. Jane Kokan, "Bin Laden's B.C. helper," *Toronto National Post*, October 13, 2005.

19. British Broadcasting Corporation, "Suicide Bombers' 'Ordinary' Lives," *BBC News*, July 18, 2005, available at http://news.bbc.co.uk/2/hi/uk_news/4678837.stm (last accessed April 15, 2006).

20. *Daily Mail*, "Suicide Bomber Profile: The Family Man," *Daily Mail*, July 13, 2005, available at www.dailymail.co.uk/pages/live/articles/news/news.html?in_article_id=355621&in_page_id=1770&in_a_source= (last accessed April 15, 2006).

21. British Broadcasting Corporation, "Suicide Bombers' 'Ordinary' Lives," *BBC News*, July 18, 2005, available at http://news.bbc.co.uk/2/hi/uk_news/4678837.stm (last accessed April 15, 2006).

22. Abd Samad Moussaoui, *Zacarias, My Brother* (New York: Seven Stories Press, 2003).

23. Kate McGeown, "Jack Roche: The Naïve Militant," *BBC*, June 1, 2002, available at http://news.bbc.co.uk/2/hi/asia-pacific/3757017.stm (last accessed March 10, 2005).

24. Michael Elliot, "The Shoe Bomber's World," *Time*, February 16, 2002, available at www.time.com/time/world/printout/0.8816.203478.00.html (last accessed March 10, 2005).

25. Alan Cowell, "Newsmaker Profile: Richard C. Reid." *SF Gate*, December 29, 2001, available at www.sfgate.com/cgi-bin/article.cgi?f=/c/a/2001/12/29/MN198887.DTL (last accessed March 10, 2005).

26. Terence McKenna, "Trail of a Terrorist," *Frontline*, 2001, available at www.pbs.org/wgbh/pages/frontline/shows/trail (last accessed March 10, 2005).

27. Patrick Bellamy, "Chosen Path," *Court TV*, July 10, 2005, available at www.crimelibrary.com/terrorists_spies/terrorists/hambali/index.html (last accessed April 15, 2006).

28. Bellamy, "Chosen Path."

29. Jeffrey Gettleman, "Zarqawi's Journey: From Dropout to Prisoner to Insurgent Leader," *Middle East Information Center*, July 13, 2004, available at http://middleeastinfo.org/article4619.html (last accessed March 10, 2005).

30. Jean Charles Brisard, *Zarqawi: The New Face of Al-Qaida* (New York: Other Press, 2005).

31. Brisard, *Zarqawi*.

32. Martha Cottam, *Images and Intervention* (Pittsburgh, PA: University of Pittsburgh Press, 2004).

33. Cottam, *Images and Intervention*, 26.

34. Mike Barber, "Video Records Soldier's Plans to Join al-Qaida," *Seattle Post-Intelligencer*, May 13, 2004.

35. Julian Borger, "Chilling, Defiant: The Video Suicide Message of September 11 Killer, *Guardian*, April 16, 2002, available at www.guardian.co.uk/international/story/0,3604,685102,00.html (last accessed January 23, 2007).

36. Middle East Media Research Institute, "Mohammed Sadiq, One of the Suicide Bombers Who Carried Out the London Bombings in a Videotaped Message: Our Words Are Dead until We Give Them Life with Our Blood," MEMRI TV Monitor Project, *MEMRI*, September 1, 2005, available at www.memritv.org/Transcript.asp?P1=835 (last accessed April 15, 2006).

37. Middle East Media Research Institute, "English-Speaking Al-Qaeda Terrorist: Oh People of the West . . . It Is Time for Us to Be Equals—As You Kill Us, You Will be Killed," *MEMRI TV Monitor Project*, *MEMRI*, August 9, 2005, available at www.memritv.org/Transcript.asp?P1=802 (last accessed April 15, 2006).

38. "Bin Laden 'a Very Nice Man'—Terror Plot Accused," *The Scotsman*, March 2000, available at www.jihadwatch.org/archives/002001.php (last accessed April 15, 2006).

39. Middle East Media Research Institute, "Saudi Al-Qaeda Terrorists Recount Their Experiences in Afghanistan," *MEMRI TV Monitor Project*, *MEMRI*, November 29, 2005, available at www.memritv.org/Transcript.asp?P1=947 (last accessed April 15, 2006).

CHAPTER 5

Methods: The Pull to Extremism

I tell you: we are in a battle, and more than half of it is taking place in the battlefield of the media. We are in a media battle in a race for the hearts and minds of the Ummah. However far our capabilities reach, they will never be equal to one-thousandth of the capabilities of the kingdom of Satan that is waging war on us. We can kill our captives by bullets. That would achieve what we're seeking without exposing ourselves to questions. We don't need that.

—Ayman al-Zawahiri in a letter to Abu Musab al-Zarqawi

Methods and locations are the second part of the recruitment story. As was explained in chapter 4, individuals must first have various personal, economic, social, and political motivations to make changes in their lives before the information provided to them through the various methods described below will have an impact on them. Due to a particular motivation or motivations, these individuals are already vulnerable to the message urging them to adopt the al-Qaida network's point of view. If a motivated recruit meets with a message that resonates, an individual may in turn desire membership in the network.

The particular methods addressed in this chapter include speeches, fatwas, religious opinions and instruction, cassette and other audio recordings, videos and DVDs, websites, chat rooms, magazines, books and essays, interviews, statements, letters, pamphlets and leaflets, poetry, cartoons, and the personal approach. These represent only some of the methods used and were chosen for their illustrative purposes. Therefore, our list is by no means exhaustive. Throughout the chapter, we note some of the locations where these methods can be found. Again, like methods, these examples are not an exhaustive representation of all places where the methods discussed here are found.

The Information Content

The methods discussed in this chapter serve the aim of the al-Qaida network, which is to "educate" individuals about what behavior it considers proper, political events, social policy, and religion, among other issues and subjects, including the network's exploits.

A spectrum of themes is associated with these methods, Generally, some of the more consistent themes are anti-American, anti-Western, anti-Christian, anti-Israeli, and anti-Jewish in character. Notably, the United States is depicted as an imperial power, while the Israelis are the U.S.-supported enemy. Both are accused of committing atrocities against Muslims. Other Western governments are added into the mix, especially because of the Iraq war. Many of these themes take aim at Arab and Muslim governments deemed corrupt and which the United States stands accused of supporting. In addition, jihad is often referred to as an honorable duty. Some of the methods openly call for jihad against the United States and Americans, as well as their allies, such as other Western countries or corrupt Arab and Muslim regimes, and the network makes Muslims aware of how they can participate in jihad. Other information simply broadcasts events impacting Muslims, such as United States involvement in Iraq. Finally, a dedicated propaganda effort informs the public of the network's nature and pursuits.

The network also clearly informs individuals that it is responding to ills perpetrated on Muslims throughout the world. Thus, activities are not so much offensive as defensive in nature. The imperial West, as well as corrupt Arab regimes, Israel, and many other enemies, started the fight.

By these methods, al-Qaida can provide their spin on, or interpretation of, behavior, events, policies, and so forth, while offering violence as the principal solution. Thus, these sources of information are influential in shaping the views of others and can cause those on the receiving end of the message to act in support of such views. It is in this way that al-Qaida can provide an outlet for pursuing this solution of violence.

Notably, the source of the information disseminated through these methods may not originate, or be directly associated, with the al-Qaida network and its supporters. However, the information itself can be useful to them in supporting or bolstering the views they advocate. The information can also be used to support the network's aim to bring individuals around to their extremist way of thinking. Even if the network does not directly use this type of information in the above-mentioned ways, the information still exists and therefore provides another confirmatory perspective that indirectly aids the network.

Like the motivations discussed in chapter 4, the methods outlined are not mutually exclusive. Multiple methods are often used or relevant in a given situation. For example, a potential recruit can be enticed by videos of jihad in Iraq, as well as by information provided on a website. In addition, many of the categories overlap, and it is impossible to treat each method as a completely separate entity. Thus, a fatwa, religious sermon, or opinion can be presented on a cassette or videotape, all of which are discussed as separate methods. In other words, methods are embedded in methods. Furthermore, multiple methods can be used at a single location; for instance, articles and videos may be posted on the Internet. One method can also be used at several locations; for instance, a cartoon may be located in both a newspaper and on the Internet. Let's now turn to some of the specific methods used.

Fatwas, Sermons, and Religious Opinions and Instruction

One of the most significant methods is the use of Friday sermons, fatwas, and other types of religious instruction and training, which can be found in numerous locations. For example, sermons can be given in a mosque, broadcast on television or the radio, or posted on the Internet. Fatwas can be printed, posted, and advertised in multiple locations, including mosques, cultural centers, religious schools, universities, and the Internet. Finally, religious instruction and training can also occur in locations such as mosques, cultural centers, religious schools, universities, and even on the Internet. That these methods can be found in multiple locations indicates their ability to reach a wide audience.

Authoritative figures tied to these methods are often referred to as shaykhs (men of religion) or imams (individuals who lead prayers). While many of these individuals may not have formal religious training or possess serious religious credentials, they are perceived by many as sources of authority. Thus, while outsiders may see them as unaccredited sources, their significant influence in certain circles should not be taken for granted or overlooked.

The content of the sermons, fatwas, and instruction can advocate an extremist viewpoint, whether reinforcing the extremist platform or calling for support for extremist activities. Popularizing these views as part of religious sermons provides support to, or justification by a religious authority for, the al-Qaida network's platform.

Friday sermons are sermons given on Friday by a religious leader. These sermons are important and influential, address many topics, and serve to instruct others on proper Islamic behavior. They can pertain to personal conduct or to more politically charged issues. The particular sermons noted here are those that demonize an enemy, notably Israel or the Jews, the United States or Americans, and at times Christians. Those giving the Friday sermons may also advocate support for the mujahidin or encourage jihad. Obviously, these views and those supporting the mujahidin and jihad are also central to the al-Qaida network.

The following are excerpts from Friday sermons broadcast in various countries in the Middle East. All of the sermons were broadcast on state-controlled television.

O God, strengthen Islam and Muslims, humiliate infidelity and infidels, destroy the enemies of Islam, and give safety to this country and to the other Islamic countries. O God, give us safety in our homelands and give wisdom to our leaders. . . . O God, give victory to our mujahidin brothers everywhere. Oh God, give them victory in Palestine, Kashmir, and Chechnya. O God, protect Al-Aqsa Mosque from the Zionist aggressors. O God, humiliate them and force them to leave.[1]

O God, support the mujahidin for your sake everywhere, support them in Palestine, Kashmir, and Chechnya. O God, make fate turn against their enemies. O God, deal with the occupier and usurper Jews, as they have tyrannized, corrupted, killed, and destroyed.[2]

O God, protect Islam and Muslims and destroy enemies of Islam, the tyrants, and the corrupt. O God, help Muslims close their ranks. O God, give wisdom to the Muslims' leaders. O God, support our leader and promote Islam through him. O God, help the mujahidin elevate your religion and your word. O God, support them in Palestine. O God, destroy the tyrant Jews, for they are within your power. O God, defeat these tyrant Jews.[3]

O God, deal with the enemies of Islam, including the Zionists and Americans, shake the land under their feet, instill fear in their heart, and make fate turn against them.[4]

O God, support our brother mujahidin. O God, grant them final victory and make them triumph over their enemies. . . . O God, deal with the enemies of Islam, including Jews and Americans. O God, shake the land under their feet and instill fear in their hearts.[5]

Syria has stood, and continues to stand, by our loyal Muslim people in occupied Iraq until they regain their sovereignty, freedom, honor, and territorial integrity.[6]

Fatwas are religious opinions. The word "fatwa" means an answer to a question. The answer is not binding; rather, it is a recommendation. Yet, the purpose of fatwas is often misunderstood or even deliberately misrepresented so that they are actually taken as binding truths. Many extremists who are deemed, or think of themselves as, religious authorities see fit to issue fatwas, even if they don't have the authority or credentials to do so. As a result, they portray fatwas as their rulings on the proper conduct of others and to justify their own actions. Those individuals vulnerable to recruitment are told that they must follow fatwas, which are therefore taken as authoritative doctrine. Others might not issue fatwas but nevertheless give their opinions on matters of importance to serve as guidance to others.

This particular fatwa was issued by Shaykh Abdullah al-Jibrin and was posted in many locations, including mosques and the Internet.

> Praise be to Allah and that suffices, and peace be upon His chosen slaves. To proceed: When the Muslims throughout the world come to know that a group from their brothers have been oppressed and harmed, it becomes obligatory upon them to aid them and to strive to help them with whatever they can from the wealth, persons, opinions and statements. [Especially] when we know of the State of Taliban in Afghanistan that it rules with the Laws of Allah, establishes the Islamic education [system], prevents the means to Shirk [association], demolishes worshipped objects and idols, exhibits the manifestation of Islam by announcing the call for prayers, establishes the Friday [prayers] and congregational [prayers], prohibits sins and the forbidden acts, as indeed these are all apparent signs of their good intentions and sound faith. And since the Kafir [disbelief in Allah] states, such as the Christians, the Jews, the Communists, and the Atheists, all of them, are against the correct [version of] Islam, and similarly the Kafir innovators, for verily it is obligatory upon the Muslims to help their brothers in this [Taliban] State of Muslims, and to endeavour to repel the plots of their enemies, those who seek to cripple the Muslims' movement and to exterminate them. For Allah the Exhaulted [sic] has said: "And co-operate upon righteousness and piety" and in the Hadeeth: "Make Jihaad against the Mushrikeen [people who practice shirk] with your wealth, your persons and your tongues." The Muslims should aid their brothers with wealth and men and should increase in the supplications for them, for victory and dominion, as Allah is the one who responds to calls of those who supplicate, and indeed He is All-Hearing and Near.[7]

In addition to sermons and fatwas, there is religious instruction and training, which there are plenty of opportunities all over the world to obtain. Like any other Muslims, extremists can set up their own schools and provide their own training, offering their own beliefs about Islam. They are also able to provide confirmatory and authoritative sources of information when engaging in religious instruction and training. Instruction by extremists can occur in Islamic centers, mosques, religious schools, training camps, and even on the Internet.

Cassettes and Audio Recordings

Cassettes and other types of audio recordings, such as CDs, are effective audio methods. They convey a powerful message in a nonwritten format. There is also a significant emotional component to the message that is conveyed to the recipient. These methods can be widely distributed and sold at a variety of locations, such as at bookstores, mosques, and cultural centers, on the Internet, or at news and radio outlets.

Cassettes and other audio recordings are used to record individuals' views (for example, sermons, lectures, lessons, Koranic recitations, and discussions) on a variety of subjects. Speakers can quote authoritative sources, such as books, documents, and letters, and discuss various social and political issues.[8] As is the case with other methods, the views of some of the individuals recorded can encourage violence, or their words can be used as justifications to incite violence. This is particularly true of those recordings released by members of the al-Qaida network who praise jihad and encourage participation in it. The views on those recordings are also frequently anti-Israeli, anti-American, and anti-Western.

In 2005, the Saudi daily *Al-Iqtisadiyaa* reported on the numerous cassettes circulating in the kingdom. The cassettes ranged from promoting jihad to discussing the rewards for participating in jihad. According to the daily, "so ubiquitous are the religious cassette shops that they are outnumbered only by groceries. . . . The bulk of the cassettes sold in these stalls are motivational. On closer scrutiny, you will realize that their contents are confined to a system of thought that serves to prepare youth to accept its ideas, yield to them, and adopt its jihad problem." With regard to the cassettes promoting jihad, "these cassettes mostly urge people to carry out Jihad through taking up arms, without specifying the zero hour or the Jihad battlefield. As such they advocate Jihad for Jihad's sake. It's a mobilization campaign in which Jihad becomes a state of mind, a mode of living. They want you to give up this foul and mean earthly life, renounce world pleasures, devote your life to Jihad, and seek to die in the Jihad battlefield so as to win martyrdom."[9]

While cassettes are very popular, after 9/11 many of the leaders in the al-Qaida network including bin Ladin, al-Zawahiri, and al-Zarqawi used audio recordings to convey their messages about U.S. policy and the Islamic resistance. In October 2004, Ayman al-Zawahiri released an audio tape that stressed the need for Islamic Resistance worldwide.

> Defending Palestine is a duty for all Muslims. You should never give up Palestine, even if the whole world let it down. In Palestine we don't face the Jews only, but the anti-Muslim world coalition led by America the Crusader and the Zionist. We do know who killed Ahmad Yassin and Rantissi; it wasn't Israel alone that killed them. The U.S., Europe and our [Arab] leaders supported them in their act. This is the century of the Islamic resistance after the governments have weakened and kneeled down before the invading crusader. Let's learn a lesson from Chechnya, Afghanistan, Iraq, Palestine, where the authority has vanished or was removed from power, but the resistance remained. The governments in Chechnya and Afghanistan were transformed into resistance leadership. We shouldn't wait for the American, English, French, Jewish, Hungarian, Polish, and South Korean forces to invade Egypt, the Arabian Peninsula, Yemen, and Algeria and then start the resistance after the occupier had already invaded us. We should start now. The interests of America, Britain, Australia, France, Norway, Poland, South Korea, and Japan are everywhere. All of them participated in the invasion of Afghanistan, Iraq, and Chechnya; they also facilitated a raison d'etre for Israel. We should not wait any more than we have already or else we will be devoured one country at a time as they have occupied us in the last two centuries. The Islamic world has entered the period of occupation and division. The resistance foiled the crusaders' and Jews' plans and put them on an embarrassing defensive, and they're looking for a way out. If the mujahideen acted like cowards in Iraq, Afghanistan, Chechnya, and Palestine, the enemy would have taken control of those countries. The people of experience and wisdom should gather forces to create a leadership for the resistance to face the crusaders' campaign as the mujahideen has done in Afghanistan and Chechnya against the will of the occupier and the agent government. Oh young men of Islam, here is our message to you: if we are killed or captured, you should carry on the fight.[10]

The following month bin Ladin also released an audio tape in which he discussed U.S. policy and also explained the reason for the attacks on 9/11.

> People of America this talk of mine is for you and concerns the ideal way to prevent another Manhattan, and deals with the war and its causes and results.
>
> Before I begin, I say to you that security is an indispensable pillar of human life and that free men do not forfeit their security, contrary to Bush's claim that we hate freedom.
>
> If so, then let him explain to us why we don't strike, for example, Sweden? And we know that freedom-haters don't possess defiant spirits like those of the 19—may Allah have mercy on them.

No, we fight because we are free men who don't sleep under oppression. We want to restore freedom to our nation, just as you lay waste to our nation. So shall we lay waste to yours.

No one except a dumb thief plays with the security of others and then makes himself believe he will be secure. Whereas thinking people, when disaster strikes, make it their priority to look for its causes, in order to prevent it happening again.

But I am amazed at you. Even though we are in the fourth year after the events of September 11th, Bush is still engaged in distortion, deception, and hiding from you the real causes. And thus, the reasons are still there for a repeat of what occurred.

So I shall talk to you about the story behind those events and shall tell you truthfully about the moments in which the decision was taken, for you to consider.

I say to you, Allah knows that it had never occurred to us to strike the towers. But after it became unbearable, and we witnessed the oppression and tyranny of the American/Israeli coalition against our people in Palestine and Lebanon, it came to my mind. . . .

The situation was like a crocodile meeting a helpless child, powerless except for his screams. Does the crocodile understand a conversation that doesn't include a weapon? And the whole world saw and heard, but it didn't respond.

In those difficult moments, many hard-to-describe ideas bubbled in my soul, but in the end they produced an intense feeling of rejection of tyranny and gave birth to a strong resolve to punish the oppressors.

And as I looked at those demolished towers in Lebanon, it entered my mind that we should punish the oppressor in kind and that we should destroy towers in America in order that they taste some of what we tasted and so that they be deterred from killing our women and children.

And that day, it was confirmed to me that oppression and the intentional killing of innocent women and children is a deliberate American policy. Destruction is freedom and democracy, while resistance is terrorism and intolerance.

This means the oppressing and embargoing to death of millions, as Bush Sr did in Iraq in the greatest mass slaughter of children mankind has ever known, and it means the throwing of millions of pounds of bombs and explosives at millions of children—also in Iraq—as Bush Jr did, in order to remove an old agent and replace him with a new puppet to assist in the pilfering of Iraq's oil and other outrages.

So with these images and their like as their background, the events of September 11th came as a reply to those great wrongs. Should a man be blamed for defending his sanctuary?

Is defending oneself and punishing the aggressor in kind objectionable terrorism? If it is such, then it is unavoidable for us.

This is the message which I sought to communicate to you in word and deed, repeatedly, for years before September 11th. . . .

You can observe it practically, if you wish, in Kenya and Tanzania and in Aden. And you can read it in my interview with Abdul Bari Atwan, as well as my interviews with Robert Fisk.

The latter is one of your compatriots and coreligionists, and I consider him to be neutral. So, are the pretenders of freedom at the White House and the channels controlled by them able to run an interview with him? So that he may relay to the American people what he has understood from us to be the reasons for our fight against you?

If you were to avoid these reasons, you will have taken the correct path that will lead America to the security that it was in before September 11th. This concerned the causes of the war.

As for its results, they have been, by the grace of Allah, positive and enormous and have, by all standards, exceeded all expectations. This is due to many factors, chief among them, that we have found it difficult to deal with the Bush administration in light of the resemblance it bears to the regimes in our countries, half of which are ruled by the military and the other half which are ruled by the sons of kings and presidents.

Our experience with them is lengthy, and both types are replete with those who are characterised by pride, arrogance, greed, and misappropriation of wealth. This resemblance began after the visits of Bush Sr to the region.

At a time when some of our compatriots were dazzled by America and hoping that these visits would have an effect on our countries, all of a sudden he was affected by those monarchies and military regimes, and became envious of their remaining decades in their positions, to embezzle the public wealth of the nation without supervision or accounting.

So, he took dictatorship and suppression of freedoms to his son, and they named it the Patriot Act, under the pretence of fighting terrorism. In addition, Bush sanctioned the installing of sons as state governors, and didn't forget to import expertise in election fraud from the region's presidents to Florida to be made use of in moments of difficulty.

All that we have mentioned has made it easy for us to provoke and bait this administration. All that we have to do is to send two mujahidin to the furthest point east to raise a piece of cloth on which is written al-Qaida, in order to make the generals race there to cause America to suffer human, economic, and political losses without their achieving for it anything of note other than some benefits for their private companies.

This is in addition to our having experience in using guerrilla warfare and the war of attrition to fight tyrannical superpowers, as we, alongside the mujahidin, bled Russia for 10 years, until it went bankrupt and was forced to withdraw in defeat.

All Praise is due to Allah.

So we are continuing this policy in bleeding America to the point of bankruptcy. Allah willing, and nothing is too great for Allah.

That being said, those who say that al-Qaida has won against the adminis-tration in the White House or that the administration has lost in this war have not been precise, because when one scrutinises the results, one cannot say that al-Qaida is the sole factor in achieving those spectacular gains.

Rather, the policy of the White House that demands the opening of war fronts to keep busy their various corporations—whether they be working in the field of arms or oil or reconstruction—has helped al-Qaida to achieve these enormous results.

And so, it has appeared to some analysts and diplomats that the White House and us are playing as one team towards the economic goals of the United States, even if the intentions differ.

And it was to these sorts of notions and their like that the British diplomat and others were referring in their lectures at the Royal Institute of International Affairs. When they pointed out that for example, al-Qaida spent $500,000 on the event, while America, in the incident and its aftermath, lost—according to the lowest estimate—more than $500 billion.

Meaning that every dollar of al-Qaida defeated a million dollars by the per-mission of Allah, besides the loss of a huge number of jobs.

As for the size of the economic deficit, it has reached record astronomical numbers estimated to total more than a trillion dollars.

And even more dangerous and bitter for America is that the mujahidin recently forced Bush to resort to emergency funds to continue the fight in Afghanistan and Iraq, which is evidence of the success of the bleed-until-bankruptcy plan—with Allah's permission.

It is true that this shows that al-Qaida has gained, but on the other hand, it shows that the Bush administration has also gained, something of which anyone who looks at the size of the contracts acquired by the shady Bush ad-ministration-linked mega-corporations, like Halliburton and its kind, will be convinced. And it all shows that the real loser is . . . you.

It is the American people and their economy. And for the record, we had agreed with the Commander-General Muhammad Atta, Allah have mercy on him, that all the operations should be carried out within 20 minutes, before Bush and his administration notice.

It never occurred to us that the commander-in-chief of the American armed forces would abandon 50,000 of his citizens in the twin towers to face those great horrors alone, the time when they most needed him.

But because it seemed to him that occupying himself by talking to the little girl about the goat and its butting was more important than occupying himself with the planes and their butting of the skyscrapers, we were given three times the period required to execute the operations—all praise is due to Allah.

And it's no secret to you that the thinkers and perceptive ones from among the Americans warned Bush before the war and told him: "All that you want for securing America and removing the weapons of mass destruction—assuming they exist—is available to you, and the nations of the world are with you in the inspections, and it is in the interest of America that it not be thrust into an unjustified war with an unknown outcome."

But the darkness of the black gold blurred his vision and insight, and he gave priority to private interests over the public interests of America.

So the war went ahead, the death toll rose, the American economy bled, and Bush became embroiled in the swamps of Iraq that threaten his future. He fits the saying "like the naughty she-goat who used her hoof to dig up a knife from under the earth."

So I say to you, over 15,000 of our people have been killed and tens of thousands injured, while more than a thousand of you have been killed and more than 10,000 injured. And Bush's hands are stained with the blood of all those killed from both sides, all for the sake of oil and keeping their private companies in business.[11]

Abu Musab al-Zarqawi released his first audiotape in January 2004, which was then posted on the Internet. This audiotape included multiple themes and was organized in three sections: citations of Quranic verses and hadiths that praise jihad and martyrdom, a tribute to a fellow al-Qaida member who was killed by U.S. forces, and an attack on Muslim clerics. Al-Zarqawi concluded his tape with a speech on how jihad is the only solution. Below is an excerpt from his speech "Jihad Is the Only Way."

Oh people, the wheels of war have begun to move; the caller has already declared Jihad and the gates of heaven are open [to the martyrs]. If you are unwilling to be one of the knights of war, make way for the women so they can run the war, and you take the cooking utensils and makeup [brushes] in their stead. If you are not women in turbans and beards, go to the horses and seize their harnesses and their reins. . . .

Oh Allah, America came with its horses and knights to challenge Allah and his Messenger [Muhammad]. . . . Oh Allah, rend the kingdom of Bush as you rent the kingdom of Caesar. . . . Oh Allah, curse the Arab tyrants and the foreign tyrants; Oh Allah, strike the apostate rulers; Oh Allah, kill them one after the other, sparing none.[12]

Videos and DVDs

Two other powerful tools in the network's propaganda efforts, videos and DVDs, appeal to individuals' visual and auditory senses and therefore can engage them on multiple levels compared to a written or audio format. Like cassettes and CDs, videos and DVDs can be distributed from a variety of locations, including bookstores, mosques, religious schools, or the Internet.

Videos can be used to record and display a lecture or statement. For example, as we have seen, bin Ladin, al-Zawahiri, and others in the al-Qaida network have released plenty of videos to offer their views of the world and world events. Other extremist figures have used them as well.

In addition to individual tapes, some videos show actual footage of jihads that have been, or are being, waged on behalf of Muslims. They illustrate the successes that can be attained against what those in the network deem to be a far more powerful imperial country or a formidable enemy. In this regard, they can be used to influence potential recruits and to demonstrate how they can join an organization that has achieved such successes.

Other videos are compilations of events and are more directly and purposefully focused on propaganda and recruitment. These depict the network's direct successes in attacking their enemies and present statements made by al-Qaida members about the cause. Finally, music videos can be used to entice individuals to join the network as well.

Videos also depict the basic and more specialized training the network conducts. They can be used not only to instruct but also, more importantly, to demonstrate the prowess, skills, and abilities of network members. Thus, they can be shown to potential recruits as part of the effort to influence them.

Numerous videos depicting jihads across the world, from Iraq to Chechnya, are available. A notable example includes the widely distributed, violent Chechen videos of the ambush of Russian soldiers and convoys, the torture and execution of Russian soldiers, and other combat situations. A training video illustrating an alleged Bosnian camp is posted on the Internet with a series of other recruitment videos taped at the Finsbury Park Mosque in London, England. The training video shows recruits participating in physical training, including jumping out of windows, crawling under barbed wire, walking across makeshift monkey bars, running with their weapons, and rapelling off of platforms. In the background, music plays, and the narrator states that the viewer is seeing the formation of a power that will terrorize the enemies of Allah. The training portion of the video lasts for approximately a minute, then phases into a speech by Abu Hamza al-Masri, the mosque's imam, justifying the use of suicide bombers.[13]

Emulating the Chechen example, the Iraq insurgency is using videotapes to depict their successes against the United States as well. For example, circulating on the Internet is a video depicting the killing of an American soldier in Iraq.[14] Additionally, posted all over the Internet are videos of members of the Iraq insurgency beheading Americans and their allies. For example, the brutal murder of American Eugene Armstrong is posted. During his beheading, his kidnappers read a statement in front of the camera, then decapitated him. These beheading videos are meant to illustrate the strength of the insurgency in defeating the Americans and to deter other governments from assisting the United States in rebuilding Iraq. Even more disturbing is the impact these videos are having on children. The clearest indication of their impact is the posting of a video where children are imitating the be-headings. Three children, using pretend weapons, emulate the insurgents by pretending to saw off the head of another child.[15]

Music videos have also become a popular type of video that is able to capture the attention of the target audience. For example, *Dirty Kuffar* is a rap music video performed by Shaykh Terra and the Soul Salah Crew. The video opens with the killing of an Iraqi civilian, then cuts to a U.S. Marine saying that the experience was awesome, and he wanted to do it again. The rap portion of the video then commences and visually depicts, among other things, jihad flashing across the screen, various world leaders transforming into pigs and devils, al-Zawahiri turning into a lion, and certain leaders and groups being referred to as "dirty kuffars." The video ends with the burning of the World Trade Center towers.[16]

Websites and Chat Rooms

Among the most significant methods used by the al-Qaida network to dis-seminate information are websites and chat rooms. Their use is the most telling example of how the network exploits modern technology in the recruitment environment. Websites and chat rooms are unique, as compared with the other methods already discussed, in that they can only be found in a single location, the Internet. Since websites and chat rooms are important methods being used by the al-Qaida network in recruitment, the Internet has become one of the most significant locations.

Websites offer many advantages. First, extremists are able to disseminate their message to a global audience. For example, information can be posted on a website in London and a viewed by an individual in New York. Also, websites are able to accommodate a multinational audience by providing information in multiple languages. This further extends the network's global reach. Many extremists use the tactic of writing English homepages in a more moderate tone and writing Arabic homepages in a more extreme one. This prohibits Westerners who do not read or speak Arabic from detecting the content and context of what is being presented on the Arabic sites. Second, websites are extremely flexible in that their Internet location can be constantly changed. This is important for extremists who continually have to adapt to government crackdowns, when websites may be blocked or monitored. In fact, many of the websites we discuss here may have already changed locations. Websites are also flexible because the information contained on them can be continually updated or changed. This allows extremists to exploit current events. Finally, websites are cost effective. It takes very little in the way of financial resources to start and maintain a website.

There are numerous websites on the Internet that are being used by the network. Al-Qaida's level of sophistication in exploiting the Internet is evident in the website al-Neda (The Call), a network website that has been shut down, then resurfaced, many times. The key to al-Neda's success is that it attacks other websites and uses these temporary hosts as a location to post its information, only to then disappear again. The identifier of the website is al-Qaida's logo, a horseman with a rifle and the Arabic slogan "No honor except for jihad."[17] Maktab al-Jihad (Jihad Organization) is also a website of the al-Qaida network. Its significance is that it serves as a centralizing node. In other words, it provides links to many other websites. Many of these websites provide anti-American and pro-al-Qaida propaganda. For example, one of the links connects a user to a site that displays graphic pictures of children who have been killed or seriously injured under the caption "Victims of so called American war on Terrorism." Another link connects the user to a site that offers information about prisoners held at the U.S. base in Guantánamo Bay, Cuba. One posting to the site announced the release of Guantánamo detainees Feroz Abassi, Moazzam Begg, Richard Belmar, and Martin Mubanga. The website also has a message board where visitors could respond to the news of the release of these four men. Another site that deals with the detainee issue is Cage Prisoners. Cage Prisoners is a self-proclaimed "human rights" website that discusses detainees who are currently being held or have been released. It primarily focuses on the U.S. base in Guantánamo Bay, Cuba. The website provides stories about the detainees and their allegations of abuse at the prison. While the site is allegedly not connected to al-Qaida, it does provide powerful visual and audio propaganda for the network. The site incorporates many methods, including interviews, videos, audio clips, cartoons, poetry, leaflets, articles, and a discussion board. There is a picture gallery of detainees, along with pictures of the prison. For example, one powerful picture is of a half-clothed prisoner up against a wire fence with military personnel next to him. The graphic is accompanied by a caption that reads "cruelty to lone prisoner." Another feature posts articles on alleged cases of abuse. One posted article from a new "source" discusses how a British prisoner claimed he was sexually assaulted, nearly drowned, and almost blinded during an attack.[18]

Supporters of Shariah is the website of the organization with the same name, which is allegedly affiliated with the al-Qaida network. The organization was started by Abu Hamza al-Masri, an imam who used this website to distribute his sermons and literature. This website offers visitors the choice of several different languages, including English, Arabic, Bosnian, Swedish, and Albanian. The English portion provides choices between articles and books, videos and audio clips, news, a question-and-answer section, and links to other sites. The information contains anti-U.S. propaganda and stresses to Muslims the importance of practicing jihad. For example, one of the sections is titled "Our Projects" and has a feature called "The Disasters Inflicted by the Bloody U.S.-Led Crusade," a Flash presentation of men, women, and children dead or with missing body parts who have allegedly suffered these injuries or death due to American operations in Iraq. The presentation concludes with the statement that the only solution is jihad in the name of Allah.

Websites can also provide training and education. For example, In 2003, the *Al-Sharq al-Awsat* newspaper published an article on the establishment of Al-Qaida University for Jihad Sciences on the Internet, a virtual university providing colleges in "electronic jihad," car bombs, and arms practice.[19] The website not only can be used to recruit individuals directly into the network but also to indoctrinate and train recruits for specific roles within the organization.

In September 2002, the website Azzam.com, which provided news on the jihads in Afghanistan and Chechnya, announced its closure. The information posted on the website pertaining to its closure provides considerable insight into how this particular method was kept up and running and the tactics it used to disseminate its message when faced with considerable attempts to shut it down. The following message was posted on the website:

> By the Grace of Allah, upon its launch in 1996, Azzam.com was one of the first Islamic web-sites on the Internet and the first web-site dedicated to Jihad and Muhajideen news and information. Allah has enabled us, with meager resources and little technological experience, to provide information on the Mujahideen and to provide daily news and interviews from the Jihad in Chechnya (September 1999 to August 2001) and the Jihad in Afghanistan from November 2001 until today.

The website also informed its readers of attempts by the Americans and Zionists to damage its site and provided numerous examples of attempts to close or infiltrate the site.

Our web-site also has not been spared damage. We have had to change through a number of servers and hosting companies over the years in order to keep the site open. In the times when the site has been shut, we have been emailing out news bulletins to keep the World informed.

After the events of 11 September 2001, our site was shut down after the American hosting company received numerous emails from viewers upset at the attacks. . . . A few weeks later, our site reappeared on the servers of a Muslim hosting company in Canada, who also duly shut the site down, after receiving a written order from the local law enforcement authorities. . . .

Also after 11 September, a group of Zionist Jews surfaced on the Internet, led by a British individual who goes by the pen-name of Johnathan R. Galt. . . . Mr. Galt organised a collective, concerted campaign, to have a number of Islamic web-sites shut down, by complaining to and putting emotional pressure on the hosting and service-providing companies. . . .

A number of discussion boards specific to web hosting companies . . . revealed threads stating that companies wanted to shut down service to the web-hosting companies hosting our sites, but they were specifically instructed by the FBI that 'this site must remain open at any cost.' We concluded that US Intelligence wanted our site to remain open for two reasons:

    (i) To use it for gathering intelligence on events happening on the ground in Afghanistan and perhaps that our news bulletins might lead them to capture "Mujahideen suspects."

    (ii) To gather intelligence on the infrastructure behind the site.

The website also warned its readers of attempts by the Americans and Zionists to hijack websites for their own purposes and offered the following predications.

1. The American authorities will attempt to take control of our domain, Az-zam.com, and use it in their "War Against Terror/Islam" in order to provide false propaganda. It will be easy to spot fake sites because we will email each other, established web-sites and organisations . . . and inform them of which site is genuine and which site is not.

2. The authorities will create new "Jihadi" web-sites in order to "steal the show." Some characteristics of these sites will be:

    a. They will portray themselves as Jihad-linked and informed on the Mujahideen and some of their content will undoubtedly be pro-Jihad and Muhahideen;

    b. They will never be forced down and will only go offline for maintenance upgrades;

    c. They will not have correspondents whose credibility can be confirmed on the ground;

    d. They will have sizeable resources and expertise at their disposable, un-like most Islamic web-sites that are run on pennies and a "best-efforts" basis by unskilled web operators;

    e. They will not really be targetted by Zionist web groups (although after this statement of ours, the authorities may infiltrate the Zionist web groups and instruct them to target the fake sites in order to establish credibility for them in the eyes of the Muslims).

    f. They will attempt to dampen emotions within the Muslims and create confusion amongst them as regards to issues that have already been clari-fied by ourselves.

3. The Zionist web groups will continue their campaigns to shut down Islamic web-sites until Muslims begin doing the same and start complaining to web hosting companies of inflammatory Zionist web-sites. . . .

4. The authorities will sponsor further "Boycott Azzam" campaigns amongst the Muslims, similar to the "Boycott Azzam" campaign that was launched by a Doctor from the "Islamic Society of Britain" . . . complete with leaflets and radio announcements.

5. Our site will continue to go online and offline until more Muslim Internet Service Providers appear who are prepared to legally challenge any attempts made to shut down our site.[20]

Chatrooms are very similar to websites in that they allow extremists to distribute information globally through the use of modern technology. They can also be very cost-effective. Furthermore, they allow members to communicate and voice their opinions to others anonymously. When individuals join a chat room hosted or infiltrated by al-Qaida network members, they can be directly exposed to al-Qaida propaganda from a member of the network.

There are many al-Qaida chat rooms available through al-Qaida-affiliated websites. For example, the Maktab al-Jihad website has a chat room. However, it is also important to realize that extremists do not need an al-Qaida chat room to spread their propaganda. An extremist can simply go to mainstream rooms and distribute information as well.

Magazines

The al-Qaida network hosts a variety of magazines that aim to disseminate their extremist message to the public in a written format. These magazines cover their views on various issues, from codes of behavior and world events to training for jihad. The network has also attempted to reach different target audiences, including women. Al-Qaida magazines can be found in and distributed from a wide variety of locations, including the Internet.

Zurwat al-Sanam (The Tip of the Camel's Hump) is the online magazine for al-Qaida in Iraq. The group's logo is an AK-47 standing on an open Koran; there is a globe in the background, and an arm points upward. The first issue was forty-three pages long and was posted in February 2005 by Abu Maysara al-Iraqi.[21] Included in this initial issue are statements by al-Zarqawi pledging his allegiance to bin Ladin, as well as bin Ladin's recognition of the now deceased al-Zarqawi as emir (leader) of al-Qaida in Iraq. Thus, the Iraqi network is attempting to use bin Ladin's blessing to attain further support and more recruits for the Iraqi network. The issue also discussed Abu Anas al-Shami, an aide to al-Zarqawi, who was killed.

Sawt al-Jihad (The Voice of Jihad) is al-Qaida in Saudi Arabia's online magazine; it was first posted on October 17, 2003. The magazine provides vast amounts of anti-U.S. propaganda and encourages readers to print out or burn CD copies of the magazine to distribute to others during the hajj. *Muaskar al-Battar* (Battar Training Camp) is a biweekly magazine that stresses the importance of military training. The magazine seeks to aid individuals in their preparation for battle. The magazine was named after deceased Saudi al-Qaida member Shaykh Yusuf al-Ayiri (a.k.a. al-Battar). *Dhuwat Sanam al-Islam* (The Crest of the Summit of Islam) is issued by the Department of Indoctrination of the al-Qaida in Iraq organization. This magazine provides information on the background and aims of the organization. Finally, *Al-Khansa* is a magazine named after an Arab poetess that targets another demographic, women. The monthly magazine is published by the Women's Bureau in the Arabian Peninsula and deals with the role of women in jihad, instructing them on how to maintain a balance between family life and jihad activities.

A weekly magazine published by Great East Islamic Front entitled *Kaide* (al-Qaida in Turkish) is being distributed in Turkey. It praises Usama bin Ladin, includes al-Qaida announcements, and is legally published in Istanbul. In an interview with *Kaide* executive Ali Osman Zor given to the Turkish weekly *Tempo*, Zor had this to say about bin Ladin:

TEMPO: What are your thoughts about Osama bin Laden?

KAIDE: We pray for all those who fight for Islam's world domination. Bin Laden is a heroic fighter of Islam. Like many Muslims, we are proud of him. Bin Laden expresses the accumulated anger felt by Muslims for centuries against the "infidel." We believe that bin Laden, like our commander Mirzabeyouglu and our soul-mate Carlos the Jackal, is one of the architects of the new world that will be built following the triumph of Islam. May Allah protect bin Laden from the evil of his enemies.[22]

Books and Essays

Books and essays are also widely available and can be used to promulgate al-Qaida's views. Some works are widely referenced, particularly those by individuals who served as foundational thinkers for the network, such as Ibn Taymiyyah and Sayyid Qutb. Members of the network have written numerous books as well, including Ayman al-Zawahiri. These books and essays are, for the most part, well argued and comprehensive. They serve to explain the network's position on, and rationale for, participation in jihad and clearly define the enemy or imperial power for the reader. Books and essays can be purchased in locations such as bookstores, mosques, and cultural centers and are oftentimes located on the Internet.

A book titled *Orator of the Peninsula: The Great Yusuf al-Ayiri in the Age of Humiliation and Insult* was released and served as a tribute to deceased Saudi al-Qaida member al-Ayiri. The compilation was posted on the Internet.[23] Al-Ayiri served as bin Ladin's bodyguard and died during a confrontation with Saudi security forces in 2003. This book is a compilation of essays by Shawq al-Mujahid written in tribute to al-Ayiri's dedication to jihad

In the following passage, the author dedicates the book to Abdullah Azzam, Usama bin Ladin, and deceased Chechen leader Khattab; the mujahidin in Iraq, Palestine, Lebanon, and the Philippines; and those who died trying to rid the Arabian Peninsula of the infidels.

> I dedicate my humble effort
>   To those who taught the world the spirit of jihad and sacrifice
>   To mujahid Abdallah Azzam, may God have mercy on him
>   To Shaykh Usama bin Ladin in Afghanistan
>   To mujahid and martyr, God willing, Khattab
>   To the valiant mujahidin in Iraq, Palestine, Lebanon, and the Philippines
>   To those who died trying to get the infidels out of the Arabian Peninsula

The author then traces al-Ayiri's life, mentioning his dedication to and support of various mujahidin causes, beginning with Soviet Afghanistan. The author praises al-Ayiri's prolific writings, which include books and articles on various subjects, such as the Taliban, the U.S. involvement in Iraq, and the role of women in jihad. The author also praises al-Ayiri's notable qualities, which include, in part, his memorization of the Koran in full, his use of the Internet, his ethics and modesty, his imprisonment in Saudi Arabia, and his own participation in jihad.

Another book entitled *39 Ways to Serve and Participate in Jihad* was posted on the Internet and begins with a religious justification for jihad.[24] It reads, in part, "Jihad today is the only option for the Islamic community, for the enemy has come to occupy the countries of Muslims one after the other. As God said in the Koran: 'Nor will they cease fighting you until they turn you back from your faith if they can'" [2:217].

The reader is then provided with the listing and detailed explanation of thirty-nine ways to participate in jihad. The following are excerpts from numbers 1, 5, 31, and 36.

1. Deciding on Jihad: Making up one's mind to start fighting is a real decision. It requires the resolve to respond to the appeal of jihad when the voice calls out, "O cavalry of God, ride!" A person must prepare himself mentally and ready his soul for fighting and bearing arms when his brothers call upon him, following the saying of the prophet as cited in al-Bukhari: "If you are called upon, ride out."

5. Outfitting a Fighter: One of the ways to take part in jihad in the path of God and serve the mujahidin is to equip fighters for jihad. Numerous well-attested sayings of the prophet note the virtue of such acts. . . . "Whoever has equipped a fighter in the path of God will receive a like reward that is no less than the fighter's reward" (16).

31. Hostility and Hatred of the Infidels: This is already a firmly fixed part of the believers' creed. Intense hatred of the infidels is in and of itself support for the mujahidin. The sworn enemies of the infidels are the mujahidin allies of God. They impose grief and defeat on the infidels. When the creed of enmity toward the infidels faded and the call sounded for tolerance and coexistence, its supporters combined animosity toward the mujahidin with a desire to reduce the people's acceptance of the mujahidin and their leaders. The message of coexistence and the internal front is best described as: "Mercy for the infidels and cruelty toward the mujahidin."

36. Raising Children to Love Jihad and Those Who Wage It: Children and the family are the promise of the future. They will drive the stage that is to come. He who will raise the next generation is already among us, and he stands on what his father taught him. Children must be raised to love jihad and the mujahidin and to know the meaning of martyrdom and sacrifice for their faith. This way, if they want to set out in the path of God, they will be a boon to Him in their obedience.

Interviews, Statements, and Letters

Interviews, statements, and letters are also methods widely used by the al-Qaida network. They are published by many other sources, such as magazines, newspapers, and websites, and are distributed widely to a variety of locations, such as newsstands and bookstores, and on the Internet.

Interviews are an important method because they derive their authority from the premise that the interviewees are deemed important enough to be called upon to discuss their beliefs. They also give those being interviewed a forum in which to articulate their beliefs. Some interviews are spontaneous, while others are planned in advance and much more carefully crafted. Those interviewed are important religious figures and members of the network, among others. They all have in common the fact that through their views, they are advocating parochial perspectives that can potentially influence already motivated individuals.

In a television interview, Saudi cleric al-Fawzan gave his views on jihad and Iraq and argued for the use of defensive jihad.

> Defensive Jihad must be authorized by the leader, if the Muslims have a legal leader. It is possible that the leader, along with the leading jurisprudents and the nation's leaders, will think that the Jihad should be postponed due to certain interests. But if they don't have a leader, as is the case, unfortunately, in some Muslim countries, should the Muslims surrender to the occupying enemy? No cleric would allow such a thing. The clerics have all agreed that if an enemy invades a Muslim country, Jihad against the enemy becomes an individual duty applying to anyone who can wage Jihad. . . .
>
> Jihad is an individual duty applying to the people of that country. If they cannot defend themselves against this enemy, then it applies to the next in line, to the next in line after them, and so on, and it is possible that it will eventually apply to all countries of Islam. But this does not mean that if an enemy enters Iraq, for instance, then all the Muslims in all the countries of the world need to come to Iraq to fight. No one has said so. Only an ignorant would say so.
>
> Jihad is an individual duty applying to the Iraqi people. They need to wage this Jihad against this enemy until it leaves their country, especially as this enemy hurts their honor, blood, and property.[25]

In November 2001 al-Jazirah Interview conducted an interview with al-Qaida senior leader Abu Hafs, the Mauritanian:

> QUESTION: Now, after America has gone to war against you [i.e., al-Qa'ida] and against Afghanistan, are you promising anything?
>
> ABU HAFS: We are not promising anything, and we do not need to promise. We are now engaged in open war. We declared [war] on the Americans and the Americans declared [war] on us. The Americans are sparing no means. So far, the [amount of explosives in the] bombs and missiles that have fallen on Afghanistan is many times greater than the atom bombs that the U.S. dropped on Japan during World War II. If you count up all the explosives that have

fallen in over a month on Afghanistan, the amount is double. America has used weapons it never used before in any previous war. But so far America has not managed to accomplish any of the goals it set for itself when it declared its Crusader war against Afghanistan.

QUESTION: What is your view regarding the future of the al-Qaida organization, considering the conditions and the open war declared against you by the U.S., the strongest country in the world?

ABU HAFS: In our opinion, America has entered the phase of the beginning of the end. America is talking about wanting to uproot terrorism in Afghanistan, but the truth is that those in Afghanistan have succeeded in uprooting America from its fortresses and bases and have dragged it, humiliated and shame-faced, to Afghanistan, where their hands, bayonets, and weapons can reach her. America lost even before it entered into battle.

QUESTION: [W]hy don't you fight a Jihad in Palestine or another Arab country, such as Mauritania?

ABU HAFS: You are probing an open wound in my heart. There is no doubt that the Palestine problem is the most important problem for every Muslim. This is the Holy Land, the land of the Night Journey [of the prophet Muhammad], the land of the Ascension into the Heavens; it is the first direction of prayer and the third [most holy] site [in Islam]. It is the land of the Prophets. No people has suffered [the likes of] the barbaric Jewish crimes from which the Palestinian people has suffered, with American and British Crusader support. The Jihad in Palestine does not need encouragement; it is a Jihad that is the personal obligation of every Muslim. But how will we fight Jihad in Palestine? If you stand on each of the borders of the Arab states [i.e., Israel's borders] and fire a single shot at the Jews within Palestine, many times more shots will be fired at you—not by the Jews but by the Arab states that guard these borders. We maintain that the Jihad is an obligation, and that Jihad in Palestine is a personal obligation [applying to every Muslim]. We see Palestine as the most important Islamic issue in the entire Islamic world. But so far, we have not had a chance to engage in it. But we strike at the Jews, we strike at the Americans, and we are acting to establish an extensive Islamic state beginning in Afghanistan. We are serving all the Islamic causes, and, first and foremost, the cause of Palestine.[26]

Statements can be used to inform others of a set of beliefs, views on certain topics, or to announce that a particular action has taken place. When published, they give the impression that the views of the individual giving the statement are important enough to be publicized. The leadership of the al-Qaida network and others who openly support them make the statements. Other statements not made by the network can be seized upon as evidence of support for its views.

Finally, many individuals write letters to express their views or to inform others of a particular action. Oftentimes, these letters are written to a specific individual, questioning that individual's views or policies, or they are used more generally to voice views and beliefs. In addition, these letters can also be the last wills and testaments of individuals who have committed suicide for the cause. The letters serve as explanations of these individuals' actions. For example, a statement was posted on the Internet by Jamaat al-Tandheem al-Sierri (Organization of al-Qaeda in Europe) that claimed responsibility for the July 2005 London Bombings.

In the name of God the most merciful. . . .

Rejoice, the nation of Islam, rejoice nation of Arabs, the time of revenge has come for the crusaders' Zionist British government.

As retaliation for the massacres which the British commit in Iraq and Afghanistan, the mujahideen have successfully done it this time in London.

And this is Britain now burning from fear and panic from the north to the south, from the east to the west. We have warned the brutish governments and British nation many times.

And here we are, we have done what we promised. We have done a military operation after heavy work and planning, which the mujahideen have done, and it has taken a long time to ensure the success of this operation.

And we still warn the government of Denmark and Italy, all the crusader governments, that they will have the same punishment if they do not pull their forces out of Iraq and Afghanistan.

So beware.

Thursday 7/7/2005[27]

Pamphlets and Leaflets

Pamphlets and leaflets are visually effective methods that deliver simple, yet powerful, messages through words, pictures, or both. Their messages vary from simply broadcasting support for the network to openly inciting violence. They can also be used to counter propaganda aimed at discrediting their cause. Similar to many of the other methods discussed, they can be widely distributed in mosques, religious schools, towns, and villages, as well as posted on the Internet.

For example, pamphlets distributed in Afghanistan advertised a $100,000 reward from al-Qaida supporters to anyone who captured or killed Westerners.[28] Other pamphlets providing instructions on kidnapping and urban guerilla warfare were posted on an Arabic website.[29]

Leaflets have been found in a variety of locations as well. For example, leaflets labeled "Al-Qaida of Mesopotamia," supporting the insurgency, were distributed in mosques in Mosul, Iraq. They stated that if Sunnis aided the infidel crusader, jihad would lose its meaning.[30] Leaflets found in 2004 in a section of London promoted al-Qaida propaganda by condemning Britain and America's efforts in the war on terror and justifying the 9/11 attacks and Madrid bombings.[31] Other leaflets found in London called upon British Muslims to "kill the Jews." The leaflets provided contact information for the founder of al-Muhajiroun.[32]

Poetry

Another interesting method used is poetry, which is an extremely creative way to express the views, feelings, and positions of the network through language. Poetry is widely used as part of other methods. For example, bin Ladin uses it in his statements, and it can be widely found embedded in books and essays.

The following is a poem by Abd al-Aziz bin Mushrif al-Bakri in the book *Orator of the Peninsula* eulogizing deceased Saudi al-Qaida member Yusuf al-Ayiri.[33]

> A lion has roared at dawn
> And the dogs of humanity trembled
> And kept their heads down as dogs do when tracking someone
> But the heroic lion lied in wait for them,
> Peeking through piles of rocks
> Then bullets were fired, taking a life away
> And the herd shouted that a lion has stood fast;
> He rejected injustice and infidels and declared jihad as the only path forever
> A treacherous wolf accompanied by soldiers pounced on the steadfast lion
> They killed him, and the soul of the martyr went to its Glorious Lord
> Oh God: Accept the honorable Shaykh Yusuf and find us an honorable
>   replacement for him
> And give our nation the patience until it realizes that blood will have to be
>   shed one day
> And that jihad is the only option

Bin Ladin also used poems to express his reasoning for using "the language of the gun." The following is a poem used by bin Ladin to express his reasoning for using "the language of the gun," as expressed by his bodyguard in a 2002 interview[34]:

> We said—and our listeners gave us their ears and heard us—let the sword oc-
> cupy the pulpit. Whoever seeks his rights, must eventually find the sword to be

his best guide. When they refused to respond to our demands, we turned our saber rattling into songs.

On a videotape released after 9/11, where bin Ladin takes credit for the attacks, he recites lines from a poem written by Yousef Abu Helaleh entitled "The Believers." According to Abu Helaleh, he sent a series of poems, including "The Believers" to bin Ladin during the early 1990s. In an interview, Abu Helaleh professed, "I respect bin Laden and consider him to be a sincere and smart holy warrior." Below are the lines from the poem "The Believers," quoted by bin Ladin on the videotape.[35]

> I witness that against the sharp blade
> They always faced difficulties and stood together. . . .
> When the darkness comes upon us and we are bitten by a
> Sharp tooth, I say . . .
> 'Our homes are flooded with blood and the tyrant
> Is freely wandering in our homes.' . . .
> And from the battlefield vanished
> The brightness of swords and the horses . . .
> And over weeping sounds now
> We hear the beats of drums and rhythm. . . .
> They are storming his forts
> And shouting: 'We will not stop our raids
> Until you free our lands'

Cartoons

Cartoons are a unique method because they deliver a message simply, through a picture that may or may not be accompanied by writing. The phrase "a picture is worth a thousand words" truly articulates the strength of this method. This method enables the author to communicate his or her message to an audience without the restrictions imposed by cultural and language barriers. For example, not everyone may be able to read or understand an Arabic magazine or newspaper article promoting anti-American propaganda. However, cartoons can create a visualization of this propaganda, which simplifies the message. Newspapers, magazines, and websites are some of the methods that contain cartoons. These methods are found in various locations, including newsstands and bookstores, and on the Internet.

For example, in their attempt to educate the public about the nature of the extremist propaganda, *The Middle East Media Research Institute* gathers and posts cartoons, which are found in Middle Eastern newspapers. One cartoon shows an American hand pushing a rock labeled "democracy" down on a globe. Another depicts an Uncle Sam figure holding the world and oil pouring out of it into his mouth. These provide compelling images that can influence potential recruits.

In our discussion on the Cage Prisoners website, we mentioned it posts cartoons, one of which shows prisoners at Guantánamo Bay, Cuba, on one side of a fence and a U.S. guard on the other side. In front of the entrance is a doormat with the words "Geneva Convention," and a sign pointing to the doormat states, "U.S. personnel wipe before entering." Another cartoon on the website shows a U.S. soldier using a blindfolded and tied-up prisoner as a human swing so he can swing from a tree.

Personal Appeals

The personal method is exceptionally important. We discuss this method last because the personal approach relies on all of the other methods, as well as on the charisma of the individual providing the information. Those employing the personal method are skilled at argumentation and draw upon sources of information to make their case. They are also good at assessing and homing in on recruits' vulnerabilities. Some have religious credentials; others have credibility based on their past participation in jihad. Those employing the personal approach explain to potential recruits that they can blame their misfortunes on the imperialist qualities and corruption of the United States, Israel, and other enemies. They stress the injustice and play upon outrage. They offer potential recruits an extremist solution to their current life situations.

Perhaps one of the most famous recruiters is Abu Hamza al-Masri, the fiery imam at London's Finsbury Park Mosque. Al-Masri is currently incarcerated in Great Britain. Abu Hamza stood out for his ability to captivate his audience when he spoke. His sermons were renowned and were taped and distributed in mosques throughout Britain.[36] In one statement discussing suicide bombings, Abu Hamza stated that his followers were destined to become martyrs and that they should bring jihad to their doors.[37] While Abu Hamza was the most prominent figure at Finsbury, others also preached jihad at the mosque, including his son Mustapha Kamal and his close associate James Ujamma. In one videotaped speech, Mustapha calls upon Muslims to celebrate when Americans are killed because Americans have champagne parties when they killed Muslims in Iraq.[38] Thus, Abu Hamza's "extended family" played an integral role in furthering his cause.

Abu Hamza's speeches and written works are posted on many websites on the Internet. This allows individuals to listen to his speeches or watch his sermons videotaped at the Finsbury Park Mosque. Thus, even outside of the mosque, his fiery rhetoric calling Muslims to engage in jihad against the West is disseminated. Abu Hamza also recognized the importance of exploiting the Internet. Various websites further spread his message of global jihad.

A recruiter tied to al-Masri was Djamal Beghal. Beghal, who is now incarcerated, appeared to be a traveling Salafist who went to various mosques throughout Europe to do al-Qaida's bidding. His persuasive skills eventually enticed many individuals to join the network. One of the mosques that Beghal worked out of was the Finsbury Park Mosque in London. There he was able to put his people skills to work. Beghal recognized the importance of going the extra step in personally connecting with these individuals in order to recruit them for the network. He would work the room by approaching individuals who came to hear Abu Hamza al-Masri's sermons and invite them to attend "study groups."[39] Furthermore, he invited those who had no place to go to stay with him at the mosque. Some notable individuals who frequented the Finsbury Mosque include Richard Reid, Nizar Trabelsi, Feroz Abassi, Ahmed Ressam, and Zacarias Moussaoui.[40]

Another example of a recruiter is Muhammad Haydar Zammar. Zammar is a German citizen of Syrian origin and birth. Zammar was member of the Syrian Muslim Brotherhood, an outlawed group that threatened the Syrian regime. As a result, he fled his country of birth. Known for his views advocating jihad in a Hamburg mosque, Zammar is thought to be the individual who recruited 9/11 hijacker Muhammad Atta, as well as the other individuals in the Hamburg cell, and sent them to Afghanistan for training.[41] Zammar was seized in Morocco by Moroccan authorities and flown to Syria for questioning. Another recruiter, Abu Zubaydah, who was captured in Pakistan in March 2002, is a veteran of the al-Qaida network. A Palestinian born in Saudi Arabia, he traveled to Pakistan in the 1980s to participate in the Soviet jihad. He rose up the ranks in the organization to become, until his capture, one of the central figures in the network. He was considered al-Qaida's chief recruiter and was responsible for the vetting of recruits that came through the al-Qaida camps in Afghanistan. He also had a key role in operational planning.[42] Recruiters in other parts of the world were also busy at work. Abu Bakar Bashir is accused of being the spiritual leader of Jemaah Islamiyah. Bashir was born in East Java and evolved to become a well-known religious figure in Southeast Asia, particularly among extremists. In the late 1970s, he was jailed for subversion. While Bashir claims that he is simply a religious teacher (he taught at the religious schools where some of the 2002 Bali bombers attended), he is accused of being connected to several plots and attacks by Jemaah Islamiyah, including plotting the assassination of former Indonesian president Megawati Sukarnoputri.

Joining the Group

This book is about the backgrounds and motivations of the individuals in the network, not about how they actually get into the network. However, it is useful to address briefly how this process may generally work based on what we have pieced together from various accounts. This will help provide a fuller picture of the recruits. It is essential to point out that there is no one single process, no one "path" to recruitment. Individuals can have very different, specific experiences. The discussion below serves to provide a general representation of the process.

When a motivated recruit encounters a resonating message, the recruit becomes ready to take the next step. The recruit may then seek out someone—perhaps a family member, a personal or social acquaintance, or a religious figure—he knows is associated with the network or can likely provide a connection to someone who is. On the other hand, a recruit noticed at a particular location, such as a mosque, bookstore, or university, may be approached by a spotter for the network, questioned, and then determined to be suitable for further probing. This can occur, for example, when the recruit has attended a lecture that expressed an extremist viewpoint. The spotter can assume that the target has been primed by the lecture's message.

However, it is important to remember that the al-Qaida network is an exclusive, extremist organization. Therefore, a person cannot just walk in off the street and expect to be given immediate membership. Because it is secretive, individuals have to go through a screening process even after this first step is taken to ensure that the group will not be infiltrated or left vulnerable. The vetting of recruits continues until the network is satisfied that the recruit is trustworthy and ready. A potential recruit may even be sent to fight jihad to prove his trustworthiness or sent to a camp to receive training. During this time, the types of messages focused on in this chapter are continually reinforced, and perhaps the recruit is even provided with new information. With reinforcement and justification for participation in the network, the recruit is brought deeper and deeper into the group. Here, both the pressure and desire to conform to the group's norms and rules are probably brought to bear. Committed individuals will adhere to these rules, norms, and messages of indoctrination. Eventually, the recruit will pass a perceived point of no return.

Conclusion

This chapter has surveyed the types of methods used to entice potential recruits and demonstrated that the types of information used by the al-Qaida network can be disseminated to individuals in various locations. Once motivated recruits come into contact with this information, it is not difficult to imagine how they eventually join the network. Having laid out our case in the first five chapters, the discussion now turns to our suggestions for dealing with this complex problem.

Notes

1. Independent Media Review Analysis, "O God, Deal with the Occupier and Usurper Jews," *IMRA*, October 28, 2002, available at www.imra.org.il/story.php3?id=14241 (last accessed March 10, 2005). This sermon was given at the Holy Mosque, Mecca, Saudi Arabia, by Shaykh Abd al-Rahman bin Abd al-Aziz al-Sudays on October 4, 2002.

2. Independent Media Review Analysis, "God, Support the Mujahidin for Your Sake Everywhere." This sermon was given at the Holy Mosque, Mecca, Saudi Arabia, by Shaykh Salih Bin-Abdullah Bin Humayd on October 28, 2002.

3. Independent Media Review Analysis, "O God, Protect Islam and Muslims and Destroy Enemies of Islam, the Tyrants, and the Corrupt." This sermon was given at the Holy Mosque, Mecca, Saudi Arabia, by Shaykh Usamah Abdallah Khayyat on November 15, 2002.

4. Independent Media Review Analysis, "O God, Destroy the Zionist, American, and British Aggressors." *IMRA*, March 10, 2003, available at www.imra.org.il/story.php3?id=16389 (last accessed March 10, 2005). This sermon was given at the Grand Mosque, Sanaa, Yemen, by Shaykh Akram Abd al-Razzaq al Ruqayhi on November 21, 2003.

5. Independent Media Review Analysis, "O God, Support Our Brother Mujahidin." This sermon was given at the Grand Mosque, Sanaa, Yemen, by Shaykh Akram Abd al-Razzaq al Ruqayhi on December 5, 2003.

6. Independent Media Review Analysis, 2003. This sermon was given at Abdallah al-Uthman Mosque, Damascus, Syria, by Shaykh Dr. Abdallah Rabih on November 7, 2003.

7. *Three Sides Tripod*, "The Two Senior Scholars—Who Dared to Speak," *Three Sides Tripod*, available at http://3sides.tripod.com/terrorism/IslamicTerror/fatwa.html (last accessed March 10, 2005).

8. Peter Molan, *Arabic Religious Rhetoric: The Radical Saudi Sheikhs. A Reader* (Kensington, Maryland: Dunwoody Press, 1997).

9. Middle East Media Research Institute, "Reformist Saudi Author: Religious Cassettes Advocate Jihad by Emphasizing Martyr's Sexual Rewards," Special Dispatch Series No. 1032, *MEMRI*, November 23, 2005, available at http://memri.org/bin/articles.cgi?Page=archives&Area=sd&ID=SP103205 (last accessed April 15, 2006).

10. Cable News Network, "Voice Seems to Be al Qaeda Leader Calling for Uprising," *CNN*, October 1, 2004, available at www.cnn.com/2004/WORLD/meast/10/01/zawahiri.transcript (last accessed March 10, 2005).

11. Usama Bin Ladin, "Full Transcript of bin Ladin's Speech," *Al Jazeera*, November 1, 2004, available at http://english.aljazeera.net/NR/exeres/79C6AF22-98FB-4A1C-B21F-2BC36E87F61F.htm (last accessed March 10, 2005).

12. Middle East Media Research Institute, "First Audio Recording by Al-Qa'ida Leader in Iraq Abu Mus'ab Al-Zarqawi," Special Dispatch Series No. 639, *MEMRI*, January 7, 2004, available at http://memri.org/bin/articles.cgi?Page=archives&Area=sd&ID=SP63904 (last accessed March 10, 2005).

13. Bosnian training video, available at www.ropma.net/alqaeda-exposed.htm (last accessed April 15, 2006).

14. Iraq video, available at www.cracker.com (last accessed March 10, 2005).

15. Arab Kids Play Beheading Game video, available at http://inhonor.net/videos.php (last accessed April 15, 2006).

16. Dirty Kuffar video, available at www.ratatak.com/modules/mydownloads/singlefile.php?lid=14 (last accessed April 15, 2006).

17. Scott Shane, "The Web as al-Qaida's Safety Net," *Baltimore Sun*, March 28, 2003, available at http://siteinstitute.org/bin/articles.cgi?ID=inthenews2703&Category=inthenews&Subcategory=0 (last accessed March 10, 2005).

18. Severin Carrell, "U.S. Guards at Guantánamo Tortured Me," *Independent*, April 24, 2005, available at www.cageprisoners.com/articles.php?id=6944.

19. Muhammad Al-Shafi, "Al-Qaeda Reportedly Establishing Open 'Internet University' to Recruit Terrorists," *Al-Sharq al-Awsat*, November 20, 2003, available at www.borrull.org/e/noticia.php?id=24090&PHPSESSID=89285ba9175e1bbd8f56eb050e946102 (last accessed March 10, 2005).

20. "Statement from Azzam.com Regarding Closure of Its Website," *Qoqaz*, September 25, 2002, available at www.qoqaz.net (last accessed November 3, 2002).

21. *Khaleej Times Online*, "Al Qaeda in Iraq Launches Internet Magazine Urging Muslims to Join Jihad," *Free Muslims Coalition*, March 5, 2005, available at www.freemuslims.org/news/article.php?article=474 (last accessed March 10, 2005).

22. Middle East Media Research Institute, "'Kaide' ('Al-Qaeda') Magazine Published Openly in Turkey," Special Dispatch Series No. 951, *MEMRI*, August 7, 2005, available at http://memri.org/bin/articles.cgi?Page=archives&Area=sd&ID=SP95105 (last accessed March 10, 2005).

23. Shawq Al-Mujahid, "The Orator of the Peninsula: The Great Yusuf Al-Ayiri in the Age of Humiliation and Insult," August 1, 2003, available at www.cybcity.com/news/index.htm (last accessed March 10, 2005).

24. "39 Ways to Serve and Participate in Jihad," November 29, 2003, available at www.almaqdese.com/a?I=278 (last accessed December 10, 2003).

25. Middle East Media Research Institute, "Saudi Cleric Al-Fawzan: Jihad in Iraq an Individual Duty Incumbent upon Iraqis," *MEMRI TV Monitor Project*, *MEMRI*, November 21, 2004, available at http://memritv.org/Transcript.asp?P1=375 (last accessed March 10, 2005).

26. Middle East Media Research Institute, "Terror in America (29) Al-Jazeera Interview with Top Al-Qa'ida Leader Abu Hafs 'The Mauritanian,'" Special Dispatch Series No. 313, *MEMRI*, December 14, 2001, available at http://memri.org/bin/articles.cgi?Page=archives&Area=sd&ID=SP31301 (last accessed March 10, 2005).

27. Back to Iraq, "London Blasts Claimed by Al Qaeda," *Back to Iraq*, July 7, 2005, available at www.back-to-iraq.com/archives/2005/07/london_blasts_claimed_by_al_qa.php (last accessed April 15, 2006).

28. Michelle Boorstein, "U.S. Finds Pamphlets Targeting Westerners," *Times Union*, April 6, 2002, available at www.timesunion.com/AspStories/story.asp?storyID=48219 (last accessed March 10, 2005).

29. Patrick Radden Keefe, "Digital Underground. Exposing the 'Darknet': Are Al Qaeda Terrorists Using Your Personal Computer?" *Village Voice*, February 15, 2005, available at www.villagevoice.com/news/0507.essay.61085.2.html (last accessed March 10, 2005).

30. Dexter Filkins, "Demonstrators in Iraq Demand That U.S. Leave," *New York Times*, April 10, 2005, available at www.nytimes.com/2005/04/10/international/middleeast/10iraq.html?ex=1270785600&en=82ca88b462c267af&ei=5090&partner=rssuserland (last accessed April 15, 2006).

31. Rachel Clarke, "Shoppers Outraged by Offensive Leaflets," *This Is Local London*, available at www.thisislocallondon.co.uk/search/display.var.156092.0.shoppers_outraged_by_offensive_leaflets.php (last accessed March 10, 2005).

32. Peter Foster, "Militants of Al-Muhajiroun Seek World Islamic State," *Telegraph*, October 31, 2001, available at www.telegraph.co.uk/news/main.jhtml?xml=%2Fnews%2F2001%2F10%2F31%2Fnmus231.xml (last accessed March 10, 2005).

33. Faris Bin-Hazzam, "Abd-al-Aziz al-Muqrin, Leader of Al-Qaida in Saudi Arabia, Smuggled Weapons from Spain to Algeria, Was Arrested in Somalia, and Fought in Afghanistan and Bosnia," *Al-Sharq al-Awsat*, December 10, 2003.

34. Mattar, Shafika, "Jordanian Flattered That Osama bin Laden Recited His Poem in Videotape," Associated Press, June 1, 2002, available at http://multimedia.belointeractive.com/attack/binladen/0106poet.html (last accessed March 10, 2005).

35. Shafica Mattar, "Jordanian Flattered That Osama Bin Laden Recited His Poem in Videotape," *Associated Press*, June 1, 2002, available at http://multimedia.belointeractive.com/attack/binladen/0106poet.html (last accessed March 10, 2005).

36. Robert Leiken, "Europe's Itinerant Imams: Can the Radical Mosques Be Tamed with Homegrown, Moderate Clerics?" *Weekly Standard*, July 19, 2004.

37. *Evening Standard*, "British Imam: 'Bring Jihad to Your Own Door,'" *This Is London*, April 26, 2004, available at www.thisislondon.co.uk/news/articles/10435138?source=Evening%20Standard (last accessed March 10, 2005).

38. Mustapha Kamal video, available at www.militantislammonitor.org (last accessed April 15, 2006).

39. Robert Leiken, "Europe's Itinerant Imams: Can the Radical Mosques Be Tamed with Homegrown, Moderate Clerics?" *Weekly Standard*, July 19, 2004.

40. Leiken, "Europe's Itinerant Imams."

41. Mark Hosenball, "The Syrian Connection," *Newsweek*, January 26, 2005.

42. British Broadcasting Corporation, "Profile: Abu Zubaydah," *BBC News*, April 2, 2002, available at http://news.bbc.co.uk/1/hi/world/south_asia/1907462.stm (last accessed March 10, 2005).

CHAPTER 6

The Way Ahead

France has betrayed the young people of the suburbs. When you're called Ali, you can't get a job. The French don't accept Islam. Politicians promise us mosques and so on, but at the same time they smear us and call us terrorists.

—Ali, a twenty-four-year-old, unemployed, French Muslim

Our intention in writing this book has been to bring attention to an aspect of the al-Qaida network that has not been studied comprehensively, individuals' motivation for joining. Recruitment into the al-Qaida network is a challenging problem that will not likely simply cease to exist in the near future. Individuals will continue to face issues in their lives that motivate them to seek alternatives, and it is highly probable that the extremist message will continue to exist and be disseminated through various methods and at numerous locations. That being said, this chapter suggests five different paths to address the al-Qaida recruitment problem:

1. Internal regime reform
2. Changing U.S. policy
3. Focusing on the message
4. Targeting the group
5. Encouraging personal interaction

Let's take a look at each of these in more detail.

The first two paths, internal regime reform and changing U.S. policy, connect primarily to chapter 4's discussion of motivation. However, elements from chapter 5 on methods are also relevant to these two strategies. The third option, focusing on the message, connects to the discussion in chapter 5. The fourth strategy, targeting the group, addresses the internal group dynamics of the al-Qaida network. As a result, it concerns discrediting both the network and its leaders to undermine the network in the eyes of potential recruits. This path is related both to the third strategy, focusing on the message, and chapter 4. Finally, encouraging personal interaction means just that—encouraging and sustaining the positive interaction already taking place between Americans and others in the Arab and Muslim world. There is actually a sixth path—to continue along the present path and do nothing. Given what is already known about recruitment, however, we cannot seriously advocate nonaction. This issue is serious enough to warrant attention and merit action.

The five categories, internal regime reform, changing U.S. policy, focusing on the message, targeting the group, and encouraging personal interaction are just our suggested paths for addressing the recruitment issue; any one of these options contains certain drawbacks. Indeed, many are very challenging to implement. None should be taken as a magic bullet for stopping individuals from joining the al-Qaida network. Furthermore, each is exceedingly complex and raises an equal number of what-if questions and concerns. In addition, pursuing one option doesn't necessarily preclude following another or all of the others. On the whole, these are options to better focus the issues raised in the previous chapters and to offer suggestions for potentially dealing with these issues. They are at least worth entertaining and perhaps even adopting on some level. Now, let's take a more detailed look at these options and what they entail.

Internal Regime Reform

Internal regime reform represents one of the ways to deal with recruitment. It targets the motivations described in chapter 4, barring one categorical exception, personal motivations. Individuals will always have numerous personal problems in their lives, and it is exceptionally difficult to mediate those problems in any society. On the other hand, mediating social, economic, and political motivations can potentially remove them from the lives of individuals. Here, we are not confining our discussion to Arab and Muslim states. The United States and other Western countries must also address many of these problems as well. Therefore, they are not immune to any of the problems outlined below.

Social motivations can be addressed on a variety of levels. Even if they cannot be completely solved, raising awareness can direct attention to the potential recruitment pool. For example, drug abuse is an evident problem for some, and a few examples are noted in this book of individuals whose lives were tainted by it. Those engaged in counternarcotics activities are aware of the places these vulnerable individuals frequent and gather. These individuals need alternatives to their situation that do not involve the extremist solution. Additionally, governments could invest more in social service programs for neighborhoods with higher substance-abuse rates. Such programs can help individuals to cope better with deeper problems and prevent them from seeking out paths that lead them to the al-Qaida network.

Another significant social issue requiring serious attention, especially in countries where this problem is pervasive, is the cultural alienation felt by generations of immigrant communities. Governments could take steps to create and enforce policies that would better integrate minorities into the wider community and take them out of second-class-citizen status. If individuals believe that they are a part of a community, they will feel less alienated and less inclined to join groups in their quest to fill this social void. Additionally, governments need to make a real effort to ensure that individuals in these communities receive the same rights and opportunities as individuals from the majority of the population.

Chapter 4 noted many examples of this type of alienation; Zacarias Moussaoui and Kamel Daoudi both experienced it, as did the perpetrators of the July 7, 2005, attacks in London. Three of the individuals who carried out the attacks were British-born Muslims of Pakistani descent, and the fourth was a naturalized citizen of Jamaican descent, one of whom was used as an example in chapter 4.

The French riots, a response to long-festering problems in France, which took place over three weeks during October and November 2005, are probably one of the best examples of what happens when issues of cultural alienation aren't dealt with properly. These issues had already been well illustrated by researchers and journalists. As Sarah Wildman points out,

> the French National Assembly passed, by an overwhelming majority, a law banning the headscarf and other "conspicuous symbols" of religiosity in French public schools. The French government believes that banning the headscarf will reduce radicalism and facilitate the integration of the Muslim population of France into the public school system. But the reason that Muslims aren't better integrated into French society has little to do with the headscarf. And, if anything, the ban will only make France's "Muslim problem" worse.

Probably the chief accomplishment of the uproar over the veil has been to obscure the socioeconomic problems—such as astronomical unemployment, miserable housing conditions, and entrenched racism—that are the true obstacles to Muslim integration in France. Since the early 1990s, Islam has drawn strength from the problems of the *banlieue*, the gritty urban suburbs that house the poor outside French cities. The unemployment rate in the *banlieue* hovers above 25 percent, and reaches as high as 40 percent in some areas. Only four percent of the *beur*—French slang for "Arab"—boys who grow up there reach university. For most, job prospects are dim. As one Tunisian Muslim woman told me recently, young Arab men turn to Islam because it is the only thing that gives them a sense of pride or honor. The future seems bleak, and the laws of the *cite*, as the housing projects are called, seem unrelated to life in Paris or Lyon. We won't find jobs, boys complain, so why look for them?[1]

During the riots, more than two hundred buildings were set on fire, ten thousand cars were damaged, and forty-five hundred people were taken into custody.[2] Because of the riots, French and international newspapers brought to light the issue of discrimination against Muslims living in France. Many saw widespread discrimination as contributing to unemployment, crime, and substandard housing situations. The French response to the riots has been mixed, both in terms of verbal discussion and implementation of policies.

Verbally, there were those French officials who claimed that France must address the problems of the poor and alienated Muslim communities. In a speech in mid-November 2005, the French president Jacques Chirac promised to create more opportunities for young people.[3] Others said the problems were found in the communities themselves. For example, some government ministers claimed that polygamy might have been one of the causes of the riots because the children of these large polygamous families were having difficulty integrating into society.[4] Interior Minister Nicolas Sarkozy said that the crime-ridden neighborhoods needed to be "cleaned with a power hose."[5] Later, after being criticized for those remarks, he claimed that France had failed to properly integrate its immigrant communities.[6]

At the same time, the French government has pursued measures, which, in their eyes, will ameliorate the perceived problems in the country. In mid-November Interior Minister Sarkozy announced that those foreign nationals who took part in the riot would be deported.[7] Prime Minister Dominique de Villepin also announced that certain reform measures were being pursued. For example, the age of apprenticeships would be lowered from sixteen to fourteen. But, this was met with opposition from teaching unions. The government also announced that it would restore credits to local associations and seek to create jobs. Interior Minister Sarkozy later announced that France would initiate measures to deal with criminal activity. Hopefully, the French did not fail to see the riots as a long-term problem existing because of alienation. Their perception of the problem is very important because it impacts how they will ultimately deal with their ethnically diverse population.

As already noted, the French riots demonstrate how important it is for governments to address cultural alienation. We mentioned above that governments can address this issue by creating and enforcing policies that integrate minorities into the wider community. Mosques are a focal point in Muslim communities and will play a central role in any attempts to successfully implement this strategy. For instance, as was mentioned in chapter 4, Richard Reid and Hasib Mir Husayn, one of the London bombers, experienced cultural alienation and, in their search for an identity, turned to local mosques. One possible solution in implementing this strategy is for governments to team up with local mosques to create programs that bridge differences between minority communities and the wider society. Governments could provide the funding, and mosques could organize programs encouraging interaction between minority individuals in these communities and members of the mainstream community. For example, the wider community could be educated about the ethnic backgrounds of those in the minority communities. Mosques could sponsor a festival recognizing the history and culture of these different ethnic groups. This would provide an opportunity for minorities and the wider community to interact and for minorities to share their diverse and rich backgrounds.

Another solution could be for governments to include local mosques in plans to improve housing conditions in minority neighborhoods. Mosques could be responsible for identifying what individuals would like to see in their neighborhoods and for organizing groups of volunteers to participate in efforts to rebuild their communities. This would send the message that the government has a vested interest in the community's welfare and wants individuals within the community to play a role in building for the future.

While most mosques are peaceful places of worship, there are those that promote the extremist message. In dealing with these mosques, the government usually uses law-enforcement mechanisms or other operational counterterrorism responses. However, these operations should be followed by efforts to address the underlying issues, such as cultural alienation, that are drawing individuals to these mosques in the first place. If the government cannot work directly with these mosques, then perhaps the neighborhoods in which they are located can be the focus of significant efforts to address cultural alienation. This will help to counter the extremist message and reduce the network's ability to exploit feelings of cultural alienation.

Coupled with the government's responsibility noted above is the accountability of society. If the individuals in these respective countries make no effort to integrate minorities into their society, then any government efforts to eliminate alienation will fall short. Communities have to recognize their responsibility in all of this. For example, since the Madrid attacks, some Moroccans in Spain have faced further cultural alienation. One young Moroccan living in Spain stated, "The economic situation is worse in Morocco, but they treat you like a person there. Here you lose your dignity."[8] As these words demonstrate, society plays a crucial role in preventing cultural alienation following attacks and subsequent counterterrorism operations. Racist leaflets circulated by the National Front in London in 2002 near the Baitul Futuh Mosque are another case in point, as is the jailing of seven members of the National Front after police found out about a plot to kidnap and torture a Somali youth.[9] These examples demonstrate that spreading hatred only serves to bolster claims that outside cultures are not welcome.

While anger and fear are common feelings following attacks, it is imperative that these emotions not be directed at minority communities and that citizens do not isolate or stereotype the communities from which the responsible individuals come. Instead, communities need to see these events as an opportunity to reach out to minorities and integrate them into their society. This will decrease the likelihood that individuals will be motivated in the future to join extremist groups because of cultural alienation.

Eradicating cultural alienation requires a combined effort by both governments and Muslim organizations. Already, many in the Muslim community recognize the importance of promoting the message that they are a part of the larger society. For example, as part of the Islamic holiday Eid al-Adha, Muslims generally slaughter an animal and give a portion of it to the poor. In 2005, the Montgomery County Muslim Council in Maryland provided seven hundred pounds of meat to the Manna Food Center, and the 2006 goal was to donate five thousand pounds.[10] Irma Hafeez, the council's general secretary, claimed, "especially after 9-11, we need to be a more obvious part of society."[11] Other efforts by Muslim communities are important as well. As Julia Hieber notes,

> Incentives also take place at the local level, where mosques and prayer room associations provide family counselling, tutorials and job application assistance. As such, these local-level self-help groups, often financed by their members, are

an important resource for Muslim youth who often face discrimination in the employment market and in applying for internships that lead to jobs. Certain cities like Paris, London, Frankfurt and Munich have started to see their Muslim associations cooperate with local city authorities in order to facilitate the support of Muslim youth at school and in their transition to full employment.

Muslim organizations are further complemented in their youth integration work by private non-Muslims associations, such as Lichterkette e.V in Munich, which focus on Muslims' needs by coordinating language, tuition, educational programmes, couselling, and professional training incentives. Alternative media reviews and newspapers, such as the *Islamiche Zeitung* in Germany and *Sezame* in France, provide their Muslim and non-Muslim readership a more inclusive view of Muslims in Europe, namely as integral members of society.[12]

Societal alienation is a problem as well. Frequently, governments are not able to adapt to a changing demographic makeup, and an alienated class emerges. This is especially true of young individuals who seek to challenge societal constraints. It is necessary to find better strategies for integrating and dealing with different generations. These strategies need to incorporate appealing opportunities for these different generations. Providing these individuals opportunities, as well as recognizing their uniqueness and importance as a group in society, is essential.

Another area of great concern to many countries is economics. Lack of opportunity, unemployment, underemployment, and corruption continue to plague countries. This is especially problematic in countries with a large youth bulge. A country full of young men with no sound economic opportunities is a recipe for disaster. Obviously, lack of employment opportunity leads some individuals to want to change their present situations and to seek out alternatives. By increasing economic opportunities, governments can minimize the probability that individuals will seek out an extremist group because of their financial circumstances.

In many countries, for example, internal corruption is squarely blamed for the lack of any real economic reform. In fact, one of bin Ladin's central issues is the corruption of Arab regimes. In his 1996 fatwa, bin Ladin argued that the Saudi government was not paying some of its merchants and contractors. Bin Ladin was pointing to the perceived self-serving nature of the royal family. Egypt is another case in point; many articles point to the rampant corruption that plagues that country. Muhammad Sid-Ahmed writes of the Egyptian state of affairs, "Casting light on the dark underworld of corruption is no easy matter, however, given the vested interest of its beneficiaries to keep it shrouded in secrecy, but every effort must be made to expose its stranglehold on our economic, political and moral well-being."[13]

While there have been public efforts to deal with such pervasive corruption, there are always examples of setbacks or attempts to thwart such efforts. For example, Joseph Krauss has noted that Egyptian President Hosni Mubarak "stripped four prominent and outspoken judges of their legal immunity. The judges were investigating allegations of vote-rigging during last fall's parliamentary elections and were part of a growing movement calling for a new law that would provide for more judicial independence."[14]

Other countries grapple with corruption as well, including Morocco, which holds an annual anticorruption day. Well-known scholar Abdeslam Maghraoui has written of the situation, "Corruption is pervasive and systemic in Morocco. It permeates every aspect of public life, from elections to establishing a business, from routing state services to taxes. It is an integral part of the political, economic, judiciary, and administrative systems that has been normalized and institutionalized during decades of authoritarian rule under Hassan II."[15]

Local newspapers have also focused at great length on this issue and the need for a proactive government response to combat it.[16] As one newspaper commented,

> There is no doubt that the lack of a firm policy against corruption is at the origin of its development. The State does not shoulder its responsibilities in this matter as the legislation, an indispensable tool to fight this plague, does not protect the public, leaving it in a weak position to face an omnipotent and arrogant administration.[17]

While the Moroccan government has unveiled an anticorruption plan, it has been met with skepticism from Moroccans themselves. One student commented, "We keep hearing the same old tune played over and over."[18]

Corruption's negative impact on society cannot be overstated. It has contributed to a haves-versus-have-nots scenario, resulting in an underclass that suffers at the expense of the ruling elite. The underclass traces its economic suffering, to include a subpar health-care system, to the ruling elite. It is an unfortunate situation. Governments need to take steps to eradicate corruption, ensuring transparency and helping to create better conditions for their citizens.

At times, unemployment and underemployment are correlated with a lack of education. It follows that if governments invent alternative ways to create employment opportunities, as well as provide for educational reform, the pool of recruits may be decreased. However, in some regions of the world where the general population is educated, there are still limited employment opportunities, resulting in an educated and unemployed workforce, which can be a very problematic combination.

Job opportunities do exist in many countries, notably Gulf Arab states. Unfortunately, however, many Gulf Arab states have created a situation where certain jobs are left to workers drawn from outside of the country. These foreign workers perform jobs that are otherwise seen as "undesirable" by the Gulf Arabs themselves. As a result, getting individuals to take these "undesirable" jobs has not been very successful, adding to already existing employment problems. One solution could be for governments to improve the appeal of these less-than-desirable jobs by offering increased remuneration. Furthermore, individuals who take them could be offered other incentives. For example, governments could offer to finance their own or their family members' educations. Obviously, a significant benefit of this option is that a good education will provide individuals with the knowledge and skills required for more "attractive" and competitive jobs.

Adding to the economic problems of countries is the failure of oil-producing states, particularly Saudi Arabia, to diversify their economies. As a result, new types of jobs that would spark economic growth are not being created. Some Gulf Arab oil-producing countries, such as Oman, Bahrain, and the United Arab Emirates (UAE), are attempting to invest in tourism in order to mitigate their reliance on a single resource that will not last indefinitely. For example, while Abu Dhabi is an oil-rich Emirate (it has 95 percent of the oil and gas resources in the UAE), it is pursuing development opportunities to diversity its economy and cope with downturns in oil prices.[19] Abu Dhabi also started its own airline and is in the process of building another airport to deal with the hoped-for increase in tourist traffic. In order to attract tourism, the Emirates Palace, boasted to be a world-class, seven-star hotel, was built.

In addition to unemployment, crime is another important economic issue. As was discussed in chapter 3, some individuals convert to Islam in prison and are later recruited into the network. One example highlighted was Richard Reid. The prison subculture offers a recruitment pool for networks such as al-Qaida. Given their bleak circumstances, these individuals often lack purpose and are easily influenced by others. Prison systems need to work at rehabilitating individuals so that upon their release they can go on to become contributing members of society, rather than contributing members of the al-Qaida network. This means identifying the reasons these individuals became involved in criminal activities in the first place, then providing them with the tools necessary to succeed in the world upon their reentry to society. Perhaps if Richard Reid had been instilled with life skills and further guidance while serving his time, he might have chosen an alternative path after prison. It is true that prisons, especially those in the United States, are limited in their capabilities to focus on rehabilitation for a variety of reasons; however, this topic is outside the scope of this book. Nevertheless, it is important to mention the role that rehabilitation could play in preventing extremist recruitment.

Also governments need to monitor extremist influences within their prison systems. Although we did not specifically mention prisons as a location in chapter 5, their role in providing a place for extremists to recruit individuals into the network should be recognized. This problem is clearly illustrated by an example from the United States. As Frank Gaffney writes,

> One year ago, prisoners in the New Folsom State Prison—a maximum-security facility outside Sacramento, California—reportedly began plotting terrorist attacks against three National Guard facilities, an Israeli consulate and several synagogues in the Los Angeles area. The attacks are believed to have been planned for the fourth anniversary of September 11 or the Jewish holidays. According to ABC news, a law enforcement report has determined that the plotters intended to "kill everyone at the target[s]," potentially resulting in dozens of casualties inflicted on innocents as part of the *jihad* (holy war) the prisoners were determined to wage against the United States. The frightening thing is that the would-be-assailants were not terrorist adherents to the political ideology of Islamofascism when they went to jail. *They became Islamists while in prison*—thanks to the sort of recruitment opportunities afforded clerics usually selected by Saudi-backed Muslim-American organizations.[20]

The criminal justice system must work to identify these individuals and take steps to limit their ability to influence others to join the network. Furthermore, once identified, these individuals should be isolated from others. One need only think back to the example of Abu Musab al-Zarqawi and the network he built inside Jordan's prison walls. A proactive approach to this issue will prevent the network from further infiltrating prisons.

While the indicators in the political-motivation categories predominantly focus on the United States and Israel, the negative perception of those in power in many countries extends to the countries that potential recruits live in as well. To exacerbate the problem, the perception is that the imperial power, the United States, is bolstering corrupt Arab and Muslim governments. In addition, the Palestinian issue is a highly emotional and contentious one. Muslim countries, especially Arab ones, are criticized for their lack of substantive support for the Palestinians or for not adequately standing up to Israel, their sworn enemy. These issues will be more fully addressed in the section on changing U.S. policy below.

Internal political matters are also relevant here. Many countries in the Arab and Muslim world have less-than-perfect records of political accountability. The United States has recently begun to push for electoral reform in countries like Egypt and Saudi Arabia. Free and fair elections are a necessary part of any opening process; yet, in practice, elections have been fraught with corruption, seriously detracting from the possibility for positive change. Corrupt activities also play into the hands of the extremists who point to the dictatorial nature of many of these regimes. For example, in November 2005, during Egypt's final round of parliamentary elections, police opened fire on crowds and blocked voters from entering polling stations in areas considered to be Muslim Brotherhood and opposition strongholds.[21]

Another issue dealt with in chapter 5 is also worth mentioning here because it requires that countries take action. Clearly, the al-Qaida network has made significant use of religious schools to spread the extremist message. These schools not only function as centers of indoctrination but, if successful, provide a pool of potential recruits to the network. Countries could deal with this issue in two ways: by actively seeking out and closing down religious schools spreading extremist messages or by addressing their curricula, outlawing extremist verbiage. Yet, religious schools are not the only problem. The school curricula in countries like Saudi Arabia include materials that glorify jihad and vilify Israel and the West. Finally, bolstering already existing mainstream public schools is essential to providing alternatives to these religious schools. If the choice in poor countries is between a religious education that provides a warm meal, clothing, and shelter for a child and a public education that doesn't fulfill these basic needs, the former will invariably win out.

Changing U.S. Policy

Changing U.S. policy is the option that raises the most "what-ifs" and "what abouts." Nevertheless, for better or worse, many see U.S. policy as a major reason for the ills of the Muslim world.

As we saw in chapter 4, political issues that can be traced back to U.S. policies can provide significant motivation for many individuals, whether alone or in conjunction with other motivators. In addition, when individuals are exposed to the type of information illustrated in chapter 5, which blames the United States for a multitude of sins, they can come to believe that it is not farfetched to think that U.S. policy change may be part of the solution to the world's ills.

The most significant issue is the United States' perceived unlimited and unquestioning support for Israel. The plight of the Palestinians is broadcast, written, and talked about on a daily basis in countries worldwide. Turn on an Arab radio or television station, and this will become very evident. Fox News's use of the term "homicide bombers" may play with U.S. audiences, but others in the Muslim world are armed with examples of the perceived mistreatment and oppression of Palestinians at the hands of Israelis. Furthermore, extremists continually assert that the United States is lying when it denies its support of Israel and claims to support the Palestinians as well, and they demonstrate this favor of the Israelis with telling examples. The wall being built by the Israelis, which the United States is not seen as effectively stopping, is a case in point. All around, the United States is considered an imperial villain.

To add fuel to the fire, the United States is seen as supporting corrupt and abusive governments, especially in the Arab world. These are the same countries in which individuals are very aware that their economic and social ills fall squarely on the shoulders of the corrupt governments under which they live. The Egyptians, Pakistanis, Saudis, and Algerians are examples. As important as it is for the United States to continue working with these governments in promoting U.S. interests, it is equally important that the United States encourage and support real reform, for instance, significant economic and political reform, within these countries. This would help mediate some of the social and economic problems previously discussed.

Additionally, the United States is perceived as acting unilaterally and in an irresponsible and self-interested way. U.S. actions taken after 9/11 are clearly perceived to be against Islam. Each time the United States acts in a Muslim country, this criticism is levied loudly, again and again, in public forums. For example, the al-Qaida network and its supporters use as evidence of this fight against Islam the incidents of civilian "collateral damage" in the wars in Afghanistan and Iraq. These deaths are depicted as the intentional killing of Muslims. Oftentimes, pictures accompanying the events serve to illustrate their argument graphically. For example, the SOS website, which was discussed in chapter 5, has a flash presentation entitled "The Crusade against Iraq." This presentation provides graphic illustrations of dead and wounded bodies, including those of children, attributable to the crusaders occupying Iraq. Another presentation entitled "United Snakes, Soldiers Exposed" depicts U.S. soldiers on the streets of Iraq, as well as pictures of them seemingly "mistreating" individuals. While we cannot know for sure what story these pictures are actually telling because the context is not adequately provided, the presentation is accompanied with banners noting that these are "pictures of the crusade against Islam." Thus, the viewer is primed to believe that these pictures are negative in character.

Unfortunately, U.S. actions in Iraq have reinforced the perception that the United States is a Muslim occupier. As a result, foreign fighters from countries around the world are coming to Iraq to aid their Muslim brothers. Furthermore, the reasons for going to Iraq were first laid out in terms of weapons of mass destruction and over time evolved into other justifications. This left others, particular those with loud and extremist voices, to fill in the blanks about what the U.S. motivation actually was. Thus, many settled on the idea that the United States was once again wielding a big stick in its quest for control of Muslim oil. Eventually, these suspicions become truths in the eyes of many. The negative perception of the United States is further exacerbated each time the United States rattles its saber and threatens Muslim countries, notably Syria.

The Abu Ghraib prison scandal involving the abuse of Iraqi prisoners at the hands of their American guards only served to exacerbate an already problematic situation in Iraq. When the pictures surfaced that depicted detainee abuse, the damage done to the reputation of the United States was severe. Discussions about the scandal were widely held on the Internet and in other venues. Other allegations of detainee mistreatment in Afghanistan and Guantánamo Bay, Cuba, have also surfaced, adding fuel to the fire. These incidents and allegations have bolstered bin Ladin's argument that the United States oppresses Muslims.

In May 2005, another scandal erupted that further discredited the United States. A *Newsweek* story broke accusing U.S. military personnel of flushing the Holy Koran down toilets at Guantánamo Bay during interrogations the previous year. While the veracity of the claims has not been fully investigated, the damage was done when the story was published, and it is unlikely to be repaired. The story caused riots in Afghanistan in May 2005 in which at least fifteen people were killed and also led to anti-U.S. demonstrations throughout the Muslim world. Notably, the Cage Prisoners website discussed in chapter 5 publicized the scandal. When *Newsweek* issued a retraction of its story, a series of articles, to include those posted on the Cage Prisoners site, responded that the U.S. government pressured the magazine to do so. Cage Prisoners then posted its own study entitled "Report into the Systematic and Institutionalized U.S. Desecration of the Qur'an and other Islamic Rituals: Testimonies from Former Guantánamo Bay Detainees." Former detainees appeared in public gatherings to speak about their mistreatment by the United States. At this point, the veracity of the article is no longer the issue. All over the Muslim world, individuals vented their frustration with the United States. As a result, not only was the reputation of the United States tarnished, but the al-Qaida network was neatly provided with additional propaganda to capitalize on.

Other contentious issues remain as well. The United States still has troops in Muslim lands. As we discussed in chapter 2, this issue is central to bin Ladin's fatwas. And while the United States has removed troops from the lands of the two holy places, Mecca and Medina in Saudi Arabia, there are still troops in Muslim countries, namely, Afghanistan, Iraq, and Qatar. If the United States remains in these countries, then it needs to publicize repeatedly its "unselfish" reasons for doing so, directly personalizing them to the populations of those countries. For example, in Afghanistan, the U.S. government should broadcast its support of the Afghani people and stress not only that its troops are present in the country to engage in counterterrorism operations but also that it is committed to rebuilding the country. It is exceedingly important for the United States to state its reasons for being in Muslim lands and to keep their best interests continually in mind. Every time the United States fails to follow through on its promises to help rebuild Afghanistan and Iraq, the network notes that the infidels are only occupying Muslim lands. Added to this is the argument that the United States' real underlying motivation is to steal precious natural resources, such as oil, from Muslim countries.

Focusing on the Message

Focusing on the message is another possible avenue for dealing with recruitment. This can be addressed at both the strategic (strategic communications from government agencies) and the tactical (information operations) levels.

The United States has lost a significant amount of credibility worldwide for a variety of reasons that can be traced to U.S. policy. This is evident in opinion polls conducted throughout the world. If U.S. policy change is not seen as a viable option, then the U.S. government should at least be consistent in what it is saying, especially across agencies. However, at the strategic level, putting out a consistent message is only the first step. Not only does the message have to be consistent, but U.S. actions also need to be in sync with U.S. statements. Thus, it does no good to craft a meaningful and well-defined strategic communication plan, only to have actions discredit the message. This severely harms the credibility of the United States in the eyes of the world and fuels hatred and resentment of U.S. policy. Again, as already pointed out, this motivates many recruits to act. In addition, even if recruits are motivated by other factors, they are continually bombarded with examples of U.S. hypocrisy through various methods and in many locations.

Now, it is true that the credibility of the United States is in question. As a result, many argue that it no longer matters what the United States says because it won't be seen as credible anyway. This is a good point, but it does not mean that the United States should not put out its message and back it up with actions. There will be less opportunity to criticize if the United States clearly articulates its policy and does not deviate from it in its actions.

A recent issue involving the U.S. military and the Iraqi press is an example of U.S. deeds being out of sync with U.S. words. According to press reports, U.S. military officers were paying for pro-American newspaper, radio, and television reports to be planted in the Iraqi press.[22] While selling America was probably well intentioned, unfortunately, it also undermined one of the United States' primary messages: its support for the principles of democracy, including a free and open press. Furthermore, U.S. statements about the situation in Iraq are now extremely suspect, especially in the eyes of Arab and Muslim governments. Finally, stories such as these detract from any good the military is doing anywhere in the world.

Another possible solution to challenging the al-Qaida message and focusing the U.S. message could be for the U.S. government to set up a body whose function is to wage the so-called information war. This would require full integration of individuals across agencies and outside the government in commercial enterprises whose expertise is the business of information. The purpose of the agency would be to wage the information war on both strategic and tactical levels. Furthermore, by creating an agency that deals with the network's propaganda campaign, the government would gain a centralized and comprehensive knowledge base about the enemy's actual information capabilities. This would also help to ward off the blindsiding that often occurs when one agency is pursuing one message, while another is pursuing its own information goals. The unfortunate result is that one agency's displeasure often becomes public, further undermining U.S. credibility as a whole with regard to the message being put forth.

Yet, it also seems that those involved in the information machine need to think about how to craft the U.S. message so that it resonates with those outside the United States. For example, the sound-bite nature and constant stream of changing experts that characterize the U.S. press may not be transferable to, for example, Arab countries. These lessons may be hard ones for some but must be learned if the information war is to be waged effectively. Knowing your audience is a principle that cannot be stressed enough.

Of course, the intention here is not to single out the United States. Many of these issues need to be addressed by other countries as well. The information war needs to be a sustained, global effort on the part of those dedicated to destroying the network. Unfortunately, when all is said and done, the failure of the United States and other countries to act adequately actually demonstrates an even greater problem—bin Ladin and other extremists are defining the information playing field. The al-Qaida network has managed to amass and sustain a very effective propaganda machine and has exhaustively exploited numerous methods and locations in disseminating its message. As was illustrated in chapter 5, the network message is simple, clear, and, for the most part, consistent. This is a sophisticated foe. It is imperative that the United States and its allies exhaust all possible resources in disseminating their message and countering al-Qaida's. These countries, including the United States, should be prepared to sustain this campaign indefinitely, using the same consistent, clear, and repetitive messages.

One potential direction can be to challenge the criticisms levied against the United States and other countries directly. Doing so requires not just a response, but an immediate one. For example, when bin Ladin claims that he is for the Palestinians, the immediate response should be that he has never demonstrated any real support for the Palestinians. This assertion needs to be made clearly, with evidence and with testimonials by Palestinians themselves. This theme needs to be continually driven home. When bin Ladin claims he is the leader of all things mujahidin, the immediate response should be that he and Ayman al-Zawahiri are hiding in a cave while other young men are being sent out to die on their behalf. Evidence, evidence, and more evidence should be given. Again, these are only two of the many, many statements the United States and other countries have failed to address either effectively or consistently.

Other issues in need of greater visibility include the killing of Muslims by members of the network. These atrocities have not gone unnoticed by leaders of the Muslim world. For example, in October 2001, Prince Turki al-Faysal criticized bin Ladin for killing innocent people in Nairobi, Dar-el-Salam, New York, and Washington, including many Muslims.[23] He further condemned bin Ladin's actions by stating,

> As to Iraq and the children of Iraq, what have you ever done for them? By God, what have you ever done for the people of Afghanistan? You have only brought destruction on them. It would have been more honorable of you after having given your blessing to acts of suicide, to commit suicide yourself and sacrifice yourself for sake of saving Afghanistan from the consequences of your actions.[24]

Prince Turki's disapproval of the killing of Muslims and of bin Ladin's actions in Afghanistan is compelling for two reasons. First, it emphasizes the devastation that bin Ladin has inflicted on the Muslim world. Second, and even more importantly, this disapproval originates from an Arab and Muslim voice. Because the United States has lost significant credibility across this part of the world, its messages are often ignored. Therefore, a message from the Arab and Muslim world carries much more weight than a message originating from the United States.

The response by the Jordanian citizenry to the 2005 Jordanian hotel bombings is instructive as well. Right after the bombings, Jordanians took to the streets to protest the attacks. The protest was attended by both leftist political groups and hard-line Islamic groups who are usually critical of King Abdullah. During the protest, they chanted "burn in hell, Abu Musab al-Zarqawi."[25] Furthermore, a survey conducted of Jordanians found that seven out of ten Jordanians had changed their position and now viewed al-Qaida as a terrorist organization. Additionally, the majority of Jordanians believed the actions of al-Zarqawi and al-Qaida to be "detrimental to Arab and Islamic causes and do not serve them."[26] It is very unfortunate that such a tragic event had to happen to get individuals to rally against the atrocities committed by the al-Qaida network.

Our last example is the negative reaction of some Egyptians to the Sharm al-Shaykh bombings. This perspective is illustrated and captured by the Egyptian playwright Ali Salem, who wrote,

> First the battle was between you and the governments of the region, and now you have declared war against the Egyptian people. Because you are cowards, you choose the weakest link [of the Egyptian people], which is not protected by anyone—those working in the tourism sector. Because your souls are dark and full of animosity and hatred, you chose the time of relaxation from hard work in order to tear their bodies to shreds.[27]

The network relies on the message that they are the defenders of Muslims throughout the world, seeking to draw individuals to their cause of defending Islam. However, their public message may not be on par with their personal perspective. The following is a personal correspondence written by a Yemeni in Afghanistan in 1998 to his colleagues in Yemen. His correspondence indicates that some network members did not believe that Afghanistan was the true Muslim paradise that they were claiming to defend.

> I send you my greetings from beyond the swamps to your country, where there is progress and civilization. . . . You should excuse us for not calling. There are many reasons, the most important of which is the difficulty of calling from this country. We have to go to the city, which involves a number of stages. The first stage involves arranging for a car (as we don't have a car). Of course, we are bound by the time the car is leaving, regardless of the time we want to leave. The second stage involves waiting for the car (we wait for the car, and it may

be hours late or arrive before the agreed time). The next stage is the trip itself, when we sit like sardines in a can. Most of the time I have 1/8 of a chair, and the road is very bad. After all this suffering, the last stage is reaching a humble government communication office. Most of the time there is some kind of fail-ure—either the power is off, the lines out of order, or the neighboring country (through which the connection is made) does not reply. Only in rare cases can we make problem-free calls.[28]

Another avenue can be to publicize the effect that al-Qaida attacks have on the livelihood of the average Muslim. When the network attacks a coun-try's infrastructure, it should be broadcast that the effect on the economy is significant. These attacks not only impact the government and society but specifically the welfare of other Muslims living in that society. For example, in 2003, attacks in northern Iraq on the oil infrastructure hurt not only Iraq's economy but also the quality of life of Iraqis. Furthermore, Iraq's attempt to rectify the situation by importing kerosene, gasoline, and petroleum from Turkey and Kuwait was sabotaged when trucks were burned and stolen and drivers were even killed.[29] When attacks like this occur, it should be broad-cast all over the Muslim world that Iraqis are not able to heat their homes or put fuel in their vehicles because of the network. These stories need to be personalized and repeated consistently over time to show the long-term effects. Additionally, after the July 23, 2005, attacks in the Red Sea resort town of Sharm al-Shaykh, Egypt, local Egyptians expressed their dismay and discontent over the attacks, which ruined many local businesses and, as a re-sult, individual livelihoods. Statements and testimonials from the Egyptians who lost their livelihoods should have been broadcast and followed up on.

While a defensive strategy is fine, being ahead in the race is extremely im-portant. Thus, taking the offensive is paramount in winning the information war. If the network is to be defeated from an informational perspective, coun-tries need to set the stage and challenge the network's credibility by putting it on the defensive. Here, the negative Jordanian response to the 2005 Am-man bombings by al-Zarqawi is instructive. Following the demonstrations, al-Zarqawi was put on the defensive and was forced to justify his reasoning behind the attacks with the following statement: "People of Jordan, we did not undertake to blow up any wedding parties. For those Muslims who were killed, we ask God to show them mercy, for they were not targets."[30] Putting al-Zarqawi on the defensive caused him to spend his time and energy doing damage control. Additionally, he most likely had to rethink his strategy of attacking outside of Iraq.

Of course, everything that has been mentioned thus far cannot be strictly a government effort. Muslim communities need to be heavily engaged in these types of debates to provide at least an alternative opinion to al-Qaida. There needs to be a dialogue, one that can outlast the extremist position that relies heavily on the current motivations of the recruits.

Targeting the Group

Our next proposed strategy, targeting the group, stems from our discussion above on the information war. There are two main parts to this option: (1) tracking and capturing its members, particularly its leadership, and (2) destroying the group from within.

The first part of this strategy, capturing or killing its members, has been, in our opinion, pretty successful. Many individuals in the military, defense, and other agencies are involved in this aspect of the "war on terrorism." For example, the Saudis are being praised by the United States for their ability to track and capture members of the Saudi network. The Pakistanis, British, and Indonesians, among others, are doing their part as well. Governments are now working more closely together in counterterrorism operations. For example, Australia provided funding to the Philippines to build up its counterterrorism capabilities.

The capture or even killing of members who choose to engage the United States and its allies on various battlefields and in locations throughout the world can erode morale within the group. In addition, taking the higher-profile and more experienced leaders out of the mix can leave the network scrambling to fill the ranks, often with less experienced members. For example, the capture of Riduan Isamuddin (a.k.a. Hambali), a key operational member, dealt a significant blow to Jemaah Islamiyah. Likewise, the December 2005 death of the number-three man, Hamza Rabia, left a void in the al-Qaida network's leadership. Therefore, there is no reason not to continue to pursue this aspect of the war.

Our second strategy is much more complex than the first. The network can be targeted, but doing so demands a great deal of knowledge about the network and the dynamics of the individuals involved. The al-Qaida network, like any other group, has issues to deal with simply because it consists of individuals who have altercations and differences over strategy and tactics, as well as money and power. One way to deal with the network would be to exploit these altercations and differences, causing the individuals to turn on each other and destroy the network themselves.

In addition, the network is really composed of many subgroups. As social psychologists have taught us, the diverging agendas of different groups can potentially create dissension among them.

Individual leaders within the network can also be targeted and discredited. All of the media coverage that certain individuals in the network receive builds up their image in the eyes of potential recruits. Exploiting the information presented in chapter 4 can discredit that image. As an example, think back to the motivations that led al-Zarqawi to join the network. He was essentially a dropout who continuously found himself in trouble with the authorities. When al-Zarqawi missed his chance to fight jihad, he formed his own group in prison and fully embraced extremism. This is not exactly the story of a born leader who was going to establish an Islamic state in Iraq, and publicizing that he was nothing more than a criminal incapable of coming up with a strategy for Iraq's future, let along implementing one, could have discredited him. Even al-Zarqawi's former mentor, Abu Muhammad al-Maqdisi, broke ranks with him on the issue of killing civilians and attacking churches and Shiite mosques.[31]

Following the Amman bombings, contributors on Islamic websites criticized the attacks in al-Zarqawi's former homeland. One noted, "We are shedding tears of blood because of the many negative aspects attached to the operation. . . . I swear to God it was a big mistake in which al-Qaida will pay a heavy price." Another argued, "Go to Amman and hear, unfortunately, a lot of people cursing al-Zarqawi everywhere. With this act, al-Qaida destroyed its great assets of Jordanian appreciation for its jihad in Iraq."[32] Al-Zarqawi's family also issued the following statement: "A Jordanian doesn't stab himself with his own spear. We sever links with him until doomsday."[33] In an article in the *Jordan Times*, Musa Keilani levied several criticisms on al-Zarqawi:

> His claim that his group does not target Muslims is devoid of any truth, since we know that his people are killing Iraqi Muslims, civilians and otherwise, by the dozen everyday. . . . Zarqawi is the number one enemy of people in Jordan and the entire Arab and Muslim worlds, because the Arab and Muslims are his targets and they have suffered immensely, and continue to suffer, as a result of his actions which he seeks to justify in the name of Islam.[34]

Even his own network criticized his approach of killing Shia. In a letter to al-Zarqawi, al-Zawahiri wrote,

> Among the things which the feelings of the Muslim populace who love and support you will never find palatable—also—are the scenes of slaughtering the hostages. You shouldn't be deceived by the praise of some of the zealous young men and their description of you as the shaykh of the slaughterers, etc. They do not express the general view of the admirer and the supporter of the resistance in Iraq, and of you in particular by the favor and blessing of God.[35]

In addition to a senior leader, lower-level members have also levied criticism. In a letter written to al-Zarqawi, an insurgent complained about the Mosul leadership of his network, calling them incompetent, lacking in training, and unwilling to collaborate. He also complained of the "squandering of Muslims money on petty expenses, cars and phones."[36]

Al-Zawahiri is another individual who can easily be discredited. There are numerous indications that he is not well liked by many. Abdullah Azzam, who is revered and respected by the mujahidin for his commitment to the cause, is known to have had little regard for al-Zawahiri and his lack of leadership. For example, Azzam complained to his son-in-law that al-Zawahiri was a troublemaker and that he, along with others, only intended to create *fitna* (discord) among the mujahidin.[37] Despite al-Zawahiri's rhetoric, he divides rather than unites Muslims. Hudhayfah Abdullah Azzam, the son of Azzam, did not directly challenge al-Zawahiri but did express dissatisfaction with those who are using his father's name and work as justification for their actions. Hudhayfah condemned the Sharm al-Shaykh bombings, denying that they represented his father's thoughts.[38]

Leveraging altercations and discrediting leadership are possible paths to destroying the group. Using network members to undermine the appeal of the group can be effective, for instance, by using the testimonials of network members. The criticism of al-Zarqawi is a case in point. Furthermore, those who have left the network have significant access to information. Their stories can be used to undermine it as well.

Encouraging Personal Interaction

Americans interact with individuals from different countries on a daily basis. This includes encounters while American citizens travel as well as interactions between non-Americans and those who run or are employed by U.S. government agencies. Those interactions can occur through the State and Defense Departments, as well as other agencies. For example, the Defense Department focuses on military-to-military exchanges, while the State Department hosts a variety of educational exchange programs, which are instrumental in promoting positive interaction between Americans and foreigners. There is another type of interaction that Americans have with others on a more local level through a variety of nongovernmental organizations (NGOs), international bodies, and government aid bodies and military-assistance organizations, such as the U.S. Peace Corps, the U.S. Agency for International Development, various UN bodies, and other nonprofits that are constantly engaged in positive works. The outpouring of support by Americans during the 2005 tsunami disaster in Asia is a case in point. For example, the International Organization for Migration (IOM) primarily responds humanely to migration issues but is also involved in many other humanitarian efforts, including emergency and postcrisis relief. In the summer of 2005 in eastern Sri Lanka, IOM and twenty-nine other international agencies, UN organizations, and local NGOs sponsored a two-day children's festival for three thousand victims of the tsunami.[39] This afforded children an opportunity to experience some relief and fun following this tragic natural disaster. As a result, individuals at the local level are seeing Americans as individuals who care about the welfare of others, regardless of their age, race, ethnicity, religion, and culture. Interacting with individuals serves to break down barriers and stereotypes that would otherwise exist without that interaction. For this reason, the United States should continue to support and fund these efforts, for they are one of the most valuable tools in its arsenal.

Related to this are U.S. military's good works in some countries. There are numerous stories of troops passing out school supplies, candy, and other commodities to locals. These acts may not be widely publicized or making an impact in the international media, but their impact on a local level is enormous. Recently, the U.S. government responded to the devastating October 2005 earthquakes in Pakistan and India that caused the deaths of seventy-three thousand people. For example, the Afghan press reported that U.S.-led coalition forces in Afghanistan sent seven military helicopters and support personnel to assist with emergency operations.[40] The military also brought in significant supplies, including medical equipment, food, and blankets.

Conclusion

We have written the book in the hope that it will cause others to think differently about the individuals who are recruited into the al-Qaida network. In discussing individuals' underlying motivations and the information potential recruits are subjected to, this book has pointed to the reasons why people may eventually join the network.

We have offered some ideas about how to dissuade and counter recruitment. While the United States and its allies may never be able to defeat recruitment completely, they can reduce the number of individuals susceptible to the network's message. Thus, in decreasing the pool of recruits, we can effectively disrupt the network's capabilities in targeting Americans both at home and abroad.

Many people share different views as to how this should be done, so it is most important to keep a continuous dialogue going and an open mind on the subject. Governments need to be open to new and innovative methods in aggressively addressing the issue. This, in conjunction with our counterterrorism efforts, will lead to disrupting the network. However, the time to address this long-term threat to our national security is now, not later.

Notes

1. Sarah Wildman, "Veiled Illusion," *New Republic*. February 13, 2004, available at http://www.tnr.com/doc.mhtml?i=dispatch&s=wildman021304 (last accessed March 10, 2005).

2. Peggy Hollinger, "Sarkozy Unveils Initiatives to Stop Urban Discontent That Fuelled Riots," *Financial Times*, November 29, 2005.

3. British Broadcasting Corporation, "Timeline: French Riots," *BBC News*, November 14, 2005, available at http://news.bbc.co.uk/1/hi/world/europe/4413961.stm (last accessed April 15, 2006).

4. Cable News Network, "French Unrest at 'Normal Levels,'" *CNN*, November 17, 2005, available at www.cnn.com/2005/WORLD/europe/11/17/france.rioting.reut (last accessed April 15, 2006).

5. BBC, "Timeline."

6. Hollinger, "Sarkozy Unveils Initiatives."

7. *France Info Radio*, "Sarkozy Promises Deportations As Riots Persist in Parts of France," *France Info Radio*, November 13, 2005.

8. Bruce Crumley and Scott MacCloud, "The Madrid Bombings One Year On," *Time*, March 13, 2005, available at www.time.com/time/europe/html/050321/story.html (last accessed April 15, 2006).

9. Diane Worthy, "Anti-Mosque Leaflets Go Straight into Bins," *This Is Local London*, November 14, 2002, available at www.thisislocallondon.co.uk/display.var.230119.0.0.php (last accessed March 10, 2005).

10. Cara Anna, "Food Pantries Receive Tons of Meat during Muslim Festival," *Journal Sentinel*, January 17, 2006, available at www.jsonline.com/story/index.aspx?id=385644 (last accessed April 15, 2006).

11. Anna, "Food Pantries."

12. Julia Hieber, "Europe: Promoting Muslim Integration," *Religioscope*, December 10, 2005, available at http://religion.info/english/articles/article_214.shtml (last accessed April 15, 2006).

13. Mohamed Sid-Ahmed, "Will the Hamza Trial in London Inaugurate a New Era of Exposing Corruption in Egypt?" *Al-Ahran Weekly*, September 23–29, 2004, available at http://weekly.ahram.org.eg/2004/709/op5.htm (last accessed March 10, 2005).

14. Joseph Krauss, "U.S. Still Urging Reform in Egypt," *Christian Science Monitor*, February 23, 2006, available at www.csmonitor.com/2006/0223/p07s02-wome.html (last accessed April 15, 2006).

15. Abdeslam Maghraoui, "Morocco," *Freedom House*, 2004, available at www .freedomhouse.org, 10 (last accessed March 10, 2005).

16. *Arabic News*, "Media Criticizes 'Worsening' of Corruption in Morocco," *Arabic News*, October 22, 2004, available at www.arabicnews.com/ansub/Daily/ Day/041022/2004102223.html (last accessed March 10, 2005).

17. *Arabic News*, "Media Criticizes 'Worsening.'"

18. Andalusi Al-Amin, "Moroccans Skeptical about Anti-Corruption Plan," *Islam Online*, April 26, 2005, available at http://islamonline.net/english/news/2005-04/26/article07.shtml (last accessed April 15, 2006).

19. Roula Khalaf, "Abu Dhabi Invests to Diversify Its Economy," *Financial Times*, November 28, 2005.

20. Frank Gaffney, "The Enemy Within," *Front Page Magazine*, August 19, 2005, available at www.frontpagemag.com/Articles/ReadArticle.asp?ID=19191 (last accessed April 15, 2006).

21. British Broadcasting Corporation, "Violence Mars Egyptian Elections," *BBC News*, December 1, 2005, available at http://news.bbc.co.uk/1/hi/world/middle_east/4487128.stm (last accessed April 15, 2006).

22. Jonathan S Landay, "U.S. Pays Iraq Media for Spin," *Inquirer Washington Bureau*, 2005, available at www.philly.com/mld/inquirer/13297089.htm (last accessed April 15, 2006).

23. Prince Turki al-Faysal Bin-Abd-al-Aziz, "Bin Ladin's Allegations," *Al-Sharq al-Awsat*, October 9, 2001.

24. Al-Faysal Bin-Abd-al-Aziz, "Bin Ladin's Allegations."

25. *Toronto National Post*, "Al-Qaida's Jordanian blunder," *Toronto National Post*, November 11, 2005.

26. *Der Standard*, "Syrian Grand Mufti Sees Al-Qaida Planning to Establish State of God," *Der Standard*, November 16, 2005.

27. A. Shefa, "Egyptian Press Reactions to the Sharm Al-Sheikh Bombings," Inquiry and Analysis Series No. 233, *MEMRI*, August 10, 2005, available at http:// memri.org/bin/articles.cgi?Page=archives&Area=ia&ID=IA23305 (last accessed April 15, 2006).

28. Alan Cullison, "Inside Al-Qaeda's Hard Drive," *Atlantic Monthly*, September 2004, available at www.theatlantic.com/doc/200409/cullison (last accessed March 10, 2005).

29. Bay Fang, "Running on Empty: Attacks on Iraq's Northern Oil Facilities Create Long Gas Lines and Cut Off Exports," *U.S. News & World Report*, December 22, 2003, available at www.usnews.com/usnews/news/articles/031222/22kirkuk.htm (last accessed March 10, 2005).

30. Mark Steyn, "Listen to the Word on the Arab Street," *Daily Telegraph*, November 22, 2005.

31. Marwan Shihadah and Muyassir Al-Shamri, "Al-Maqdisi to Al-Hayah: Bin Ladin Refused Al-Zarqawi's Request to Teach My Books to His Supporters," *Al-Hayah*, July 10, 2005.

32. Maamoun Youssef, "Islamic Websites, Known for al-Qaida support, Criticize Jordan Bombings," *Associated Press*, November 15, 2005, available at http://news .tmcnet.com/news/2005/nov/1204650.htm (last accessed April 15, 2006).

33. Michael Howard, "Al-Zarqawi's Family Disown Him after Bombings," *Guardian*, November 21, 2005.

34. Musa Keilani, "Together against Misguided Miscreants," *Jordan Times*, November 20, 2005.

35. *Weekly Standard*, "English Translation of Ayman al-Zawahiri's Letter to Abu Musab al-Zarqawi," *Weekly Standard*, October 12, 2005, available at www. weeklystandard.com/Content/Public/Articles/000/000/006/203gpuul.asp?pg=2 (last accessed April 15, 2006).

36. *Al-Sharq al-Awsat*, "Letter to Zarqawi Decries Terror Leaders," *Al-Sharq al-Awsat*, August 7, 2005, available at www.asharqalawsat.com/english/news .asp?section=1&id=1127 (last accessed April 15, 2006).

37. Wright, "The Man behind Bin Laden."

38. Al-Arabiyah Television, "Statement Abdallah Azzam's Son," *Al-Arabiyah*, July 25, 2005.

39. Gina Wilkinson, "Sunshine Festival for 3,000 Children in Sri Lanka," *International Organization for Migration*, August 1, 2005, available at www.iom.int/tsunami/ stories/sr_ns_01_08_05.htm (last accessed April 15, 2006).

40. Afghan News, "Pakistan Quake Relief Effort," *Afghan News*, October 10, 2005.

Bibliography

"39 Ways to Serve and Participate in Jihad." November 29, 2003, available at www.almaqdese.com/1?I=278 (last accessed December 10, 2003).

Afghan News. "Pakistan Quake Relief Effort." *Afghan News*. October 10, 2005.

Agence France Presse. "Professor Bombmaker—and Fanatic." *AFP*. November 10, 2005.

Aglionby, John, and Maria Ressa. "Security Tightened after Bali Suicide Bombing." *CNN*. October 2, 2005, available at www.cnn.com/2005/WORLD/asiapcf/10/02/bali.blasts (last accessed April 15, 2006).

Al-Amin, Andalusi. "Moroccans Skeptical about Anti-Corruption Plan." *Islam Online*. April 26, 2005, available at islamonline.net/english/news/2005-04/26/article07.shtml (last accessed April 15, 2006).

Al-Arabiyah Television. "Statement Abdallah Azzam's Son." *Al-Arabiyah*. July 25, 2005.

Alexandar, Yonah, and Michael Swetnam. *Usama bin Laden's al-Qaida: Profile of a Terrorist Network*. Ardsley, NY: Transnational Publishers, 2002.

Al-Faysal Bin-Abd-al-Aziz, Prince Turki. "Bin Ladin's Allegations." *Al-Sharq al-Awsat*. October 9, 2001.

Al-Mujahid, Shawq. "The Orator of the Peninsula: The Great Yusef Al-Ayiri in the Age of Humiliation and Insult." August 1, 2003, available at www.cybcity.com/news/index.htm (last accessed March 10, 2005).

Al-Murshid, Abd-al-Muhsin. "Fundamentalist Websites Publish Physical Training Programs for al-Qa'ida's Women and Some of Them Urge Organization's Elements to Reduce Intake of Kabsat." *Al-Sharq al-Awsat*. October 4, 2003.

Al-Shafi, Muhammad. "Al-Qaeda Reportedly Establishing Open 'Internet University' to Recruit Terrorists." *Al-Sharq al-Awsat*. November 20, 2003, available at www.borrull.org/e/noticia.php?id=24090&PHPSESSID=89285ba9175e1bbd8f56eb050e946102 (last accessed March 10, 2005).

Al-Sharq al-Awsat. "Letter to Zarqawi Decries Terror Leaders." *Al-Sharq al-Awsat*, August 7, 2005, available at www.asharqalawsat.com/english/news.asp?section=1&id=1127 (last accessed April 15, 2006).

Al-Zawahiri, Ayman. "Knights under the Prophet's Banner." *Al-Sharq al-Awsat*. December 2, 2001.

Al-Zayyat, Montasser. *The Road to Al-Qaeda: The Story of bin Laden's Right-Hand Man*. London: Pluto Press, 2004.

Andreoli, Marcella. "Under Orders from Usama." *Panorama*. April 22, 2004.

Anna, Cara. "Food Pantries Receive Tons of Meat during Muslim Festival." *Journal Sentinel*. January 17, 2006, available at www.jsonline.com/story/index.aspx?id=385644 (last accessed April 15, 2006).

Arab kids play beheading game video, available at http://inhonor.net/videos.php (last accessed April 15, 2006).

Arabic News. "Media Criticizes 'Worsening' of Corruption in Morocco." *Arabic News*. October 22, 2004, available at www.arabicnews.com/ansub/Daily/Day/041022/2004102223.html (last accessed April 15, 2006).

Arabic News. "Prince Nayef Discloses Investigations into al-Qaida Burning Three Copters in al-Qasim." *Arabic News*. June 17, 2005, available at www.arabicnews.com/ansub/Daily/Day/050617/2005061719.html (last accessed April 15, 2006).

Argetsinger, Amy. "Muslim Teen Made Conversion to Fury." *Washington Post*. December 2, 2004, available at www.washingtonpost.com/wp-dyn/articles/A26447-2004Dec1.html (last accessed March 10, 2005).

Aziz, Roya, and Monica Lam. "Profiles the Lackwanna Cell." *Frontline*. October 16, 2003, available at www.pbs.org/wgbh/pages/frontline/shows/sleeper/inside/profiles.html (last accessed March 10, 2005).

Azzam, Abdullah. *Join the Caravan*. 1987, available at www.religioscope.com/info/doc/jihad/jihadfile.htm (last accessed March 10, 2005).

Azzam Publications. "Interview with Egyptian Islamic Jihad leader Dr. Ayman al-Zawahiri." *Qoqaz*. October 11, 2002, available at www.qoqaz.net (last accessed November 3, 2002).

Back to Iraq. "London Blasts Claimed by Al Qaeda." *Back to Iraq*. July 7, 2005, available at www.back-to-iraq.com/archives/2005/07/london_blasts_claimed_by_al_qa.php (last accessed April 15, 2006).

Baker, Peter. "A Confessed Bomber's Trail of Terror: Uzbek Details Life with Islamic Radicals, Turn Back to Violence." *Washington Post*. September 18, 2003, available at www.uzbekconsul.org/news/Trail.pdf (last accessed March 10, 2005).

Barber, Mike. "Video Records Soldier's Plans to Join al-Qaida." *Seattle Post-Intelligencer*. May 13, 2004.

Bellamy, Patrick. "Chosen Path." *Court TV*. July 10, 2005, available at www.crimelibrary.com/terrorists_spies/terrorists/hambali/index.html (last accessed April 15, 2006).

Benjamin, Daniel, and Steven Simon. *The Age of Sacred Terror*. New York: Random House, 2002.

Bergen, Peter. *Holy War, Inc*. New York: Free Press, 2001.

Bin-Hazzam, Faris. "Abd-al-Aziz al-Muqrin, Leader of Al-Qa'ida in Saudi Arabia, Smuggled Weapons from Spain to Algeria, Was Arrested in Somalia, and Fought in Afghanistan and Bosnia." *Al-Sharq al-Awsat.* December 10, 2003.

"Bin Laden 'a Very Nice Man'—Terror Plot Accused." *The Scotsman.* March 2000, available at www.jihadwatch.org/archives/002001.php (last accessed March 10, 2005).

Bin Ladin, Usama. "Bin Laden's Fatwa." *Al Quds Al Arabi.* August 1996, available at www.pbs.org/newshour/terrorism/international/fatwa_1996.html (last accessed March 10, 2005).

———. "Text of Fatwah Urging Jihad against Americans." *Al-Quds al-'Arabi.* February 23, 1998, available at www.ict.org.il/articles/fatwah.htm (last accessed March 10, 2005).

———. "Full Transcript of bin Ladin's Speech." *Al Jazeera.* November 1, 2004, available at http://english.aljazeera.net/NR/exeres/79C6AF22-98FB-4A1C-B21F-2BC36E87F61F.htm (last accessed March 10, 2005).

Bin Omar, Abdullah. "The Striving Sheik: Abdullah Azzam." *Nida'ul Islam.* July–September 1996, available at www.islam.org.au/articles/14/azzam.htm (last accessed March 10, 2005).

Bloom, Mia. "Terror's Stealth Weapon: Women." *Los Angeles Times.* November 29, 2005, available at www.latimes.com/news/opinion/commentary/la-oe-bloom29nov29,0,3416302.story?coll=la-news-comment-opinions (last accessed April 15, 2006).

Bodansky, Yossef. *Bin Ladin: The Man Who Declared War on America.* Roseville, CA: Prima Publishing, 2001.

Boggan, Steve. "Campaign against Terrorism: At the Mosque on a Terraced Street, Terror Suspects Came to Worship." *Independent.* January 19, 2002.

Boorstein, Michelle. "U.S. Finds Pamphlets Targeting Westerners." *Times Union.* April 6, 2002, available at www.timesunion.com/AspStories/story.asp?storyID=48219 (last accessed March 10, 2005).

Bosnian training video, available at www.islamic-news.co.uk (last accessed April 15, 2006).

Boucher, Richard. "U.S. Department of State Designates the Islamic Jihad Group under Executive Order 13224." *U.S. Department of State.* May 26, 2005, available at www.state.gov/r/pa/prs/ps/2005/46838.htm (last accessed April 15, 2006).

Braungart, Richard, and Margaret Braungart. "From Protest to Terrorism: The Case of SDS and the Weatheren." In *Social Movements and Violence: Participation in Underground Organizations,* ed. Donatella della Porta, 45–78. Greenwich, CT: JAI, 1992.

Brisard, Jean Charles. *Zarqawi: The New Face of al-Qaida.* New York: Other Press, 2005.

British Broadcasting Corporation. "Profile: Abu Zubaydah." *BBC News.* April 2, 2002, available at http://news.bbc.co.uk/1/hi/world/south_asia/1907462.stm (last accessed March 10, 2005).

———. "Profile: Al-Qaeda 'kingpin.'" *BBC News.* March 5, 2005, available at http://news.bbc.co.uk/2/hi/south_asia/2811855.stm (last accessed March 10, 2005).

———. "Bomb Wrecks Top Jakarta Hotel." *BBC News.* August 5, 2003, available at http://news.bbc.co.uk/2/hi/asia-pacific/3124919.stm (last accessed March 10, 2005).

———. "Spain Names 'Bomb Suspect' Group." *BBC News*. March 30, 2004, available at http://news.bbc.co.uk/1/hi/world/europe/3583113.stm (last accessed March 10, 2005).

———. "Piecing Together Madrid Bombers' Past." *BBC News*. April 5, 2004, available at http://news.bbc.co.uk/1/hi/world/europe/3600421.stm (last accessed March 10, 2005).

———. "Hamza Faces 11 U.S. Terror Charges." *BBC* News. May 27, 2004, available at http://news.bbc.co.uk/1/hi/england/london/3752257.stm (last accessed March 10, 2005).

———. "Timeline: Bali Bomb Trials." *BBC News*. August 24, 2004, available at http://news.bbc.co.uk/1/hi/world/asia-pacific/3126241.stm (last accessed March 10, 2005).

———. "Madrid Bombing Suspects." *BBC News*. March 10, 2005, available at http://news.bbc.co.uk/1/hi/world/europe/3560603.stm (last accessed March 10, 2005).

———. "Suicide Bombers' 'Ordinary' Lives." *BBC News*. July 18, 2005, available at http://news.bbc.co.uk/2/hi/uk_news/4678837.stm (last accessed April 15, 2006).

———. "Profile: Saudi al-Qaeda Leader." *BBC News*. August 19, 2005, available at http://news.bbc.co.uk/1/hi/world/middle_east/4166612.stm (last accessed April 15, 2006).

———. "Profile: Abu Bakr." *BBC News*. November 8, 2005, available at http://news.bbc.co.uk/1/hi/world/asia-pacific/4416712.stm (last accessed April 15, 2006).

———. "Bali Bomb Maker's Luck Runs Out," *BBC News*. November 10, 2005, available at http://news.bbc.co.uk/2/hi/asia-pacific/4423960.stm (last accessed April 15, 2006).

———. "Timeline: French Riots." *BBC News*. November 14, 2005, available at http://news.bbc.co.uk/1/hi/world/europe/4413964.stm (last accessed April 15, 2006).

———. "Violence Mars Egyptian Elections." *BBC News*. December 1, 2005, available at http://news.bbc.co.uk/1/hi/world/middle_east/4487128.stm (last accessed April 15, 2006).

Brown, Stephan. "White Terror." *Front Page Magazine*. July 31, 2003, available at www.frontpagemag.com/Articles/ReadArticle.asp?ID=9173 (last accessed March 10, 2005).

Burke, Jason. *Al-Qaeda: Casting a Shadow of Terror*. New York: I. B. Tauris, 2004.

Burke, Jason, Paul Harris, and Martin Bright. "Suspect Arrested in Pakistan May Hold al-Qaeda's Secrets." *Observer*. August 8, 2004, available at www.guardian.co.uk/alqaida/story/0,,1278651,00.html (last accessed March 10, 2005).

Cable News Network. "Voice Seems to Be al Qaeda Leader Calling for Uprising." *CNN*. October 1, 2004, available at www.cnn.com/2004/WORLD/meast/10/01/zawahiri.transcript (last accessed March 10, 2005).

———. "Abdullah: Al Qaeda Is 'Madness and Evil.'" *CNN*. October 13, 2005, available at http://edition.cnn.com/2005/WORLD/meast/10/13/abdullah.abcinterview (last accessed April 15, 2006).

———. "French Unrest at 'Normal Levels.'" *CNN*. November 17, 2005, available at www.cnn.com/2005/WORLD/europe/11/17/france.rioting.reut (last accessed April 15, 2006).

Campo-Flores, Arian, and Dirk Johnson. "From Taco Bell to Al Qaeda." *Time*. June 24, 2002.

Carrell, Severin. "U.S. Guards at Guantánamo Tortured Me." *Independent.* April 24, 2005, available at www.cageprisoners.com/articles.php?id=6944 (last accessed April 15, 2006).

CBS. "The Mastermind." *CBS News.* March 5, 2003, available at www.cbsnews.com/stories/2002/10/09/60II/main524947.shtml (last accessed March 10, 2005).

———. "Money-Transfer Systems, Hawala Style." *CBS News.* June 11, 2004, available at www.cbc.ca/news/background/banking/hawala.html (last accessed March 10, 2005).

ChargePadilla.org. "Padilla Indicted!" *ChargePadilla.org.* November 22, 2005, available at www.chargepadilla.org/index.html (last accessed April 15, 2006).

Chichizola, Jean. "The Afghan, the Convert, and the Unknown Kamikaze." *Le Figaro.* March 18, 2004 (last accessed March 10, 2005).

Chua-Eoan, Howard. "Is He Osama's Best Friend?" *Time.* November 12, 2001, available at www.time.com/time/archive/preview/0.10987.1001170.00.html (last accessed March 10, 2005).

Clarke, Rachel. "Shoppers Outraged by Offensive Leaflets." *This Is Local London,* available at www.thisislocallondon.co.uk/search/display.var.156092.0.shoppers_outraged_by_offensive_leaflets.php (last accessed March 10, 2005).

Coll, Steve. *Ghost Wars: The Secret History of the CIA, Afghanistan, and Bin Laden from the Soviet Invasion to September 10, 2001.* New York: Penguin Group, 2001.

Collins, Aukai. *My Jihad: One American's Journey through the World of Usama Bin Laden— as a Covert Operative for the American Government.* New York: Pocket Star, 2002.

Corbin, Jane. *Al Qaeda: In Search of the Terror Network That Threatens the World.* New York: Nation Books, 2002.

Cottam, Martha. *Images and Intervention.* Pittsburgh, PA: University of Pittsburgh Press, 2004.

Cottam, Martha, Beth Dietz-Uhler, Elena Mastors, and Tom Preston. *Introduction to Political Psychology.* Mahwah, NJ: Lawrence Erlbaum and Associates, 2004.

Cowell, Alan. "Newsmaker Profile: Richard C. Reid." *SF Gate.* December 29, 2001, available at www.sfgate.com/cgi-bin/article.cgi?f=/c/a/2001/12/29/MN198887.DTL (last accessed March 10, 2005).

Crumley, Bruce. "The Boy Next Door." *Newsweek.* November 5, 2001.

Crumley, Bruce, and Scott MacCloud. "The Madrid Bombings One Year On." *Time.* March 13, 2005, available at www.time.com/time/europe/html/050321/story.html (last accessed April 15, 2005).

Cullison, Alan. "Inside Al-Qaeda's Hard Drive." *Atlantic Monthly.* September 2004, available at www.theatlantic.com/doc/200409/cullison (last accessed March 10, 2005).

Cziesche, Dominik, Georg Mascolo, Sven Roebel, Heiner Schimmoeller, and Holger Stark. "As If You Were at War." *Der Spiegel.* March 22, 2004.

Daily Mail. "Suicide Bomber Profile: The Family Man." *Daily Mail.* July 13, 2005, available at www.dailymail.co.uk/pages/live/articles/news/news.html?in_article_id=355621&in_page_id=1770&in_a_source= (last accessed April 15, 2005).

———. "Suicide Bomber Profile: The Teenager." *Daily Mail.* July 13, 2005, available at www.mailonsunday.co.uk/pages/live/articles/news/news.html?in_article_id=355619&in_page_id=1770&in_a_source= (last accessed April 15, 2005).

Delong-Bas, Natana. *Wahhabi Islam from Revival and Reform to Global Jihad*. New York: Oxford University Press, 2004.

Dennis, Anthony. *Osama Bin Laden: A Psychological and Political Portrait*. Lima, OH: Wyndham Hall Press, 2002.

Der Spiegel. "The Warriors from Pearl Harburg." *Der Spiegel*. November 26, 2001.

Der Standard. "Syrian Grand Mufti Sees al-Qaida Planning to Establish State of God." *Der Standard*. November 16, 2005.

Dirty kuffar video, available at www.ratatat.com/modules/mydownloads/singlefile. php?lid=14 (last accessed April 15, 2006).

Elegant, Simon. "The Family behind the Bombings." *Time*. November25, 2002, available at www.time.com/time/asia/covers/1101021125/story.html (last accessed March 10, 2005).

Elegant, Simon, and Jason Tedjasukmana. "The Jihadis' Tale." *Time*. January 20, 2003, available at www.time.com/time/asia/covers/1030127/story.html (last accessed March 10, 2005).

Elliot, Michael. "Hate Club: Al-Qaeda's Web of Terror." *Time*. November 4, 2001.

———. "The Shoe Bomber's World." *Time*. February 16, 2002, available at www.time. com/time/world/printout/0,8816,203478,00.html (last accessed March 10, 2005).

Emerson, Steven. "Abdullah Assam: The Man before Osama Bin Laden." International Association for Counterterrorism and Security Professionals, available at www.iacsp. com/itobli3.html (last accessed March 10, 2005).

———. *American Jihad: The Terrorists Living among Us*. New York: Free Press Paperbacks, 2003.

Ensor, David. "Wives, Mother May Hold Key to bin Laden's Whereabouts." *CNN*. March 12, 2002, available at http://archives.cnn.com/2002/US/03/12/gen.binladen.wives (last accessed March 10, 2005).

Evening Standard. "British Imam: 'Bring Jihad to Your Own Door.'" *This Is London*. April 26, 2004, available at www.thisislondon.co.uk/news/articles/ 10435138?source=Evening%20Standard (last accessed March 10, 2005).

Fang, Bay. "Running on Empty: Attacks on Iraq's Northern Oil Facilities Create Long Gas Lines and Cut Off Exports." *U.S. News & World Report*. December 22, 2003, available at www.usnews.com/usnews/news/articles/031222/22kirkuk.htm (last accessed March 10, 2005).

Fighel, Jonathan. "Sheikh Abdullah Azzam: Bin Laden's Spiritual Mentor." *Institute for Counter-Terrorism*. September 27, 2001, available at www.ict.org.il/articles/articledet .cfm?articleid=388 (last accessed March 10, 2005).

Filkins, Dexter. "Demonstrators in Iraq Demand That U.S. Leave." *New York Times*. April 10, 2005, available at www.nytimes.com/2005/04/10/international/middleeast/10iraq. html?ex=1270785600&en=82ca88b462c267af&ei=5090&partner=rssuserland (last accessed April 15, 2006).

Finn, Peter. "German at Center of Sept. 11 Inquiry." *Washington Post*. June 12, 2002, available at http://pqasb.pqarchiver.com/washingtonpost/access/124816271.html?dids =124816271:124816271&FMT=ABS&FMTS=ABS:FT&fmac=&date=Jun+12%2C

+2002&author=Peter+Finn&desc=German+at+Center+Of+Sept.+11+Inquiry (last accessed March 10, 2005).

Firestone, Reuven. *The Origin of Holy War in Islam*. Oxford: Oxford University Press, 1999.

Foster, Peter. "Militants of Al-Muhajiroun Seek World Islamic State." *Telegraph*. October 31, 2001, available at www.telegraph.co.uk/news/main.jhtml?xml=%2Fnews%2F2001%2F10%2F31%2Fnmus231.xml (last accessed March 10, 2005).

Gaffney, Frank. "The Enemy Within." *Front Page Magazine*. August 19, 2005, available at www.frontpagemag.com/Articles/ReadArticle.asp?ID=19191 (last accessed April 15, 2006).

Gambill, Gary. "The Libyan Islamic Fighting Group (LIFG)." *Terrorism Monitor* 3, no. 6 (March 24, 2005), available at www.jamestown.org/publications_details.php?volume_id=411&issue_id=3275&article_id=2369477 (last accessed April 15, 2006).

Gettleman, Jeffrey. "Zarqawi's Journey: From Dropout to Prisoner to Insurgent Leader." *Middle East Information Center*. July 13, 2004, available at http://middleeastinfo.org/article4619.html (last accessed March 10, 2005).

Gilbert, Colleen. "War from Within." *Front Page Magazine*. July 26, 2005, available at www.frontpagemag.com/Articles/ReadArticle.asp?ID=18901 (last accessed April 15, 2006).

Global Security. "Terrorist Training Camps." *Global Security*, available at www.globalsecurity.org/military/world/para/al-qaida-camps.htm.

Global Terror Alert. "The Foreign Martyrs of Iraq." *Global Terror Alert*. 2003–2004, available at www.globalterroralert.com/pdf/0105/iraqmartyrs04.pdf (last accessed March 10, 2005).

Gunaratna, Rohan. *Inside Al Qaeda*. New York: Columbia University Press, 2002.

Halaby, Jamal. "Iraqi Woman Confesses on Jordan TV." *SF Gate*. November 13, 2005, available at http://sfgate.com/cgi-bin/article.cgi?f=/n/a/2005/11/13/international/i081557S62.DTL (last accessed April 15, 2006).

Hieber, Julia. "Europe: Promoting Muslim Integration." *Religioscope*. December 10, 2005, available at http://religion.info/english/articles/article_214.shtml (last accessed April 15, 2006).

Hollinger, Peggy. "Sarkozy Unveils Initiatives to Stop Urban Discontent That Fuelled Riots." *Financial Times*. November 29, 2005 (last accessed April 15, 2006).

Horgan, John. "The Search for the Terrorist Personality." In *Terrorists, Victims and Society: Psychological Perspectives on Terrorism and Its Consequences*, ed. Andrew Silke, 4–27. Chichester, UK: John Wiley and Sons, 2003.

Hosenball, Mark. "The Syrian Connection." *Newsweek*. January 26, 2005.

Howard, Michael. "Al-Zarqawi's Family Disown Him after Bombings." *Guardian*. November 21, 2005.

Ide, Arthur Frederick, and Jacob Arnold Auliff. *Jihad, Mujahideen, Taliban, Osama bin Laden, George W. Bush & Oil: A Study in the Evolution of Terrorism and Islam*. Garland, TX: Tangelwuld Press, 2002.

Independent Media Review Analysis. "O God, Deal with the Occupier and Usurper Jews." *IMRA*. October 28, 2002, available at www.imra.org.il/story.php3?id=14241 (last accessed March 10, 2005).

———. "O God, Destroy the Zionist, American, and British Aggressors." *IMRA*. March 10, 2003, available at www.imra.org.il/story.php3?id=16389 (last accessed March 10, 2005).

Iraq video, available at www.cracker.com (last accessed April 15, 2006).

Johnson, Zachary. "Chronology: The Plots." *Frontline*. January 25, 2005, available at www.pbs.org/wgbh/pages/frontline/shows/front/special/cron.html (last accessed March 10, 2006).

Kaplan, Abraham. "The Psychodynamics of Terrorism." In *Behavioral and Quantitative Perspectives on Terrorism*, ed. Yohan Alexander and John Gleason, 237–57. New York: Pergamon, 1981.

Keefe, Patrick Radden. "Digital Underground. Exposing the 'Darknet': Are Al Qaeda Terrorists Using Your Personal Computer?" *Village Voice*. February 15, 2005, available at www.villagevoice.com/news/0507,essay,61085,2.html (last accessed March 10, 2005).

Keilani, Musa. "Together against Misguided Miscreants." *Jordan Times*. November 20, 2005.

Khalaf, Roula. "Abu Dhabi Invests to Diversify Its Economy." *Financial Times*. November 28, 2005.

Khaleej Times Online. "Al Qaeda in Iraq Launches Internet Magazine Urging Muslims to Join Jihad." *Free Muslims Coalition*. March 5, 2005, available at www.freemuslims.org/news/article.php?article=474 (last accessed March 10, 2005).

Kohlmann, Evan F. *Al-Qaida's Jihad in Europe: The Afghan-Bosnian Network*. Oxford: Berg Publishers, 2004.

Kokan, Jane. "Bin Laden's B.C. helper." *Toronto National Post*. October 13, 2005.

Krauss, Joseph. "U.S. Still Urging Reform in Egypt." *Christian Science Monitor*. February 23, 2006, available at www.csmonitor.com/2006/0223/p07s02-wome.html (last accessed April 15, 2006).

Landau, Elaine. *Osama bin Laden*. Brookfield, CT: Twenty-first Century Books, 2002.

Landay, Jonathan S. "U.S. Pays Iraq Media for Spin." *Inquirer Washington Bureau*, 2005, available at www.philly.com/mld/inquirer/13297089.htm (last accessed April 15, 2006).

Laqueur, Walter. *The New Terrorism: Fanaticism and the Arms of Mass Destruction*. Oxford: Oxford University Press, 1999.

Lefkowitz, Josh, and Lorenzo Vidino. "Al Qaeda's New Recruits." *Wall Street Journal*. August 28, 2003, available at http://online.wsj.com/article/0,,SB106202472928168100 (last accessed March 10, 2005).

Leiby, Richard. "Taliban from Down Under." *Washington Post*. March 10, 2002, available at http://pqasb.pqarchiver.com/washingtonpost/access/110332251.html?dids=1103322 51:110332251&FMT=ABS&FMTS=ABS:FT&fmac=&date=Mar+10%2C+2002&a uthor=Richard+Leiby&desc=Taliban+From+Down+Under (last accessed March 10, 2005).

Leiken, Robert. "Europe's Itinerant Imams: Can the Radical Mosques Be Tamed with Homegrown, Moderate Clerics?" *Weekly Standard*. July 19, 2004.

"London Blasts Claimed by Al Qaeda," available at www.back-to-iraq.com/archives/000884.php (last accessed March 10, 2005).

Maghraoui, Abdeslam. "Morocco." *Freedom House*. 2004, available at www.freedomhouse
.org.

Makarenko, Tamara. "Central Asia's Opium Terrorists." *PBS*. 2005, available at www
.pbs.org/wnet/wideangle/printable/centralasia_briefing_print.html (last accessed April
15, 2006).

Manchester Evening News. "Suicide Bomber 'Had All to Live For." *Manchester Evening News*,
July 13, 2005, available at www.manchesteronline.co.uk/men/news/s/165/165813_
suicide_bomber_had_all_to_live_for.html (last accessed April 15, 2006).

Margulies, Phillip. *Al-Qaeda: Osama Bin Laden's Army of Terrorists (Inside the World's Most
Infamous Terrorist Organizations)*. New York: Rosen Publishing Group, 2003.

Marquardt, Erich. "Intelligence Brief: Aqaba Attack." *Power and Interest News Report*.
August 30, 2005, available at www.pinr.com/report.php?ac=view_report&report_
id=356 (last accessed April 15, 2006).

Mattar, Shafika. "Jordanian Flattered That Osama bin Laden Recited His Poem in Videotape." *Associated Press*. June 1, 2002, available at http://multimedia.belointeractive
.com/attack/binladen/0106poet.html (last accessed March 10, 2005).

McCauley, Clark. "The Psychology of Terrorism." In *Psychological Issues and the Response
to Terrorism*, ed. Chris Stout, 33–54. New York: Praeger Publishers, 2002.

McDonnell, Patrick J. "Al Qaeda Camp in Oregon." *Los Angeles Times*. September 22,
2002.

McEvers, Kelly. "Jemaah Islamiyah Uses Women, Marriage to Strengthen Ties." *Straits
Times*. January 19, 2004.

McGeown, Kate. "Jack Roche: The Naïve Militant." *BBC*. June 1, 2004, available at
http://news.bbc.co.uk/2/hi/asia-pacific/3757017.stm (last accessed March 10, 2005).

McKenna, Terence. "Trail of a Terrorist." *Frontline*. 2001, available at www.pbs.org/wgbh/
pages/frontline/shows/trail (last accessed March 10, 2005).

Mcpherson, Lynn. "London: Our Son Was Brainwashed to Do This Evil." *Sunday Mail*.
July 11, 2005, available at www.rickross.com/reference/alqaeda/alqaeda63.html (last
accessed April 15, 2006).

Middle East Media Research Institute. "Terror in America (29) Al-Jazeera Interview with
Top Al-Qa'ida Leader Abu Hafs 'The Mauritanian.'" Special Dispatch Series No. 313.
MEMRI. December 14, 2001, available at http://memri.org/bin/articles.cgi?Page=archi
ves&Area=sd&ID=SP31301 (last accessed March 10, 2005).

———. "First Audio Recording by Al-Qa'ida Leader in Iraq Abu Mus'ab Al-Zarqawi."
Special Dispatch Series No. 639. MEMRI. January 7, 2004, available at http://memri
.org/bin/articles.cgi?Page=archives&Area=sd&ID=SP63904 (last accessed March 10,
2005).

———. "A Letter by an Alleged Wife of a Martyr to the Wife of Paul Johnson." Special
Dispatch Series No. 75. MEMRI. August 5, 2004, available at http://memri.org/bin/
articles.cgi?Page=archives&Area=sd&ID=SP75804 (last accessed March 10, 2005).

———. "Al-Qaida Women's Magazine: Women Must Participate in Jihad." Special Dispatch Series No. 779. MEMRI. September 7, 2004, available at http://memri.org/bin/
articles.cgi?Page=archives&Area=sd&ID=SP77904 (last accessed March 10, 2005).

———. "Saudi Cleric Al-Fawzan: Jihad in Iraq an Individual Duty Incumbent upon Iraqis." MEMRI TV Monitor Project. *MEMRI*. November 21, 2004, available at http://memritv.org/Transcript.asp?P1=375 (last accessed March 10, 2005).

———. "'Kaide' ('Al-Qaeda') Magazine Published Openly in Turkey." Special Dispatch Series No. 95. *MEMRI*. August 7, 2005, available at http://memri.org/bin/articles.cgi?Page=archives&Area=sd&ID=SP95105 (last accessed April 15, 2006).

———. "English-Speaking Al-Qaeda Terrorist: Oh People of the West . . . It Is Time for Us to Be Equals—As You Kill Us, You Will be Killed." MEMRI TV Monitor Project. *MEMRI*. August 9, 2005, available at www.memritv.org/Transcript.asp?P1=802 (last accessed April 15, 2006).

———. "Mohammed Sadiq, One of the Suicide Bombers Who Carried Out the London Bombings in a Videotaped Message: Our Words Are Dead until We Give Them Life with Our Blood." MEMRI TV Monitor Project. *MEMRI*. September 1, 2005, available at www.memritv.org/Transcript.asp?P1=835 (last accessed April 15, 2006).

———. "Now Online: Swear Loyalty to Al-Qaeda Leaders." Special Dispatch Series No. 1027. *MEMRI*. November 18, 2005, available at http://memri.org/bin/articles.cgi?Page=archives&Area=sd&ID=SP102705 (last accessed April 15, 2006).

———. "Reformist Saudi Author: Religious Cassettes Advocate Jihad by Emphasizing Martyr's Sexual Rewards." Special Dispatch Series No. 1032. *MEMRI*. November 23, 2005, available at http://memri.org/bin/articles.cgi?Page=archives&Area=sd&ID=SP103205 (last accessed April 15, 2006).

———. "Saudi Al-Qaeda Terrorists Recount Their Experiences in Afghanistan." MEMRI TV Monitor Project. *MEMRI*. November 29, 2005, available at www.memritv.org/Transcript.asp?P1=947 (last accessed April 15, 2006).

Miller, John, and Michael Stone. *The Cell: Inside the 9/11 Plot, and Why the FBI and CIA Failed to Stop It*. New York: Hyperion, 2002.

Molan, Peter. *Arabic Religious Rhetoric: The Radical Saudi Sheikhs. A Reader*. Kensington, MD: Dunwoody Press, 1997.

Moussaoui, Abd Samad. *Zacarias, My Brother*. New York: Seven Stories Press, 2003.

MSNBC. "Purported bin Laden Tape Posted on Web." *MSNBC*. December 17, 2004, available at www.msnbc.msn.com/id/6722361 (last accessed March 10, 2005).

Mustapha Kamal video, available at www.militantislammonitor.org (last accessed April 15, 2006).

Napoleoni, Loretta. *Modern Jihad: Tracing the Dollars behind the Terror Networks*. Sterling: Pluto Press, 2003.

News24. "'Al Qaeda Financed Casablanca.'" *News24*. August 5, 2004, available at www.news24.com/News24/World/News/0,,2-10-1462_1523957,00.html (last accessed March 10, 2005).

Newsweek. "Bin Laden's Invisible Network." *Newsweek*. October 29, 2002, available at www.msnbc.com/news/645596.asp (last accessed March 10, 2005).

Noorani, A. G. *Islam and Jihad*. New Delhi: Left Word Books, 2002.

Orbach, Benjamin. "Usama Bin Ladin and Al-Qai'da: Origins and Doctrines." *Middle East Review of International Affairs* 5, no. 4 (December 2001), available at http://meria.idc.ac.il/journal/2001/issue4/jv5n4a3.htm (last accessed March 10, 2005).

PBS. Open Sermon to the Militant Iraqi People. *Frontline*, available at www.pbs.org/wgbh/pages/frontline/shows/saud/etc/fatwa.html (last accessed April 15, 2006).

Pearlstein, Richard M. *The Mind of the Political Terrorist*. Wilmington, DE: Scholarly Resources, 1991.

Perrin, Andrew. "One More Down." *Time*. December 9, 2002, available at www.time.com/time/asia/magazine/printout/0,13675,501021216-397545,00.html (last accessed March 10, 2005).

Post, Jerrold. "Terrorist Psycho-logic: Terrorist Behavior as a Product of Psychological Forces." In *Origins of Terrorism*, ed. Walter Reich, 25–40. Baltimore: Johns Hopkins University Press, 1998.

Priest, Dana. "British Raids Net a Leader of Al Qaeda." *Washington Post*. August 5, 2004, available at www.washingtonpost.com/wp-dyn/articles/A40921-2004Aug4.html (last accessed March 10, 2005).

Qutb, Sayyid. *In the Shade of the Quran*. Maclean, VA: Wamy International, 1995.

———. *Social Justice in Islam*. Oneonta, NY: Islamic Publications, 2000.

———. *Milestones*. Burr Ridge, IL: American Trust Publications, 2002.

Randal, Jonathan. *Osama: The Making of a Terrorist*. New York: Knopf, 2004.

Raphaeli, Nimrod. "Al-Zawahiri: The Making of an Arch Terrorist." Inquiry and Analysis Series No.127. *MEMRI*. March 11, 2003, available at http://memri.org/bin/articles.cgi?Page=archives&Area=ia&ID=IA12703 (last accessed March 10, 2005).

Rashid, Ahmed. *Taliban: Militant Islam, Oil and Fundamentalism in Central Asia*. New Haven, CT: Yale University Press, 2001.

———. *Jihad: The Rise of Militant Islam in Central Asia*. New York: Penguin Books, 2003.

Ressa, Maria. "JI 'Claims Jakarta Bombing': Website Says Blast Targeted Australia for Iraq Policy." *CNN*. September 9, 2004, available at www.cnn.com/2004/WORLD/asiapcf/09/09/indonesia.blast (last accessed March 10, 2005).

Reuters. "Uzbekistan Arrests Blast Suspects: Suicide Bombers Hit U.S., Israeli Embassies; Death Toll Rises to 3." *Reuters*. July 31, 2004, available at www.msnbc.msn.com/id/5558327 (last accessed March 10, 2005).

Ross, Brian, and David Scott. "An American Married to Al Qaeda." *ABC News*. December 23, 2004, available at www.abcnews.go.com (last accessed March 10, 2005).

Rotella, Sebastian, and David Zucchino. "Embassy Plot Offers Insight into Terrorist Recruitment, Training." *Los Angeles Times*. October 22, 2001, available at http://www.norwalkadvocate.com/news/nationworld/sns-worldtrade-embassyplot-lat,0,3646484.story?page=1&coll=sns-newsnation-headlines (last accessed March 10, 2005).

Rumsfeld, Donald. "Rumsfeld Says Stop Recruitment of New Terrorists." *United States Embassy, Tokyo, Japan*. November 2, 2003, available at http://japan.usembassy.gov/e/p/tp-20031104a5.html (last accessed March 10, 2005).

Sabbagh-Gargour, Rana. "Failed Suicide Bomber 'Acted out of Revenge.'" *The Times*. November 15, 2005, available at www.timesonline.co.uk/article/0,,251-1872491,00.html (last accessed April 15, 2006).

Sageman, Marc. *Understanding Terror Networks*. Philadelphia: University of Pennsylvania Press, 2004.

Scheuer, Michael. *Imperial Hubris: Why the West Is Losing the War on Terror.* Dulles, VA: Potomac Books, 2004.

Sciolino, Elaine. "Kamel Daoudi." *New York Times.* September 22, 2002.

Shane, Scott. "The Web as al-Qaida's Safety Net." *Baltimore Sun.* March 28, 2003, available at http://siteinstitute.org/bin/articles.cgi?ID=inthenews2703&Category=inthene ws&Subcategory=0 (last accessed March 10, 2005).

Shaul, Shay. *The Endless Jihad: The Mujahidin, the Taliban and Bin Laden.* Jerusalem: Gefen Publishing House, 2002.

Shefa, A. "Egyptian Press Reactions to the Sharm Al-Sheikh Bombings." Inquiry and Analysis Series No. 233. *MEMRI.* August 10, 2005, available at http://memri.org/bin/ articles.cgi?Page=archives&Area=ia&ID=IA23305 (last accessed April 15, 2006).

Shihadah, Marwan, and Muyassir al-Shamri. "Al-Maqdisi to Al-Hayah: Bin Ladin Refused Al-Zarqawi's Request to Teach My Books to His Supporters." *Al-Hayah.* July 10, 2005.

Sid-Ahmed, Mohamed. "Will the Hamza Trial in London Inaugurate a New Era of Exposing Corruption in Egypt." *Al-Ahran Weekly.* September 2004, 23–29, available at http://weekly.ahram.org.eg/2004/709/op5.htm (last accessed March 10, 2005).

Sifaoui, Muhammad. *Inside Al Qaeda: How I Infiltrated the World's Deadliest Terrorist Organization.* New York: Thunder's Mouth Press, 2004.

Silke, Andrew. "Cheshire-Cat Logic: The Recurring Theme of Terrorist Abnormality in Psychological Research." *Psychology of Crime and Law* 4 (1998): 51–69.

———. "Becoming a Terrorist." In *Terrorists, Victims and Society: Psychological Perspectives on Terrorism and Its Consequences,* ed. Andrew Silke, 29–53. Chichester, UK: John Wiley and Sons, 2003.

———. "Courage in Dark Places: Reflections on Terrorist Psychology." *Social Research* (spring 2004): 177–98.

Smolar, Piotr. "Converts to Radical Islam, a Growing Minority of Activists." *Le Monde.* June 4, 2004.

Spencer, Robert. "Why American Muslim Converts Turn to Terrorism." *Human Events,* June 3, 2004, available at www.humaneventsonline.com/article.php?id+4063 (last accessed March 10, 2005).

"Statement from Azzam.com Regarding Closure of Its Website." *Qoqaz.* September 25, 2002, available at www.qoqaz.net (last accessed November 3, 2002).

Strange, Hannah. "British Muslims Called to Take Up Jihad." *United Press International.* January 11, 2005, available at www.washtimes.com/upi-breaking/20050110-082616-6312r.htm (last accessed March 10, 2005).

Steyn, Mark. "Listen to the Word on the Arab Street." *Daily Telegraph.* November 21, 2005.

Tashkent Uzbek Radio 1. "Ex-Militant Reveals Details about Uzbek Islamic Movement." *Tashkent Uzbek Radio 1.* September 7, 2003.

Taylor, Maxwell. *The Fanatics: A Behavioral Approach to Political Violence.* London: Bassey's, 1991.

Tazghart, Uthman. "Al-Majallah Goes to Minguettes, the Neighborhood of Islamic Radicalism in France." *Al-Majallah.* January 25, 2004.

This Is Local London. "Leaflets Promote Al Qaeda Propaganda." *This Is Local London.* April 28, 2004, available at www.thisislocallondon.co.uk/search/display.var.484526.0.leaflets_promote_al_qaeda_propaganda.php (last accessed March 10, 2005).

Thomas, Evan. "Cracking the Terror Code." *Newsweek.* October 15, 2001, available at http://msnbc.msn.com/id/3668484 (last accessed March 10, 2005).

Three Sides Tripod. "The Two Senior Scholars—Who Dared to Speak." *Three Sides Tripod,* available at http://3sides.tripod.com/terrorism/IslamicTerror/fatwa.html (last accessed March 10, 2005).

Toronto National Post. "Al-Qaida's Jordanian Blunder." *Toronto National Post.* November 11, 2005.

"Unknown Islamic Jihad Group Assumes Responsibility for Uzbekistan Attacks." April 12, 2004, available at www.muslim.uzbekistan.com (last accessed March 10, 2005).

U.S. Department of State, Washington File. "The 4,000 Jews Rumor." *U.S. Department of State.* October 30, 2004, available at http://usinfo.state.gov/media/Archive/2005/Jan/14-260933.html (last accessed March 10, 2005).

U.S. News & World Report. "Letter to the Editor—Zapping Zarqawi." *U.S. News & World Report.* December 5, 2005.

Ware, Michael. "Meet the New Jihad." *Time.* June 27, 2004, available at www.mafhoum.com/press7/200S30.htm (last accessed March 10, 2005).

Weekly Standard. "English Translation of Ayman al-Zawahiri's Letter to Abu Musab al-Zarqawi." *Weekly Standard.* October 12, 2005, available at www.weeklystandard.com/Content/Public/Articles/000/000/006/203gpuul.asp?pg=2 (last accessed April 15, 2006).

Weiser, Benjamin, and Tim Golden. "Who and Where Are al-Qaida?" *Houston Chronicle.* October 17, 2001, available at www.chron.com/cs/CDA/printstory.mpl/side/1074253 (last accessed March 10, 2005).

Whitlock, Craig. "Saudis Facing Return of Radicals: Young Iraq Veterans Join Underground." *Washington Post Foreign Service.* July 11, 2004, available at www.washingtonpost.com/wp-dyn/articles/A41375-2004Jul10.html (last accessed March 10, 2005).

Wiktorowicz, Quintan. *Radical Islam Rising: Muslim Extremism in the West.* Lanham, MD: Rowman & Littlefield Publishers, 2005.

Wiktorowicz, Qunitan, and John Kaltner. "Killing in the Name of Islam: Al-Qaeda's Justification for September 11." *Middle East Policy* 10, no. 2 (summer 2003): 76–92.

Wildman, Sarah. "Veiled Illusion." *New Republic.* February 13, 2004, available at www.tnr.com/doc.mhtml?i=dispatch&s=wildman021304 (last accessed March 10, 2005).

Wilkinson, Gina. "Sunshine Festival for 3,000 Children in Sri Lanka." *International Organization for Migration.* August 1, 2005, available at www.iom.int/tsunami/stories/sr_ns_01_08_05.htm (last accessed April 15, 2006).

Woolf, Alex. *Osama Bin Laden* (A&E Biography). Minneapolis: Lerner Publishing Group, 2003.

Worthy, Diane. "Anti-Mosque Leaflets Go Straight into Bins." *This Is Local London.* November 14, 2002, available at www.thisislocallondon.co.uk/display.var.230119.0.0.php (last accessed March 10, 2005).

Wright, Lawrence. "The Man behind Bin Laden." *New Yorker*. September 9, 2002, available at www.newyorker.com/printables/fact/020916fa_fact2 (last accessed March 10, 2005).

Youssef, Maamoum. "Islamic Websites, Known for al-Qaida support, Criticize Jordan Bombings," *Associated Press*, November 15, 2005, available at http://news.tmcnet.com/news/2005/nov/1204650.htm (last accessed April 15, 2006).

Zahab, Mariam, and Olivier Roy. *Islamist Networks: The Afghan-Pakistan Connection*. New York: Columbia University Press, 2004.

Index

About the Authors

Elena Mastors is associate professor at the Naval War College in Newport, Rhode Island. She received her Ph.D. in political science and political psychology from Washington State University, where she focused on conflict and terrorism. She has published books and articles and written papers in the area of conflict and terrorism from a political-psychological perspective. She is also a frequent lecturer on the important role of individuals in extremist groups.

Alyssa Deffenbaugh is a program analyst with ManTech International Corporation. Prior to her current position, she worked for the Defense Intelligence Agency as a terrorism analyst, then as a regional analyst covering Middle East issues. She received her B.A. from Temple University in criminal justice and psychology in May 2002.